SERIOUS
ENTERTAINMENTS

SERIOUS ENTERTAINMENTS

The Writing of History in Twelfth-Century England

NANCY F. PARTNER

THE UNIVERSITY OF CHICAGO PRESS
CHICAGO AND LONDON

NANCY F. PARTNER is assistant professor of history at the
State University of New York
College at Purchase.

THE UNIVERSITY OF CHICAGO PRESS, CHICAGO 60637
THE UNIVERSITY OF CHICAGO PRESS, LTD., LONDON
© 1977 by The University of Chicago
All rights reserved. Published 1977
Printed in the United States of America
81 80 79 78 77   9 8 7 6 5 4 3 2 1

Library of Congress Cataloging in Publication Data

Partner, Nancy F
  Serious entertainments.

  Bibliography: p.
  Includes index.
  1. Henry of Huntingdon, 1084?–1155. The chronicle
of Henry of Huntingdon.   2. William of Newburgh,
1136–1198? Historia rerum anglicarum Wilhelmi rerum
englicarum Wilhelmi Parvi.   3. Richard of Devizes, fl,
1191. Chronicon Ricardi Divisiensis de rebus gestis
Ricardi Primi regis Angliae.   4. Great Britain—History
To 1066.   5. Great Britain—History—Norman period,
1066–1154.   6. Great Britain—History—Richard I,
1189–1199.   7. Great Britain—History—To 1485—
Historiography.   I. Title.
DA130.H413P37   1977   942'.007'2   77-4402
ISBN 0-226-64763-3

For J. A. L.

"Come, Miss Morland, let us leave him to meditate over our faults in the utmost propriety of diction, while we praise Udolpho in whatever terms we like best. It is a most interesting work. You are fond of that kind of reading?"

"To say the truth, I do not much like any other."

"Indeed!"

"That is, I can read poetry and plays, and things of that sort, and do not dislike travels. But history, real solemn history, I cannot be interested in. Can you?"

"Yes, I am fond of history."

"I wish I were too. I read it a little as a duty, but it tells me nothing that does not either vex or weary me. The quarrels of popes and kings, with wars and pestilences, in every page; the men all so good for nothing, and hardly any women at all—it is very tiresome: and yet I often think it odd that it should be so dull, for a great deal of it must be invention, and invention is what delights me in other books."

"Historians, you think," said Miss Tilney, "are not happy in their flights of fancy. They display imagination without raising interest. I am fond of history—and am very well contented to take the false with the true. In the principal facts they have sources of intelligence in former histories and records, which may be as much depended on, I conclude, as any thing that does not actually pass under one's own observation; and as for the little embellishments you speak of, they are embellishments and I like them as such. If a speech be well drawn up, I read it with pleasure, by whomsoever it may be made—and probably with much greater, if the production of Mr. Hume or Mr. Robertson, than if the genuine words of Caractacus, Agricola, or Alfred the Great."

"You are fond of history!—and so are Mr. Allen and my father; and I have two brothers who do not dislike it. So many instances within my small circle of friends is remarkable! At this rate, I shall not pity the writers of history any longer. If people like to read their books, it is all very well, but to be at so much trouble in filling great volumes, which, as I used to think, nobody would willingly ever look into, to be labouring only for the torment of little boys and girls, always struck me *as a hard fate; and though I know it is all very right and necessary, I have often wondered at the person's courage that could sit down on purpose to do it."*

Conversation between Catherine Morland and Eleanor Tilney,
from Jane Austen's NORTHANGER ABBEY
(composed 1798–1799; published 1818)

Contents

Acknowledgments

Although this book, in its first version, was a doctoral dissertation for the University of California at Berkeley, it was written almost entirely at the Newberry Library, Chicago, whose Midwestern romanesque walls made a wonderfully hospitable shelter for a twelfth-century endeavor. I would like the Newberry staff and its director, Mr. Lawrence Towner, to know how much I have appreciated their efficiency and courtesy and generosity.

A work composed, as this one was, from the "inside-out" like a mosaic or a crossword puzzle whose eventual design remains, long and perversely, a secret known only to its author, had to put some strain on the patience of those who consented to be its mentors and guides. Professor Paul J. Alexander encountered the odd pieces of text that descended on him at uncertain intervals with imperturbable courtesy, and gave in return much excellent advice and kind encouragement.

Though I cannot presume that the reader can discover it without being told, this book was intended to be in the historical style, of density and texture and "style" in the best sense, of my dissertation director, Professor Robert Brentano. It is meant to be an exploration of style of thought and personality and expression. It was written, in an important sense, for him to read, and if he can do so with any pleasure it may be considered a success.

Introduction:
THE READING
OF MEDIEVAL HISTORY

IT IS SAD TO THINK THAT HISTORY, "REAL SOLEMN HISTORY," WAS not sufficiently "horrid" to compete for Catherine Morland's attention with "Castle of Wolfenbach, Clermont, Mysterious Warnings, Necromancer of the Black Forest, Midnight Bell, Orphan of the Rhine, and Horrid Mysteries"—her holiday reading list.[1] And yet, in spite of kings and popes and pestilences (and a great deal of invention), Catherine was right; by the end of the eighteenth century, history could not very well compete with novels as popular entertainment, and during the next two centuries, it was to develop into a kind of writing more "real" and "solemn" than anything the heroine of *Northanger Abbey* could ever have imagined.

Her friend Miss Tilney, with more refined taste and extensive literary experience, defended history against the charge of being both invented and dull by asserting that history books are substantially true and thus edifying, and that where they are false the superior taste of the modern age has probably improved upon antique reality. She is easily and correctly imagined as the reader to whom, a few years before her conversation with Miss Morland, the author of a popular history of England (abridged from Hume, Smollet, and others) addressed his prefatory remarks:

> It will be sufficient, therefore, to satisfy the writer's wishes, if the present work be found a plain unaffected narrative of facts, with just ornament enough to keep attention awake, and with reflection barely sufficient to set the reader upon thinking. Very moderate abilities were equal to such an undertaking; and it is hoped the performance will satisfy such as take up books to be informed or amused.[2]

Those persons "such as take up books to be informed or amused" had, for centuries, taken up history books in expectation of just those facts, ornaments, and reflections promised by the modest historian (although any working historian may object that keeping a reader awake and thinking is not such a humble ambition after all). Both Miss Tilney and the modest historian appreciated history as a higher form of entertainment and, in so doing, may be considered among the last educated persons to accept fully a tradition of historical reading and writing continuous for nearly three thousand years and now substantially dead.

The works of Mr. Hume and Mr. Robertson are still available to us, but the serious reader, the scholarly reader, no longer chooses to read them unless he is a student of early eighteenth-century thought and letters. Certainly the student of early English history will resist the attractions of graceful prose and will approach his popes and pestilences through other sources— would prefer, in fact, those unimproved "genuine words of Caractacus, Agricola, and Alfred the Great"—if he could only get at them. Eighteenth-century works on early English history, opinionated, embellished, elegant, are, by strict scholarly standards, expendable. The histories written during much earlier centuries are fiercely biased, unconscionably invented, and often inelegant as well; they are not expendable at all but continue to be read for a variety of historical purposes and in a variety of scholarly moods. The reader whose mood is one of realistic sympathy is constantly (and abruptly and funnily) taught to remember that the first and best readers of medieval histories, the learned patrons, for example, without whose interest many historical works might never have been written, held those books up to a standard not very different, in modern eyes, from the "horridness" that so distinguished *The Mysteries of Udolpho.*

No great literary patron like Alexander of Lincoln would have been gratified to find his name conspicuously flourished in the preface to an austere catalog of events and dates, however accurate. Serious and skillful medieval writers did not all attempt universal histories, but if their ambition rose beyond the modest annal to the dignity of high literature, their work had to arrest the attention and divert the imagination with scenes of great triumphs and failures, inside information about princes both secular and ecclesiastical, matters of provincial but intense interest, scandalous gossip, tales of exotic places, and, of course, accounts of exemplary lives and evidences of God's continuing interest in human affairs to elevate the mind—and all this in as beautiful a style as the writer could command. Not many historians could manage to satisfy thoroughly all contemporary requirements for information, morality, amusement, and beauty of language, especially at the ample length their generations of leisurely readers admired. Current standards for historical scholarship and composition have changed irrevocably and drastically from the informal, expansive canons medieval historians hoped to meet. Readers have changed as well: we now demand "hard" information, disdain amusement, resist morality, and we no longer read at leisure.

The eighteenth-century Miss Tilney who took pleasure in reading history found it perfectly natural and proper that historians of the highest literary and intellectual character should include much in their works that was "false," with the implicit assumption that such falseness was not intended to deceive or corrupt the reader's mind. She assumed, as readers and writers had for centuries, that literary embellishment was a beneficent and welcome mediator between boredom and historical narrative; she knew quite well how unlikely it was that a modern history should contain the very words of Alfred the Great, but she had no objection to reading a good speech if an historian could write one. Alexander of Lincoln revealed a similar feeling in 1124 when he commissioned a history of England from a poet. One authority whom Alexander would have accepted, Isidore of Seville, maker of august and useful clichés on every subject, had distinguished history from other forms of prose on the basis of its truthfulness of content, but he had considered that to be a fairly minor distinction.[3] Prose in the high style constituted a literary endeavor essentially undivided by the fictional or nonfictional character of its subject matter. The chief events of *historia* were to be received or observed, not invented, but in every other respect of verbal play and elaboration history had to resemble fiction if it aspired to dignity. History was left, for centuries, in an informal and capacious antechamber of the arts, with few restrictions but the accumulating weight of tradition. During the whole of the Middle Ages, history enjoyed many of the freedoms of fiction; and fiction, in turn, conventionally masqueraded as fact—no serious deception was intended by either.[4]

Odd as it may seem to jump precipitately from the Middle

3

Ages to the eighteenth century, there was throughout that span of time (with various exceptions and developments) an essential continuity of assumptions that could be brought to the reading of history. By the eighteenth century, histories were more orderly and less rambling than their venerable and, by then, uncouth-sounding ancestors and saints and miracles had given way before statesmen and parliaments. Nevertheless, the educated Christian of the eighteenth century was not yet ready to relinquish belief in the miraculous (however skeptical about individual cases), and he could still read Alfred's speeches with pleasure. By the end of the century, the change to modern rigor and persevering inquiry was already well begun; it would soon be ludicrous for an historian, like the self-effacing person quoted above, to dismiss, for example, the Britons before the arrival of the Romans with blithe contempt: "It is fortunate for mankind, that those periods of history which are the least serviceable, are the least known."[5] That remark was made in 1771. Some 570 years earlier, William of Newburgh had been of much the same opinion; one hundred years later, such an opinion would be held in utter contempt.

We have simply lost contact, albeit willingly and rightly, with everything that could allow us to approach medieval histories naturally and directly. And yet those works have continued to be read by scholars variously puzzled, bored, critical, and intrigued, because they are the sources for information otherwise unavailable. They have been plumbed and sifted, often brilliantly, for the nugget of truth in the swamp of "falseness," and that ruthless and methodical dissection of medieval histories has been the first step of modern scholarship on its way to rewriting the past in newly persuasive, dispassionate, and verifiable modes. But even that austere undertaking, like any other, contains the beginnings of its own special absurdity, as shown by one intriguing study that compares eclipses noted in medieval chronicles with modern astronomical charts and proposes establishing thereby a sort of correctness quotient with which to evaluate the usefulness of medieval histories[6] — harmless enough, or perhaps a small further hardening of modern sensibilities to the past.

The older, longer tradition of history as serious entertainment was a particularly rich one in England, as is most recently witnessed by the impressive size, among other impressive things, of Antonia Gransden's survey of English historical writing from 550 to 1307 (and always by those Rolls Series volumes, shelved and awesomely endless); that tradition has been examined with particular depth and elegance in essays by C. N. L. Brooke and Sir Richard Southern.[7] The hovering, magisterial presence of Bede in English intellectual life made history writing important and dignified; it inspired imitation and suggested possibilities for form and meaning in human history to many generations of new historians. The Norman Conquest, which brought to England men with no English traditions or loyalties and thus threatened to erase English memories of saints and saintly kings, had its quickening effect on the notable twelfth-century English gift for memory-keeping, history-writing.[8] The English wrote a great deal of history in the twelfth century, much of it of fine quality, all of it worth attention. I chose three historians: Henry of Huntingdon (writing during 1125–1154), William of Newburgh, and Richard of Devizes (both writing around 1200)—three who are interesting representatives of the best possibilities in twelfth-century English historiography. Each was an ecclesiastic by profession (Henry an archdeacon; William an Augustinian canon; Richard a Benedictine monk), intellectual and literary in his education and tastes, and each wrote a history of England at the request of a friend or patron. Diversity of subjects, leisurely digressive avenues, and open possibilities of historical interpretation characterize the books these men wrote, and I have tried to examine them as carefully and sensitively and flexibly as I have been able. My choice of these three historians required no unusual discovery or discernment; I did not intend making an ultimate selection, but an interesting one. Each of the three simply "works," and works with and against the others effectively.

All medieval histories contain more that is valuable to us than scraps of verifiable information, although what that "more" is, exactly, varies from book to book and is sometimes difficult to describe. The history of written history is a peculiarly modern study in its mirror-gazing self-consciousness; much of the fascination of the subject focuses on the authors—sometimes totally obscured behind copied "authorities" and personal reticence, sometimes daringly present. There are, from the twelfth century—that period which is distinctively one of reemerging personality and even idiosyncrasy—a variety of authorial voices asserting themselves over annal–anonymity and tempting the reader to the reconstruction, in mosaic bits, of a mind and a personality.[9] Twelfth-century historians increasingly tended to record many things other than their ostensible subjects: best of all, their own voices. These minds and emotions in the act of observing, registering, sifting impressions make the really irresistible object for our minds; these were, after all, the men who would, in later centuries, be academics. They were educated and reasonably articulate, and they were writing in a genre that encouraged digression and quiet idiosyncrasy. They have unexpected things to tell about themselves and their part of their world.

But, if the objects of historiographical study press forward in hospitable invitation, the most suitable manner for accepting that invitation is not entirely clear. There is no single method to bring to historiographical studies. Too many ready-made tasks executed firmly on the text threaten to overwhelm the vulnerable past with the aggressive present; a too-little-disciplined attention may result in nothing but a mildly appreciative reading. History during the twelfth century and long after did not constitute an intellectual specialization and it forces—often happily—much of its own wayward variety on its students. It has been nicely observed that the history of history is a subject in which there is "a fantastic miscellany of strange and unexpected things which, after being kicked out the door, are summoned back by the window—all of them to be absorbed into the history of historiography."[10] But only a little experiment is necessary before one learns that no matter how fantastic and miscellaneous the instruments one brings to the opening of a twelfth-century text, they are never enough. The subjects that came under the author's attention may range from crusades, through medical prescriptions, to demonical toads, and one is hard pressed to keep in sight the travels of a curious and wide-ranging mind. Then there is the intriguing imponderability of sensibility: changes in taste, in basic reactions and expectations concerning the world, habits of mind, the universal absence of the laws of physics (in the way that things unknown *are*, in a very real sense, absent), the universal belief in supernatural events. Unable to reproduce in ourselves the unconsidered assumptions of past minds, we can only attempt a discriminating sympathy.

I attempted to read my histories as thoroughly as I could, with the intention of acquiring a live sense of the writer's mind and personality and a palpable sense of his book—of its texture, its intellectual style, its appeal—and all this, with the conviction that every man who writes a book, whatever its subject, is capturing in some way an image of his world and that it, too, can be "read." It was not my intention to move from the particular historians to generalized abstractions about the philosophy of history, but to move back and forth, to shift focus between the foreground of the text and the middle distance of its special world and thus to capture both. I wanted to trace the connecting lines between the historian and his book and the world he watched and cared about (and took for granted and ignored) and to describe what I had found so as to invite the reader to go back to Henry and William and Richard and see them again—but perhaps not quite the same as before. The student of historiography does not (I am thankful) begin quite alone. For English medieval history, there is now Antonia Gransden's compendious and exact *Historical Writing in England, c. 550 to c. 1307* (the second volume is in preparation), which must be the best starting point for historiographical studies.[11] Robert Hanning's *Vision of History in Early Britain from Gildas to Geoffrey of Monmouth* is a particularly successful study of a major theme in early English history.[12] Beryl Smalley's essay, "Sallust in the Middle Ages," makes sharply observed and useful comments on the tone and style of medieval historians,[13] as does her book, *Historians in the Middle Ages*. There are the invaluable essays of Eric Auerbach in *Mimesis;* and all of Arnaldo Momigliano's standard-setting essays, but especially those on late Roman historiography.[14] I mentioned above the work of C. N. L. Brooke and of Sir Richard Southern, but note especially Sir Richard's four presidential addresses to the Royal Historical Society (1970–1973) on *Aspects of the European Tradition of Historical Writing*.

But even with admirable aid in the work of others, the student of medieval historians is left peculiarly alone with his author and must willingly follow wherever he eccentrically leads, gathering his tools along the way, and must inevitably see, as scholars

7

always have, "that it is too late to look for instruments when the work calls for execution, and that whatever abilities I had brought to my task, with those I must finally perform it."[15] I have hoped to say something plausible and useful to others about three twelfth-century histories of England in a way that is orderly enough for intelligibility yet does not betray the characteristic informality of the originals by imposed patterns; I have also attempted to build, out of whatever came workably to hand, three portraits of twelfth-century historians that must remain necessarily unfinished, but are perhaps distinguishable.

I

HENRY OF HUNTINGDON

One
HISTORY AND CONTEMPT
OF THE WORLD

NOT MUCH IS KNOWN ABOUT HENRY, THE ARCHDEACON OF Huntingdon in the diocese of Lincoln from 1110 to about 1154; no personal correspondence or anecdotes survive from his long life, and no one, evidently, considered him important enough for a written memorial. His biography depends upon a few notices scattered through his own works and in a few more places (preserved in cartularies) where he left his name in the course of his official duties. Still, the small quantity of information about him is concrete and suggestive, the condensed distillation from a successful life lived just below the first ranks of property and talent in an age of personal reticence. He mentions Lanfranc as having been "famous in our own time," which places Henry's birthdate a few years before 1089, when Lanfranc died.[1] The *Historia Anglorum* leaves off in 1154 with the promise of another book for the new reign; since that book was never written it may be assumed that Henry died shortly after 1154, at about seventy years of age.[2]

He wrote an obituary in the *Historia* for his father, named Nicholas, who was the first archdeacon of Huntingdon and therefore a clerk in holy orders (but not necessarily a priest):

> In the same year [1110] Nicholas, father of the one who wrote this history, yielded to the law of death and was buried at Lincoln. Of him it is written:
> Stella cadit cleri, splendor marcet Nicholai;
> Stella cadens cleri, splendeat arce Dei.
> The writer has inserted this into his work that he might obtain a corresponding labor from his readers, insofar as it is a suitable task of piety to say, "May his soul rest in peace. Amen."[3]

Nicholas was probably a native of Cambridgeshire or Huntingdonshire and, since Henry speaks of Aldwin, abbot of Ramsey, as "dominus meus," his Rolls Series editor Thomas Arnold reasonably speculates that Nicholas held land of the abbey. Nicholas was a canon of Lincoln Cathedral and held the archdeaconry of Cambridge, Huntingdon, and Hereford (Cambridge was assigned to the newly created see of Ely in 1009). The first archdeacon of Huntingdon was clearly an important man in his neighborhood in his day; his son, with warm filial hyperbole, calls him a man "than whom no one was handsomer in body, nor was his character less beautiful than his person."[4] Nicholas was present at Ely in 1106 for the second translation of Saint Etheldreda and was one of the few witnesses mentioned by name, along with notables like Herbert, bishop of Norwich, and the abbots of Ramsey and Saint Albans; he donated a bible in two volumes to the library of Lincoln Cathedral.[5] Nicholas evidently had enough influence with his superior, the bishop of Lincoln, to secure the succession to his archdeaconry for Henry —quite a substantial inheritance for a young man of about twenty-five. Henry does not mention his mother. Clerical marriage, although common enough, was uncanonical by the late eleventh century, and efforts to enforce celibacy, a central part of the Gregorian reform program, were growing frequent and increasingly stringent during Henry's lifetime. The English clergy, far from Continental centers of reform, were particularly recalcitrant on the issue of marriage, and there is no reason to suppose that a married archdeacon of Henry's father's generation would have suffered in his reputation or prosperity on that account. Nonetheless, by 1127–1129, when the *Historia* was being composed, the whole question of clerical celibacy had become a live issue in England and a source of peculiar irritation for Henry, and he was understandably discreet.[6]

He was received as a little boy, *puerulus*, into the *familia* of Bishop Robert Bloet of Lincoln and grew up amidst luxury.[7] As a child, youth, and young man, he lived in the wealth and extravagant splendor of England's richest episcopal court—the very memory of which so dazzled him that, as a man about fifty years old, in a treatise advocating contempt for the world, he could scarcely find language sumptuous enough to convey his sense of the glittering past: "I saw the most handsome knights, noble young men, the costliest horses, gold and gilded baggage, the numbers of carts and the splendid guards, the silk and purple garments; surely I could think no one more blessed."[8] He could hardly in his youth, he reasonably excuses himself, have learned contempt for the world. In later years he did learn to feel, about the world and its pleasures and their passing, a certain recoil of distrust which he called *contemptus mundi,* and that feeling pervades much of his mature literary work.

Robert Bloet, whose splendid entourage lured the young Henry into thinking well of worldly success, gave him the archdeaconry of Huntingdon in 1110, the benefice he held all his life. He was also a canon of Lincoln[9] and thus one of the *familia* of the bishop of Lincoln—first Robert Bloet, later Alexander, and for a long time, Robert de Querceto—attached by family tradition and gratitude to the interests of lavish, powerful, ecclesiastical statesmen. He dedicated an epistle to Henry I and perhaps was part of the king's entourage in Normandy once. He traveled with Archbishop Theobald to Rome in 1139 and visited Robert de Thorigny at Bec, where he discovered Geoffrey of Monmouth's history of Britain.[10]

Archdeacons were traditionally close to their bishops and very important men in their administrative areas: "He was the *oculus episcopi* through which the state of the diocese was brought to the bishop's notice, and his authority was thus almost equivalent to that of the bishop in matters the transaction of which did not require episcopal order." The fact that archdeacons were proverbially greedy, even rapacious, is a sad but not, in itself, a sufficient comment about them; theirs was not an office designed for popularity. Their duties, once nicely described as those of "ecclesiastical police,"[11] involved the scrutiny and correction of every sort of conduct of clerks and laymen directly at the parish level. The "eye of the bishop" was responsible for peering into everything and everybody's business, making public accusations in the court or rural chapter, and assigning punishment. By the twelfth century, those archdeacons who, like Henry, had been assigned a specific area of jurisdiction, often corresponding to a county, were local powers backed by the full delegated authority of the bishop; the scope and detail of their business made them often rich and never well loved.[12] Their instruments for maintaining the Church's material and moral fabric were the visitation tour, during which inquiries were made of any transgression against morality or Church property, and the chapter, at which accusations were made public, judgment brought, and punishment assigned. The rural chapter was a vigorous, pragmatical institution: swift, detailed, *13* and humiliating in its accusations, insistent and expensive in its corrections. It was the setting for the promulgation and enforcement of new council decrees as well as of established law,[13] and no detail of conduct, no matter how private, was safe from its jurisdiction.

Archdeacons' wealth, their general unpopularity, and their crucial necessity to the Church seem inextricably mixed and it is understandable why a preacher, in 1190, "could find no more effective parable to demonstrate the mutability of human fortunes than to declare to his congregation that even popes and archdeacons died."[14] It is frequently, however, a long and misleading way from the general to the particular, and Henry of Huntingdon never wrote about his official duties, nor did anyone write about him, and his share in the traditions peculiar to his order cannot be fairly assessed. Perhaps it is in his favor (a refinement of taste, of choice of friends) that he seems to have been well and amicably acquainted with the major monasteries in his archdeaconry and that he always spoke well of monks.

As the son of an archdeacon and as an official under Bishop Robert Bloet whose son was dean of Lincoln,[15] Henry moved in ecclesiastical circles in which the traditional English acceptance of clerical marriage was still much stronger than the comparatively recent insistence on celibacy. In England, Anselm must be acknowledged the first archbishop to have made serious and repeated efforts to enforce the canons enjoining celibacy on men in higher orders. Earlier efforts had been sporadic and without effect except, of course, to make increasing numbers of clerks understand, to some reluctant degree, that their domestic arrangements were not strictly in accord with the current law of the Church.[16] Considering the particular circumstances in which he lived, the influence of custom, and the example set by his closest relatives and benefactors, it is not in the least surprising to find that Henry was himself married. Documents from a cartulary of Ramsey Abbey in the archdeaconry of Huntingdon reveal the names of Henry's son, grandson, and great-grandson and show that he was, if not demonstrably a married man, certainly a family man.[17] His pointed use, however, in the *Historia*, of the word *uxor* indicates that, in his eyes, priests had wives and not concubines or worse.

14   Ramsey Abbey had a great deal of demesne land in its own

county of Huntingdon, a part of which, the manor (now parish) of Stukeley (Stivecle, Styvecle, Stiveclea, and so forth), was held in farm by Archdeacon Henry who was also the abbot's tenant in the nearby parish of Gidding.[18] He was succeeded as *firmarius* of Stukeley by his son Master Adam, whom the scribe of an extent of Stukeley carefully identified as "Master Adam who succeeded archdeacon Henry in the farm of Stukeley," and, in another extent, as "Adam, son of archdeacon Henry."[19] The title of "Master" (*magister*) commonly indicated a man in minor orders. An "Adam of Stukeley" is recorded as a tenant of Ramsey in the nearby parish of Abbot's Rypton.[20] The family can be traced for two more generations ᴀs contention over the Stukeley manor caused names to surface. Henry's grandson appears when "Adam of Stukeley and his son Aristotle" (elsewhere mentioned as "Aristotle of Stukeley") agreed with Robert Trianel, abbot of Ramsey 1180–1200, to farm Stukeley for one hundred *solidi*.[21] Abbot Richard de Selby, 1214–1216, reassigned Stukeley to the maintenance of Ramsey,[22] despite the claims of Aristotle's son Nicholas, who entered into litigation for it. The outcome of Nicholas's suit is recorded by several documents in the Ramsey Cartulary and also in the Feet of Fines (12 Hen. 3): "Nicholas of Stukeley, son of Aristotle," upon a settlement of thirty marks of silver, relinquished all claim to Stukeley and to his holdings in Gidding where his great-grandfather had been a tenant. The record in the Feet of Fines is endorsed with the quit-claim of Adam of Stukeley. One document notices slightly a niece of Master Adam.[23] The scattered notices all point to a respectable, prosperous, ecclesiastical family that suffered no penalty for its uncanonical succession of generations.

The archdeacon was a man of literary tastes, well appreciated by his patron, the cultivated Bishop Alexander (who also received the dedication of Geoffrey of Monmouth's history of Britain); Henry was chosen about 1127 by Alexander to write a history.[24] He had established his reputation for letters earlier as a poet. Some epigrams remain from his eight books of them, six *jocunda* and two *seria;* and even in the epistle *De contemptu mundi* he cannot resist mentioning his "carmen . . . in amorem," composed "acceptabile" and, sadly, no longer extant.[25] There exist three formal epistles: one is to Henry I, written between

15

1131 and 1135, consisting of lists of patriarchs, legislators, judges, and kings of the Old Testament, the monarchies of Babylonia, Persia, Greece, and Rome, and a list of the Frankish emperors. A second, addressed to Warin the Briton, is a list of kings of Britain from Brutus to Julius Caesar (abbreviated from a copy of Geoffrey of Monmouth's *Historia Britonum* shown to Henry at Bec by Robert de Thorigny in 1139).[26] The third, written in 1135, is an epistle called *De contemptu mundi*, addressed to his friend and *consors* Walter. It is discussed below. A book, *De miraculis*, consists of miracles of English saints abstracted from Bede, with additional material about contemporary saints and shrines.[27] Works no longer extant, ascribed to him by Leland, are: *De herbis*, *De aromatibus*, *De gemmis*, *De ponderibus et mensuris*, and *De lege Domine*, which is addressed to the monks of Peterborough.[28] Henry was a man of elegant taste and wide if perhaps facile learning, prosperous and important enough to gratify any reasonable ambition, and a traditionalist in Church matters.

The *Historia Anglorum* was written because Alexander of Lincoln asked Henry to write it; that is what Henry says in the prologue: "I undertook that the events of the kingdom and the origins of our nation be traversed at your command, Prelate Alexander—you who will appear as the flower and pinnacle of the kingdom and the nation."[29] Taking, it would seem, as few chances as possible with his commission, Alexander had given a number of working instructions: to follow Bede's *Ecclesiastical History* as far as possible, then to use the chronicles preserved in old libraries up to the point at which his author had firsthand material—nothing adventurous, but sound enough. Unfortunately, these personal instructions ("tuo quidem consilio") from the flower of the realm were sufficiently banal for the author's conventional gratitude to slip nearly into comic (and surely unintended) excess. Whether or not he needed such beginner's rules, Henry was a good choice for the project. Literary ornaments in an amplified, dignified style built over a basic, plausible narrative of events made the kind of history that was worth the attention and patronage of a great man whose attention would never linger over plain annals kept dutifully, cursorily, by monks. And Henry did have, by all prevailing standards, every qualification for writing history that the cultivated bishop could have been aware of: an easy gift for language; knowledge of classical literature; familiar access to important monastic libraries.

The *Historia Anglorum* must impress the reader as a carefully planned work, the divisions into books determined, not fortuitously, but by a scheme that energetically attempted to unify and articulate the mass of event. The narrative is clear and vigorous and moves at a good pace, with brief pauses for excursuses of aesthetic and moral effect. The first edition of the *Historia*, in seven books, began with Bede's famous description of Britain and ended with events of 1129, noting the death of the young Philip of France.[30] The ending in 1129 was a logical conclusion (with an epilogue on the lessons of history), and the work was obviously considered complete. But Henry was never content to leave his project; he continued to work on it, bringing it up to date with the passing years and rearranging its original structure to accommodate the new material.

A second edition brought the narrative to 1135 and the death of Henry I by simply extending Book VII a little. Four years later, a third edition brought the work to the end of 1138, further lengthening Book VII.

The fourth edition, of 1147, written when Henry was in old age, shows the first major changes. The narrative ends, in this edition, in the twelfth year of Stephen's reign, with the return of Bishop Alexander from Rome. Henry evidently reconsidered the structure of the work and divided the seven books differently. Book VII then ended with the death of Henry I (as in the second edition); the next historical book began with a description of Henry I's character and funeral. Inserted between the seventh book and what Arnold chose to print as Book VIII of his Rolls Series edition, were two additional books, numbered VIII and IX (the present VIII being then number X). Book VIII consisted of the epilogue to the first edition, and the three epistles that had been composed and published years earlier (the ancient rulers; the kings of Britain; the *De contemptu mundi*). The epilogue, based on the theme of the frailty and brevity of worldly glory, was slightly altered to serve as a prologue to the genealogical epistle on ancient rulers—stressing the fact that all were dead and many nearly forgotten. Book IX was the *De miraculis*. In that enlarged edition Book X simply resumed the historical narrative with the funeral of Henry I.

The work as a whole looks very different with two genealogical lists, a moral treatise, and a book of miracles inserted, breaking the account of Henry I's death into two widely separated books. The original *Historia* had been conceived about a plan flexible enough for reasonable inclusions, but not meant to accommodate foreign substances. Arnold concludes, very reasonably I think, that Henry had decided to use his history, of whose popularity he must have had assurance, as a reliquary for his literary reputation.[31] His ideas about the ingratitude of a forgetful posterity, expressed in the *De contemptu mundi* and the epilogue/prologue, make such a motive very plausible. (And the scheme did, after all, work.)

A final, fifth, edition brought the narrative to 1154. The last book ends with a proposal, never executed, for a new book for the new king, Henry II.

Thomas Arnold's Rolls Series edition consists of the eight historical books (numbered consecutively), with the epistle *De contemptu mundi* as an appendix. The epilogue (rendered in précis and quotation in Arnold's prefatory remarks) was dropped; there must have seemed no logical place for it, especially since the history was ultimately left unfinished. Henry had himself, by 1147, left the epilogue permanently in the middle of the work (transformed to a prologue). An epilogue so casually treated by its own author may very well be considered expendable by modern historians; the epistles are another matter. Arnold has excluded entirely the two historical genealogies, and it is likely that there is not terribly much an historian misses by their absence (genealogical works based on secondhand materials indicate in broad strokes an interest in the past but rarely can be made to disclose anything more precise). The *De miraculis* should, I think, have been printed entire, although Arnold quotes substantial portions from the passages on modern saints. The *De contemptu mundi*, however, so impressed Henry's earliest editors that it has for a long time been less cavalierly handled and has been printed many times, both alone and in conjunction with the *Historia*. The *De contemptu* is specifically a formal epistolary treatise—addressed to a recipient, with frequent internal use of the forms of direct address; it consists of a series of moral reflections on persons and events of recent history. The morality is grounded firmly in historicity. In content and didactic style, it closely resembles the *Historia;* in fact, it seems a more concentrated, single-minded version of it. The impulse to use the *De contemptu* to discuss Henry as an historian is plainly reasonable and strongly compelling. And I have, of course, done so.

The formal prologue, addressed to Bishop Alexander, is composed in a floridly dense high style that allows the author to parade a bit in his own name before retreating into dutiful obscurity behind Bede and the old chroniclers, as his patron had suggested. Henry made his prologue an elaborated defense of the writing of history, designed for a graceful, if faintly overambitious, display of a fashionable education. His claims for this species of letters are unequivocally high:

> Not only have I always thought that sweet relief from labor and the highest solace of grief (during life) reside almost entirely in the pursuit of literature, but with much greater pleasure and the security of greater renown have I believed the splendor of history is embraced. For nothing is more distinguished in life than to trace and frequent the tracks left by outstanding lives.[32]

He concludes by quoting Horace, briefly, in praise of Homer, "the historian." Poets and historians (as Henry was both, perhaps he thought the distinction not worth making) are identical in their intention to teach morality through example, and both make books more palatable than philosophy taken straight. Homer, whom Henry undoubtedly knew from a very respectful distance, illustrates the happy concord of amusement and morality.

Though the pagan authors are given first place for elegance, Henry proceeds quickly ("But why do we linger among strangers?")[33] to sacred letters, which teach virtues and vices identical to those of the pagans. And so, forward to secular history, which boasts the same didactic effects as sacred and the additional attraction of discerning the future: "History, therefore, represents the past as though present to sight; it indicates the future through the past by imagination."[34] Henry seems intent, in a slightly scattershot way, to fix every possible degree of dignity to his subject, and he adds the interesting argument

19

that memory is the chief distinction between rational beings and beasts: men who willfully remain ignorant of the past are beasts by choice.

The "arguments" of the prologue are discarded and forgotten as soon as the work gets under way, and that is not a failing peculiar to Henry; most medieval historians chose to leave their philosophy and their promises behind them as soon as possible. But one lesson of history, quickly but movingly stated, ends the prologue and is never discarded. A poem of Henry's own composition concludes his prefatory remarks; it is an invocation and prayer, and suggests, at its end, that even Bishop Alexander may have something to learn from history:

> See, great father, what becomes of the powerful:
> See how the honor, the pleasure, the glory
> of the world come to nothing.[35]

Henry's sources were, on the whole, very much what Alexander had directed him toward: Bede, of course, is the only author mentioned by name in the prologue, but Nennius, Eutropius, Aurelius Victor, and Jerome and Gregory the Great (for the early books), with the Anglo-Saxon Chronicle in the Peterborough compilation for events after the time of Bede, were what "chronicles kept in old libraries" would have suggested, more or less, to any contemporary reader.[36] He incorporates local tradition, anecdotes, his own literary invention, and, after 1128, uses almost solely information he has gathered himself. He follows his major authorities (Bede, the Peterborough Chronicle) closely—sometimes, in the early books, verbatim. He was not inclined to extensive investigations after matters of fact or novelties; his chronology is unreliable.

Henry is candid and graceful in his acknowledgments to Bede—for history and holiness both: "In the same year [735] the Venerable Bede, always in sound mind, ascended to the heavenly palace; suppressing the vices of others by his own regal virtue, he was not inferior to kings themselves, and most worthily deserves to be ranked with kings as though a king himself."[37] "As though a king" is the compliment that Henry, searching for the highest, finds. His reliance on Bede is unquestioning, and when the *Ecclesiastical History* must give way to more modern books, he reassures his readers that he has followed it as closely as possible. His other great authority, the Peterborough Chronicle, having no particular author, is treated more vaguely; only rarely does he refer directly to it and then, once, to grumble at its incompleteness: "In the twelfth year of King Edward, the old writers say that there was a battle between the men of Kent and the Danes at Holme; but who the victor was, they leave undecided."[38] Elsewhere, he argues implicitly with his anonymous authority over the question of whether or not God slept during the reign of Stephen.[39]

He was impressed by the long Anglo-Saxon poem in the Chronicle describing the battle of Brunanburh between Athelstan of Mercia and Anlaf, King of Ireland. He translated the poem into Latin for his book and entered into the problems of poetic translation with serious interest: "Of the magnitude of this battle, English writers tell in poetic form, and have employed foreign language as well as foreign figures of speech; they should be given a faithful translation, so that, rendering their eloquence almost word for word, we may thoroughly learn through the dignity of the language the dignity of the deeds and minds of those people."[40]

Nonwritten information—tradition and anecdote—mostly passes as assumed and not worth special mention, although on one occasion Henry remarks that he heard about the massacre of Saint Brice's Day from an old man. And at the beginning of Book VII (1088) he asserts that henceforth all the old books will be put aside (partially true) in favor of firsthand reports: "Now those things are to be told which we either saw ourself or which we heard from those who saw them." The most original portion of the Historia begins further on, after 1128.

Thomas Arnold, in the introductory remarks to his edition, is pointedly unsatisfied with Henry's accomplishment, especially his inability or disinclination to collect enough material for the books of contemporary events: "so evident a disposition," Arnold says, "to flinch from the research and fullness of statement which become a historian."[41] There is, of course, the matter of different times and different tastes and Arnold's nineteenth-century disdain for Henry's copious "moralizing" and "effusions" in hexameter would not have been understood at all by twelfth-century readers. Still, when Arnold accuses Henry of being "so terribly curt and perfunctory" when he must have had

21

the means to be otherwise, we must, after all allowances and adjustments have been made, simply agree. Arnold's summary opinion is that Henry "formed large projects, but was too indolent to execute them satisfactorily."[42] But a kinder judgment is possible, following one who knew a little about large projects himself and considered that, "to have attempted much is always laudable, even when the enterprise is above the strength that undertakes it."[43]

The archdeacon, a man trusted with a large and diverse administration, had a well-developed sense of order. As the products of his intellect and imagination consistently demonstrate, he liked a formal structure dominating the surface of things—openly displayed. The *Historia Anglorum*, where it was built on the work of previous writers (Books I–VI, and VII in part), displays intelligible sequence, firmly linked to "meaning" in history, and a clarity of structure insistently brought to the reader's attention. But as the book moves past written authority and begins to depend on Henry's investigations and luck, that insistent order takes a dying fall into more various and digressive spaces.

Henry of Huntingdon is a writer who persists—almost to the point of insult—in telling his readers what they are reading. Book I (after Bede's description of Britain and its chief cities) presents the plan for the work. The major divisions of the *Historia* are the five plagues that God has inflicted on Britain in the form of belligerent nations: Romans, Picts and Scots, Angles, Danes, and Normans.

> Divine Vengeance inflicted five plagues on Britain from the beginning to the present time; it not only visited them on the faithful, but even singled out the unfaithful. First were the Romans who conquered Britain but later withdrew; second were the Picts and Scots who harassed Britain bitterly in war but did not conquer; third were the Angles who fought and conquered Britain; fourth were the Danes who prevailed in war but afterwards perished; fifth were the Normans who conquered, and the English are dominated by them to the present day.[44]

Since the Picts and Scots, however like a plague, were not precisely an invasion, they are included in the first book, which ends when the reprobate Britons decide to call in the Saxons (used synonymously with Angles) for aid.

Book II traces the military history of the Saxons or Angles to a time when each king in the heptarchy was Christian. It ends with a summary of its contents and a proposal for the next book:

> In this book which we call "The Arrival of the Angles," the deeds of the Angles [infidels, up to this point] have been recorded—with a certain disorder, we think. We have gone, step by step, from the invasion of Britain by the Saxons through each realm, illustrated by its kings, until the kings of each were enlightened by the gleam of faith.... And now must be written very carefully in the next book, who the preachers were, by whose exhortations and miracles and preaching those kings were converted to faith in our Lord.[45]

The relation between Books II and III shows Henry's rather insistent orderliness. Where Bede composed a complex, interwoven mesh of military and Christian events in gradual progression toward a kingdom united under one ruler and one Church, Henry arranges a clear separation of political and ecclesiastical history. He sifts out the various conversions of the heptarchy kings and makes Book III concurrent in time with, but distinct in theme from, Book II. A brief prologue that lists the seven kings and their respective missionaries presents the theme of the book: "This book concerns the conversion of the Angles which was accomplished by Pope Gregory in this order."[46] Book III ends with a proposal for the beginning of IV ("concerning the deeds of the Christian kings of the English")[47] and reminds the reader that the author has, at this point, accomplished exactly what he set out to do: "for all the contents of this book have been set down according to the proposed plan."[48]

Book IV opens with the synodal letter of the Council of Hatfield. Whatever reason he had for putting it in this place, Henry may have felt it was awkward because he apologizes before resuming the narrative concerning the English kingdoms and kings during the eighth century. As usual, Book IV closes with a recapitulation and the program for the next book: the arrival of the Danes and hostilities with them.

Book V has its own prologue, in which Henry reminds the reader of the five plagues and, for the particularly careless, of where they are in the series: "At the beginning of this history, we said that Britain was struck by five plagues. The fourth of those which is that of the Danes, we shall recount in this book; and indeed this one was far more savage, far more cruel than the others."[49]

After the recapitulation that ends V, Book VI is announced as the "arrival of the Normans," and it begins in the slightly awkward time, the year 1000—the middle of Ethelred's reign— with the Danish invasions left unfinished. Henry's understanding of his theme of invasions as divine vengeance directs him, however, to set off in a separate book that first crucial link between the reigning families of Normandy and England— Ethelred's decision to ask for Emma of Normandy in marriage. The conquest of England by the Normans was the ultimate result of that marriage.[50] The book ends with the death of William I (in Henry's own lifetime).

On the largest scale, Henry cast the divisions of his history, regarded equally as event or literature, into a series of moral events. He found in certain large segments of time and human history recognizable entities whose unity was neither artificial nor natural but truly divine—God's gesture. The basic idea of national sin and foreign punishment was not new; Bede had adapted a venerable convention to his own nation's history when he described the ascendancy of the Angles and Saxons as a punishment of the fallen Britons; Henry extended what had become a cliché. Nonetheless, it was an artistically and morally persusasive cliché that allowed writer and reader to discern the great spiritual moments in a nation's life.

After the Norman Conquest, the organizing theme of moral lapse and retributive invasion could not very well be continued, and the clarity of history distilled by time is disturbed by the shortsighted preoccupations of current life. Book VII (the one Henry asserts is composed only of first- or secondhand reports) proposes a new, more inclusive theme for the Norman kings: "It will soon appear how God began to afflict the Normans themselves, His own avengers, with various disasters."[51] The book ends with the death of Henry I.

Except for the interesting idea that the Normans, having served to punish the English, must, in divine justice, turn on themselves, the contemporary history Henry records here breaks loose from the thematic grid against which the account of past time is pinned. Book VIII begins with what seems the logical end of VII: a character sketch of Henry I and an account of the decomposition of his corpse, treated as an exemplum. The author's plan for including the extraneous epistles after Book VII may have had something to do with that arrangement. Toward the end of the last book, seeming to feel that his work appeared an inadequate reflection of the great events of his lifetime, Henry apologizes for not writing more, but excuses himself on the grounds that fuller treatment would take too many books.[52] Book VIII ends with the accession of Henry II: "And now a new book must be given to the new reign." But no more was ever written.

The theme of the five plagues serves to control the historical materials Henry selected from his authorities, to organize them into intelligible segments of a reasonably intelligible whole without, however, having much effect on the narrative. The expository narrative reads like the neatly arranged patchwork it is; the theme of divine intention is mostly confined to the openings and closings of the first six books. It "explains," with largeness of gesture, the course that history (or God) had taken on the island; it does not interfere very much with the details of that history as Bede and others had chosen to record them.

The history is predominantly secular in content, preoccupied with kings and conquests, and comparatively little space is given to ecclesiastical history as such. The movements of nations, directed by God against one another to fulfill some great if often unspecified purpose, fill most of the narrative. In general, Henry is cautious about assigning characteristics to whole peoples; he usually speaks from the point of view of England's welfare, and he judges its various inhabitants and invaders according to the damage they did. He simply echoes Bede in condemning the Britons for irreligiousness and the Saxons for bellicosity, but his treatment of the Danes is curiously sympathetic. He does not soften their ferocity (they are frequently noted tossing children on the points of their spears) but admires their headstrong tactics and considers them loyal and honorable. In Book VI Henry remarks that, by killing Canute, the Danes were guilty of treason for the first time,[53] and he describes Canute and Harthacanute as embodying the bravery, candor, and piety of their race.

In contrast to the honorable simplicity of the Danes, the Normans are cunning, subtle, and rapacious. They seem to Henry peculiarly well suited to be instruments of divine justice: "God chose the Normans for the displacing of the English because He saw that they held the prerogative over all other peoples for singular savagery."[54] Henry's general harshness to the Normans seems the result of his specific complaints with William II, Henry I, and Stephen—mainly over taxes, mistreatment of the Church and of his friends, and the chaos caused by the Anglo-Norman nobles during Stephen's reign. He never, however, questions the legitimacy of William I's rule. The Godwin family is presented as the very type of self-seeking treachery, covetousness, and perjury (Henry tells the anecdote of Godwin choking to death at King Edward's table after challenging God).[55] He charges that Harold swore on many relics to defend William's right to the succession and later perjured himself.[56]

Henry admired the example of the Anglo-Saxon kings who gave up their earthly crowns to win eternal ones by becoming monks; but so long as kings held the empty power of worldly scepters, Henry, an administrator himself, was prepared to respect vigorous and just rule. Canute was the only king to win his full approval for courage, energy, justice, and piety and was the only king Henry credits with abolishing a tax.[57] He is severe on William I for his greed and cruelty.[58] William II, of course, pleased no one.[59] But Henry I, during whose reign Henry was an adult, is shown to be a character full of plausible contradictions, and his sternness came to seem attractive in the confused years after his death.[60] Both of Henry I's successors appear to have been equally disastrous for England, and their respective supporters guilty of perjury, violence, self-seeking, and felony. The history ends, or rather stops, at the accession of Henry Plantagenet, who is greeted as a welcome relief from misrule and no rule.

Historians of the reign of Stephen who turn to Henry of Huntingdon as a well-placed contemporary observer tend to agree strongly enough with Thomas Arnold about Henry's being "curt and perfunctory" when he ought to have been detailed and thorough. He condenses quite a lot of event into the seventh and eighth books; the poems that decorate the text throughout begin to proliferate, along with lengthy and fairly conventional speeches. These speeches, however, are not entirely without historical interest. Given contemporary conventions of "high" literature, it is easy enough to accept the idea that Henry and his patron would have considered a bare narrative, however long and detailed, a poor job of history writing. If an historian was capable of composing in hexameter and creating interesting speeches, he brought far nobler gifts to literature than the mere ability to copy down everything he had ever heard. Still, Henry does apologize at one point for not writing more history, and he may have felt the inadequacy of his record.

Stephen enters England over broken oaths, brings chaos and suffering on the land, and breaks his own coronation oath (the only coronation oath Henry mentions) by refusing to protect the Church or to abolish the Danegeld. God finally moves in just anger to break Stephen's power and kills his only son.[61] Stephen had, after all, been violently harsh to Henry's bishop and patron, Alexander of Lincoln, and to Alexander's uncle, Roger of Salisbury. Their arrest is described as an unprovoked act of shameless oppression, and the castles Stephen appropriates from Alexander are made to seem merely pretty country retreats.[62]

The history is not heavily "ecclesiastical" in tone or content, but Henry was certainly "episcopal" in his interests and point of view. He discusses Bishop Remigius, who moved the diocesan seat from Dorchester to Lincoln, and treats the election of Robert Bloet to Lincoln at some length in order to defend his memory against a charge of simony.[63] Alexander "The Magnificent" is naturally enough a leading figure in events and is given a full character sketch at his death.[64]

The Divinity, as an actor in human history, is a distant, architectural God in the early books, building the slow alternations of sin and retribution; in the contemporary books, He becomes nearer and irritable, inclined to be partisan, and quick to send portents and meaningful death, especially during the unstable hatreds of Stephen's reign. He is, most often, the "Deus irritatus," easily angered and freely, if not always consistently, violent.

There is little suggestion in the history, or in any of his other writings, that Henry felt any particular imaginative sympathy with his theme of the five plagues. It was a useful formal device for controlling masses of information without interfering seriously with authorial freedom. Henry's use of the successive invasions (instruments of divine justice) to open and close the books of his history and to enclose chapters of diverse, even miscellaneous material was merely his variation on a commonplace device of medieval narrative literature—the placing of a frame around a great expanse of unrelated picture. The frame could be any kind of coherent beginning and end (a hero beginning and ending his adventures, for example) that allowed the author to do anything he chose with the narrative material in the middle. The device was rudimentary by modern notions of structure, but it appears to have satisfied medieval readers. This matter of narrative structure is discussed at greater length in chapter 8;[65] it is important to note here only that Henry used the invasion–plagues in a rather perfunctory manner to give his book some design, and in spite of the fact that it purports to be the key to the meaning of English history, he never expands the idea or gives it any depth or much detail. His real interest lay elsewhere.

> See, great father, what becomes of the powerful:
> See how the honor, the pleasure, the
>   glory of the world come to nothing.[66]

> Behold the great eminence, how quickly, how lightly it is annihilated.[67]

> These things, once you have gotten them, you have them;
> but once you have the world's goods, they flow away like
> water from a broken vase, and you have nothing.[68]

The first quotation is the last two lines of the invocation poem in the prologue to the history; the second is the last line of the history in its first edition; the third is the ending of the epilogue that concluded the first few editions of the history. (The "great eminence ... annihilated" refers to the accidental death of the young French prince, Philip; the other lines were intended for general application.) These particular lines were chosen, not for their singularity—similar statements virtually make up the warp of Henry's expressed thoughts about life and history and himself—nor as being particularly striking (though I rather like the one about "water from a broken vase . . ."), but for their placement in the first edition of the history. Those were the thoughts, about mutability and death, with which Henry concluded each distinct major section of the history: prologue, narrative, epilogue. And they were not only his final thoughts but his first responses, his continuing reflections, his recurring doubts about human life, especially as lived in prosperity, dignity, and good fortune.

Henry did not rely on Bishop Alexander to discover, by his own lights, how the pleasures and honors of the world come to nothing; at every reasonably appropriate spot in the history, he pauses to note in explicit and often exclamatory language that greatness declines, pomp is humiliated, fortune turns, and power has no sway over death. The excursuses on the brevity of the enjoyment of fame and power and on the inevitability of death begin with Henry's reflections on the emperors of Roman Britain:

> . . . concerning the forty-five emperors who ruled Britain as well as other parts of the world: if anyone could acquire renown in heaven, they have it, because they have none here and now . . . even a fairly long discussion of their deeds seems dry, a cause for boredom and distaste. For that reason, considering them—for whose power and majesty the whole world scarcely sufficed—we understand how our fame is nothing, and our power and pride, for whose sake we labor and sweat and rage.[69]

He notes, after recording a battle in 675 between Wulfere, king of Mercia, and Escwin of Kent, in which both armies suffered considerable loss, "It is worthwhile to observe how vile are the acts of men, how vile the glorious battles of kings and their noble exploits."[70] The vileness lay, not in the deeds themselves—the carnage or cruelty—but in the fact that one of the kings died that same year, the other the next. All their efforts came, in the end, to nothing, as Henry would say.

> Therefore, reader, observe and reflect how quickly the greatest names devolve to nothing. Pay attention, I beg of you, and study how nothing in the world endures, so that you may acquire the kingdom for yourself, and that substance which lacks nothing, that name and dignity which will not pass away, that memory and renown which will

nowhere grow old. It is the highest prudence to think about
this, the greatest wit to seek it, the greatest happiness
to acquire it.[71]

From ancient (that is, Roman Britain) through old (Anglo-
Saxon) to modern (Anglo-Norman) times, the *Historia* is woven
through with this strand of melancholy distaste. The great and
prosperous, having the most to distract them from thoughts of
loss and death, are in most urgent need of advice, and Henry's
book sometimes seems determined to become entirely a *me-
mento mori* addressed to royalty. The Anglo-Saxon kings who
set aside their crowns to become monks—Cedwalla and Ina of
Wessex, Ethelred and Cenred of Mercia—are the archetypes of
human wisdom: the noble renunciation of everything most
seductive and most vile in order to embrace that serene death in
the midst of life which was the monk's symbolic state. Their
example is urged upon living rulers (though surely the idea of
William Rufus or Henry I becoming monks had its little irony for
Henry as for us): "Therefore, present rulers of the earth, imitate
those kings, wise and blessed, not raging and wretched."[72] The
finest regal exemplum was King Ceolwulf of Northumbria, who
was so moved by Bede's conversation and writings that he too
descended from his throne to ascend, by a different route, to
another kingdom. Henry's Ceolwulf is not only a ruler but a
reader—and a reader of a fascinating transparency of mind.

Ceowulf spoke often with Bede while he was alive, and
both before and after his death, often consulted the
History with his own eyes. He began to examine the
deeds and death of each king attentively, and he saw in a
clearer light that earthly kingdoms and mortal things
are acquired in labor, possessed in fear, and lost with
grief. Some people, at the sight of beautiful and appealing
things, were foolish or weak although they had heard it
preached that those things should be forsaken and
despised, and it seemed to him frivolous and irrational,
because they did not yet grasp how the treasures of the
world sting, how they come to nothing and bear no fruit
except ultimate punishment—no king, however wise and
experienced, ever prevented it. For he felt within himself
that his own realm had been obtained laboriously and
possessed in fear, but he refused to lose it with grief.
Willingly, therefore, as the master and not the servant

of riches, as a great man, he threw away the vile things. It incensed him most of all that when boys or women and the common mob, or even the rich, pressed forward upon seeing him and marveled at his good fortune, he himself was tormented inwardly by mortal worries and betrayals and every kind of failure, and he was tortured in mind and body. And just when others judged him most blessed, he who alone inspired the secrets of his mind, judged him most wretched.[73]

Ceolwulf continued to study the lives of kings in Bede's history and to experience that uneasy revulsion from everything for which he was so ignorantly envied until, in the habit of a monk, he exchanged his false crown for a true.[74]

The idea of a king anxiously searching the pages of history for an escape from the torments of regality is, naturally, very attractive, the more so as the Normans were hardly to be found in libraries looking for spiritual peace. (The figure of Ceolwulf with his heavy scepter in one hand, his "Bede" in the other, is placed just after the account of Bede's death—an elegant tribute.) The bare, chronicled facts of Ceolwulf's life do not include his mental anguish or his reading; and the movements of his mind, most notably his ironic self-consciousness in the face of vulgar admiration, are all Henry's.

The vileness of Ceolwulf's existence resided, apparently, in his own mind—like all kings, he had much to worry about; everyone else ("boys or women and the common mob, or even the rich") was so obtuse as to think him a fortunate man. But the anguish of a sensitive mind, imagining in advance what it is "to lose with grief" is not Henry's only approach to a certain kind of lesson. He ventures the case of King Henry I, successful in all his major projects since youth, apparently free from the subtle pains of sensibility, and unfortunate only in the tragicomical contrast between his bastards and his one surviving legitimate daughter. One would not seriously think that either Henry's life or death (brought on by complications following an indigestible dinner of eels) lent itself to the high moral line, but his corpse obligingly devolved, indeed deliquesced, to a condition at once putrescent and didactic. Henry lingers over the inevitable fate of the royal remains: the intestines, brain, and eyes were given separate burial at Rouen and the rest salted down and sent on to Caen, where no amount of salt and bullhide shrouding could retard a

31

general decay too advanced to conceal and too revolting for me, though not for Henry, to describe.[75]

> Therefore, Reader, whoever you are, see the corpse of the most powerful king whose head crowned in gold and choicest gems had shone as in the light of God, whose sceptered hand had been radiant, whose person had glowed in cloth of gold, whose mouth was accustomed to the most delectable and exquisite dishes, before whom all rose up, all were in dread, all rejoiced, all marveled. See, I say, what that body has become, how horribly it has moldered away, how wretchedly it has been degraded. See the end of those things over which this judgment ever hangs, and learn contempt for anything so limited, anything doomed to annihilation.[76]

It is, at last, not the meanness or misery of life itself but the change—so saddening to witness, so fearful to anticipate—into death that matters. The effect on the shocked spectator, "Reader, whoever you are," of majesty and luxury melting into viscous horror, of the world's happiest gifts suddenly foul, gross, and filthy, is the anxious heart of Henry's book.

The epilogue (first attached to the history when it ended in 1129) leaves, in every way, the elaborate and formal prologue far behind. The artificial beauties of the prologue, the invocation of pagans and Christians to witness to the dignity of tracing famous footsteps, the utility of history, the bestial state of life without memory, all are forgotten before a plea more urgent and more personal:

> Tell me, Henry, author of this history, tell me—who were the archdeacons of former times? Who is to say if any of them was noble or ignoble, famous or obscure, praiseworthy or shameful, elevated or failed, wise or foolish? If any of them undertook some labor for the sake of praise and fame, when now no memory can remain of him any more than of his horse or his ass, why did that wretch so weary his mind?[77]

These are the sentiments which conclude with the sad image of the world slipping away like water from a broken vase, leaving nothing.

When the steadily increasing length of the history swallowed the epilogue into its middle, it was handily put to use as a preface to the genealogical epistle once intended for the edification of Henry I—its gloomy sentiments introducing the rolls of dead eminence. The concluding lines of the epilogue, about the anticipation of rotting in our graves making us turn our thoughts from the enticements of the world to the truly valuable things in God—those things that will not run out of the shattered vase of our earthly life—introduce the epistle *De regibus*, and, together, they make a new work that teaches the frailty of human greatness (set into the eighth book of the expanded edition of the history). The lists of past rulers are preceded and concluded by some pointed remarks to Henry I: asking whether he should so embrace the realm he acquired by heredity or whether there might be something further worth acquiring; reminding him how the most terrible, the most magnificent rulers all come "to nothing"; reminding him that his days of rule are not merely passing but fleeing. "Vale rex...."[78] Not perhaps the most amusing trifle to present to an aging monarch, but such words were conventional then, sermonlike, unprovocative, except to a sensitive ear.

This was a kind of literature very much to Henry's taste. As these passages should suggest, the history itself, in its didactic aspect, is not only a tale of human sin and divine punishment, but also an extended illustration of the treacherous volatility of pleasure and of the false promises of fame. In short, it is a recital of the entire array of anxieties, revulsions, longings, and resentments found in that genre of Christian letters called *contemptus mundi*. Henry's epistle *De contemptu mundi* is the only self-announced work on that theme, being a *contemptus* treatise illustrated by examples from recent history; but the *Historia Anglorum* is shot through with commands and pleas to read it as if it too were a *contemptus* treatise; the epilogue plus genealogy make up another separate treatise; the poems often play on the same ideas. Mistrust of the world's empty promises—that anything *sub coelo* will endure (including an author's reputation)—is the refrain of Henry's thoughts. All assembled, it seems a fair amount of labor to show that everything in this world comes to nothing (*nihil* being one of Henry's favorite words) in the end. Why, as Henry says, did that hypothetical forgotten archdeacon so weary his brain to write what would preserve his memory no longer than that of his horse? Ironic self-address ("Tell me,

Henry, author of this history, tell me—who were the archdeacons of former times?") comes easily to him.

Yet, to speak of irony or urgency may seem to many rather to be missing the point in a twelfth-century writer who displays the themes and attitudes characteristic of *contemptus mundi* literature. As with so many medieval genres, the very words, *contemptus mundi*, summon up regiments of conventional expression, set motifs, thoughts, and tropes so often used with so little variation as to have lost the capacity to convey any personal message. The language of *contemptus mundi* was indeed highly conventionalized by the time Henry of Huntingdon began to read or write it; from biblical and pagan antiquity through patristic times and the early centuries of the Middle Ages, writer had followed upon writer with extraordinary fidelity to the established ideas and expressions of disdain for the corrupt and evanescent world, and of longing for the pure and eternal Divine.[79] The exact subcategory into which Henry's writings fit is the *ubi sunt*—moral writings on the vanity and sin of the transitory pleasures of the world where all must pass away, with special emphasis on the rhetorical question in an early-established formula: where are the rich, the powerful, the beautiful of past years? Dead and forgotten. Therefore, mortal, place your hopes on that which will neither decay nor die, the *ubi sunt* writer always concludes.[80] This observation that even the great die, usually followed by lists of examples from the history and literature of antiquity, has been called by one major student of it, "a kind of theological banality."[81]

Certainly the recoil in disdain and fear from everything that is transitory, most notably human life and its fragile joys, was a commonplace of Christian thought—at once cliché and genuine. The literature of that spiritual cliché was also a mix of convention and sincerity. The modern scholarly impulse has mainly dwelt on the convention, tracing the motifs and language of *contemptus* literature as though they constitute a purely formal tradition. There is considerable value in that approach, but it tends to relegate all *contemptus* writings to a dead topos—a sterile convention or set-piece whose use by a long succession of writers made increasingly formulaic and banal. And the extreme degree of verbal repetition that marks *contemptus* writing does almost repel interpretation beyond elaborate cataloging. Still, medieval writers were more content than modern with ready-turned phrases and could use them to express utterly sincere and individual thoughts. Peter Damian, whose genuine revulsion from worldliness of all kinds no one doubts, was not entirely original in his *De fluxa mundi gloria et saeculi despectione,* and yet the whole course of his career and writings compels belief in the genuine impulse behind the conventional language.[82] The weight of so much tradition should not bury the occasional intensely felt work.

The scholarly problem of confronting a vision of the world so common to medieval literature that it can easily seem a formulary of dead sentiments has been discussed most thoroughly and vigorously by Francesco Lazzari, for whom the interest of the genre lies, not in its poetic continuities, but in its ability, sometimes, to reveal the intensely personal life of the very mortal Christian. Lazzari objects eloquently to the more common motif-tracing approach as tending to wash out all trace of the personal under the relentless march of analogues and influences.[83] While admitting that much of *contemptus* literature is banal and rote, he insists that that banality should not be the object of scholarly attention but, rather, the text, which is "a true document of life":[84] the commonplaces separated from original elements and the theological and literary influences from the force of experience.[85] The author's life, influences, and experience, so far as they can be known, his writings, the characteristics of his mind—all examined with close attentiveness to nuances and shades of meaning—should distinguish the *contemptus* treatise, written in response to authentic, individual feeling, from the literary exercise.

As Lazzari argues so well, literary forms and formulas are not necessarily empty. They can give expression and articulate life to feelings that otherwise might be left inchoate and silent; the feelings common to a shared culture and historical moment are not any less real because shared. Henry of Huntingdon fits easily with the newly intense and vociferous *contemptus mundi* writers of the early twelfth century, when the genre proliferated with a special new energy.[86] He was one of the true *contemptus* writers: the repetition, the variation, the continual return to one central reaction in a variety of literary settings, as well as certain special circumstances of his life, make him a *contemptus mundi* writer of more than ordinary interest.

The epistle *De contemptu mundi,* addressed to a friend,

"Walter" (speculatively identified as a fellow archdeacon of Leicester),[87] is strongly marked—rather more so than the history—with that strain of elegiac sentimentality, a "dolce malincolia" as Lazzari calls it, characteristic of much *ubi sunt* literature.[88] Walter, at the beginning, is spoken to as one with whom Henry once shared his youth, now his old age: "Walter, once the ornament of youth . . . now you are consumed with mournful grief."[89] The youth who once accepted gifts of poems from his young friend now receives the letters of one old man to another: no longer a "song about love" but a letter concerning "contempt for the world."[90] At the end of the letter, the writer learns that his friend has just died: "But before I had finished this letter, I was informed that my friend, to whom I was writing, was dead. . . . Now indeed I cannot send you a letter, but an epitaph; briefly then, let the memorial be written, with tears."[91] A case of life imitating art? Perhaps.

The epistle begins with a discussion of the diocese of Lincoln, "our church," and of the magnificence of Robert Bloet's court, in which Henry was raised. The cathedral clergy from the time of Remigius to Henry's day are listed—all now absorbed into oblivion. The second chapter describes young men who expected to rule but died before their reign; the third chapter shows that even clever and talented men cannot prevent ultimate humiliation and loss; the fourth offers noblemen, once powerful and famous, now gone. The fifth chapter shows that even kings suffer misfortune and failure. The sixth chapter, especially poignant, contains lists of deceased bishops and abbots, all men of good reputation and accomplishment, whose lives and deaths inspire Henry with bitter reflections on the treachery of life's promises. Numerous names appear both in the history and the epistle and to the same purpose.

Henry was not really old when he wrote that letter; he lived and wrote for another twenty years. But the literary exaggeration is not wholly artifice, for he seems to have left far behind him the frivolous élan that produced the "song about love," which he recalls with obvious fondness, but as the sort of thing he can no longer write. Life, he would have us know, has shown him nothing but its own lying speciousness, and that through the example of the lives of men he knew, all apparently favored and fortunate, all reduced in time by loss, disease, grief, and accident and cut down at last by death. And thus his treatise on contempt for the fool's gold of the world is based on "those things which I myself have seen"[92] and, in that respect, is a genuine innovation on the *ubi sunt* mode. To our eyes, what Henry had seen was twelfth-century life at its best, raised far above the grinding squalor of common experience. With his own, he had seen Bishop Robert Bloet weeping at dinner for the shabbiness of his servants and dying in the presence of the king whose disfavor had so reduced him to poverty and grief; he saw the succession of archdeacons of Lincoln Cathedral—all dead and "absorbed in oblivion"; the young victims of the White Ship; Simon, son of Robert Bloet, "raised like a prince," made dean of Lincoln and lifted high in royal favor—then reduced to prison, exile, and misery.[93] Nobles, scholars, crowned princes, whether raised by birth, merit, or luck, all suffer death, often preceded by pain or disgrace; even virtue and intellectual distinction are quickly forgotten. Just as in the history, but more densely assembled in the epistle, Henry watches and mourns for lives spent pursuing those things which are "acquired in labor, possessed in fear, and lost with grief."

The lesson is always there to resolve the anxieties and regrets raised by the parade of the human condition: "Therefore, Walter, think how this present life is nothing. And when we see how the powerful with their great acquired possessions have accomplished nothing, lest we too accomplish nothing, let us seek that other way of life in which we may hope and acquire blessedness."[94]

But the resolution never quite holds; however rigorously moral the contempt for them, the tears for things will reappear: "For our death . . . is continual. . . . Whatever you do, whatever we say . . . suddenly it dies. The memory of those things survives for a while about the dead. And when even that perishes, it is like a second death and all our deeds and words are utterly annihilated. . . . They come to nothing."[95] Just as Henry in the epilogue to the history hovers ironically about the absurdity of writing what no one will read or remember and has King Ceolwulf at the height of his reign inwardly racked by the knowledge that he had struggled to acquire what he was helpless to hold, the heart of this kind of contempt for the world lies in hopeless attraction to its terrible, fleeting pleasures. The things

37

of the world Henry proposes for disdain are not low indulgences, the base satisfactions of the flesh, but pride in achievement, respected office, dignity and merit rewarded. Those, as he very well knew, are the things that are most bitterly "lost with grief." The alternations of fury and resignation at the loss of the deceptively "solid" gratifications and at the loss of life itself are unmistakably genuine.

The careful historicity of the *contemptus* epistle and the painful moral vision that pervades the history, making the epistle seem a précis of the history, were the literary expressions of what seems to have been the mental and moral situation of Henry's life. He was fascinated by the cruelty of prosperity in the face of death and eternity, and with good reason. Henry had enjoyed much prosperity: Lincoln was England's richest diocese, and an archdeaconry represented a considerable share in it; his literary reputation must have been gratifying; his acquaintance extended to men of rank and position; and his family must have reflected and enhanced all of that good fortune. But comfort and security, tempered by good education and refined tastes, can produce introspection and uneasy yearnings as well as complacency. When Henry wrote the sections of the epistle in which he lists the past archdeacons of Lincoln, now gone and forgotten, as exempla teaching disdain for the world, he clearly knew just how inexorably fixed was his own name in that mortal roll call. In fact, the mark of the personal is so unmistakable in Henry's *contemptus* writing because he himself was always its central exemplum.

The concentration on contemporary history in the epistle, the author's voice in Ceolwulf's musings, the apostrophe to himself in the epilogue (and elsewhere) all point to a sensibility absorbed in the attractions and disappointments of the world and longing for stability in that tense, ambivalent way typical of *contemptus* writing in the twelfth century. Henry's reflections, whether occasioned by Roman emperors or Norman nobles, always turn back to himself and are always ironic (after all, he never did give up his office or his writing or, so far as we know, anything).

In some ways his understanding of the world's treachery ran as deep and emotional as Peter Damian's; they are not such an incongruous pair as might, at first, seem. The connection between Gregorian reform, with its emphases on simony and celibacy, and contempt for the world as a literary topos is straightforward and clear.[96] The genre *contemptus mundi*, already old by the late eleventh century, made a natural vehicle for writers like Damian who wanted to air some of the new currents of feeling and thought; revulsion was often the motive–impulse of reform. But Henry, too, son of a cleric, uncanonical inheritor of a valuable benefice, prosperous and married, had his interest in reform. He was against it. The special effect that the introduction of Gregorian reform to England—especially council decrees aimed at abolishing clerical marriage—had on passages of Henry's history is discussed at greater length in pages 41–47; but in brief, Henry reported the council's deliberations as the collective expressions of ignorant foreign interference, hypocrisy, and misguided zeal. He was not one of Archbishop Anselm's enthusiastic admirers.

Reading certain passages of the history alone, it is easy to see Henry as unequivocally antireformist. There is no question about the sincerity of his views in favor of clerical marriage—such views were still traditional and respectable in England—but the atmosphere, as it were, of reform did not leave any intelligent cleric totally unmoved. The reform movement, regarded in its broadest sense, was as much a response to restless spiritual disaffections from settled Christian institutions and modes of life as it was a program of papal ambitions. Feeling, however tepid, among educated clerics, regular and secular, ran to reform, and worldliness, ever more alluring in the prosperous twelfth century, inspired longings and disgusts proportional to that allure. Previous generations of substantial, married archdeacons who enjoyed the favor of great patrons and the comfort of sons to benefit by their possessions would not have dwelt so ironically, so lengthily on the nothingness of it all, would not have told us of literary archdeacons whose renown lasted as long as that of a horse. Those are the refinements of sensibility: they lead seldom to the monastery, often to poetry. But action is a fairly crude measure of sincerity. As one who had embraced so much of the world, Henry was perfectly aware that his favorite lament might ring false in many ears, hence the ironic strain running through the *dolce malincolia*. However ready with sarcasm and anger for legates and bishops who began, during his adult years, to bring the message of reform to England, Henry   *39* was not insensitive to the inner tensions of his own situation: his clerical father, inherited benefice, uncanonical wife and children, worldly literary ambitions, all surface in the anxiety and edginess of his "contempt" for the world. His literary preoccupation with the *contemptus mundi* theme was the outlet for spiritual restlessness and self-contempt. Henry was no Anselm, but he was of the same world.

The poems as well tell the same recurring thoughts about the world, inexorable death, delusive pleasures. A long poem on "De contemptu visibilum" begins:

> Death hastens, you linger;
> Death batters the door, you dally;
> Death enters, you wait.
>   Mortal, remember what you are.
> While you guard your possessions,
> Why lose yourself?
> Will you lose your wealth with me?
>   If not yourself, what do you have?
> You neglect yourself to care for your belongings,
>   however few.
>   I warn you: Take more care of yourself
> And less of those things.[97]

"But what do the possessions of men become, or man?" the poet inquires later in the same poem, and answers, "Food for worms." Death hastens, certainly, but the world is hard to leave, and the things that are "acquired in labor" and "possessed in fear" are so truly "lost in grief."

Contempt for the world was the informing spirit of Henry's literary work and of his spiritual life as well, but when threatened in his professional or domestic character, he was ready with another spirit. Every natural tie and lifelong habit attached Henry to the "world," in the common medieval sense of human institutions and activities and values.[98] And as his poem so ironically celebrates, he cultivated his small worldly corner very well—and half despised himself for it. Henry knew all about reform, at least in the sense that he understood its deepest impulse, but he was also a man bound by many interlacing duties, loyalties and interests to the old world of clerical life, and however coldly he might mock himself and it in the public privacy of poetry, he did not like reformers.

By the time the first edition of the history was finished, about 1129, there had been four reform councils in England whose decrees were specifically aimed at abolishing clerical marriage and its inevitable corollary, the inheritance of benefices. They made a natural subject for the history but had an awkward effect on it; Henry's angry inability to accept that central issue of Gregorian reform, modified by a wary reluctance to state his objections openly, shaped his account of the introduction of reform to England with insinuation, slander, and prevaricating silence.

Although Archbishop Anselm's adoption of the Gregorian program was the first really determined effort to impose celibacy on English clerks in higher orders, the canonical injunctions against marriage and concubinage were sufficiently well known in England to make the disapproving surprise that pervades Henry's account of the first reform council of 1102 (London) sound a little disingenuous:

> In the same year [1102] at the feast of Saint Michael, Archibishop Anselm held a council at London, in which he forbade wives to the priests of England, something formerly not prohibited. The prohibition seemed quite proper to some, but dangerous to others; for in their attempt at purity, many might fall into disgusting filth, to the great shame of the name of Christian. In that same council abbots who had acquired their abbeys in a way that God forbade, lost them just as God willed.[99]

Henry's emphatically terse remark that wives were "formerly not prohibited," while not exactly true, was a live reflection of the particular recalcitrance of the English clergy on that issue and, in a way, of the inconsistent enforcement that canons enjoining celibacy had received in England.[100] The reforming efforts of tenth-century prelates and kings, almost entirely inefficacious, may have passed into such oblivion that a twelfth-century writer, even an historian, could be honestly ignorant of them, unless he chose to find and study pre-Conquest law codes. But celibacy was urged upon the clergy in the eleventh century, even before the Conquest, with some insistence. Aelfric wrote several pastoral letters in the vernacular to persuade as many clerks as possible that marriage was not acceptable for men of their station. R. R. Darlington was convinced that clerical marriage was, in Ethelred's reign, "a burning question . . . and a   *41*

subject of acute controversy" and that Aelfric's letters on the
subject were widely read in the eleventh century. The earlier
portions of the *Historia Anglorum*, however, contain no notice
of the issue.[101]

Regardless of the extent of Henry's honest ignorance of fairly
early prohibitions, it is unlikely that he or his father was
unaware of Lanfranc's decree of 1076 which, though something
of a compromise, foretold that the Conqueror's church would
not overlook even entrenched disobedience.[102] The decree allowed married parish priests to keep their wives but flatly
forbade marriage under any circumstances to canons. One of
those who subscribed was Remigius, the bishop of Lincoln who
made Nicholas first archdeacon of Huntingdon and probably
gave him his canonry as well. Nor should the status of clerical
marriage in ecclesiastical law have been concealed from a canon
of Lincoln after Lanfranc's collection of canon law, an abridge-
ment of the False Decretals, had been dispersed to the cathedral
libraries.[103] One twelfth-century manuscript of Lanfranc's collection survives at Lincoln Cathedral, to whose library Archdeacon Nicholas donated a Bible. Though it could be argued that
no previous English council had prohibited marriage precisely as
Anselm's did, no one could pretend, then or now, that canon
law, in collections reflecting the special concerns of Gregorian
reform, was unknown or unaccepted in England by the early
twelfth century.[104] Henry's assertion that wives were "formerly
not prohibited" was the conservative's protest, a way of saying
that no one had ever seriously interfered with the domestic
arrangements of respectable men like his father, and that no one
should.

The opinions ascribed vaguely to the "others" who thought
enforced celibacy "dangerous" reveal the basic emotional protest
of the married clergy, which inevitably must sound like a
petulant threat: if they are denied marriage, they must descend
to something worse, to "disgusting filth." A similar argument
was more formally stated by the carefully anonymous Anonymous of York (or Rouen or elsewhere) about 1100 in a pamphlet
in favor of clerical marriage. He quotes Paul (1 Cor. 7 : 2),
"Because of fornication, let each have his own wife," and
comments that "as for priests, some are continent, and some are
incontinent. The ones who are continent are so by a gift of God,

and without that gift and grace they could not be continent."[105] Like the Anonymous in his caution as well, Henry does not venture to expose himself as one of those to whom celibacy seemed impossibly difficult. Interestingly, he fully accepts the attack on simony. He shows he was not ideologically anti-Gregorian and even allows that part of Anselm's campaign the accolade of divine justice.

Anselm's decrees were not obeyed. Eadmer, who has been called the official historian of the reform party,[106] wrote an account of the council, full of indignation that the canons effected nothing but mass disobedience. Anselm, in his letters to Herbert, bishop of Thetford; Archbishop Gerard of York; and William, archdeacon of Canterbury, revealed some attempts to enforce the celibacy canons but, even more clearly, revealed the ingenuity of the men who "interpreted" them into farce and the blatancy of those who did not even bother to do that. The very punctilious bowed to the letter of the law against cohabitation with a woman and simply moved their wives next door.[107] Repellent as he found compromises, Anselm had to request a dispensation from Paschal II in 1107 for advancing the sons of priests to sacred office "on account of the conditions of the time."[108]

By the time the political situation and Anselm's determination fostered another reform council, it was 1108—just two years before Henry was to succeed his father as archdeacon, and Anselm and his advisers had some stringent and sophisticated methods to introduce for enforcing the canons of 1102. The peculiar interest these methods held for archdeacons and the unlikeliness of any cathedral dignitary remaining ignorant of the decisions of a national council (especially those which concerned him directly) enable me to brave the treachery of arguments from silence. Henry simply omitted the Council of 1108 from his history, and that silence is resonant at once with rebellion and dejection.

Henry I completely supported Anselm's insistence on clerical celibacy and shared the initiative of calling the council to London because, according to Eadmer, "the king wanted to suppress the crime of incontinence."[109] The basic prohibitions had been stated clearly enough in 1102: subdeacons, deacons (who composed the order most eleventh- and twelfth-century archdeacons took), and priests were not to take wives or concubines, or were to separate from those they already had.[110] Six years later the concern was with enforcement, and that necessarily directed sharp attention on the archdeacons.

An archdeacon's chapter was the natural scene for the promulgation and enforcement of new council decrees as well as of established law. The duty of maintaining the discipline and reputation of the clergy made archdeacons take particular interest in the sexual morality of clerks; a set of visitation questions for archdeacons of the diocese of Lincoln from 1233 devotes eight of fifty questions to that subject.[111] Clearly, by his activity or neglect, an archdeacon could determine whether canon law were to stagnate as revered but dead letter or were to be assimilated to the living society.

The reformers in 1108 recognized the archdeacons' crucial power over the cause of celibacy and tried to create legislation that could persuade them to conform personally to the canons and to enforce the law on others. One decree specifically insists on celibacy for all archdeacons and canons, and another exacts an oath from all archdeacons that they not take bribes to overlook illicit situations, on pain of losing their archdeaconry if they should refuse the oath.[112] Henry's father certainly should have taken that oath, though Robert Bloet, bishop of Lincoln (in whose household Henry was raised), was himself married and may not have been an urgent reformer. Regardless of whether he took the oath or not, Nicholas did not lose his benefice and his son did inherit it. The council made such an awkwardly sensitive subject both for Nicholas in 1108 and for Henry at the time of writing, 1125–1129, that it defeated rhetoric and was excluded from the *Historia Anglorum*. It has recently been stated that the Council of 1108 brought archdeacons "an enormous accession of business—and profit" and was "the decisive factor in the emergence of the twelfth-century archdeacon as the formidable, ubiquitous, acquisitive figure which passed into contemporary proverb."[113] It is no quarrel with that position to remark that the council also brought some archdeacons considerable embarrassment.

Anselm died not long after his last council; Henry's obituary runs as follows: "Archbishop Anselm, the philosopher of Christ, died in Lent."[114] The death of Henry's father Nicholas occurred in

1110, and notice of it, in the text of the history, is separated from that of Anselm's death by only a few lines:

> In the same year Nicholas, father of the man who wrote this history, yielded to the rule of death, and was buried at Lincoln. Of him it has been said:
> "The star of clerks has fallen,
> Nicholas's light fades out;
> But the star of clerks having fallen,
> the citadel of God shines forth."
> The author has placed this in his work, that he might obtain a reciprocal labor from all his readers, since piety makes it fitting to say, "May his soul rest in peace. Amen."[115]

The contrast between the pride and warmth of Henry's obituary for his father and the cool politeness for Anselm is marked and intentional, yet Henry prudently refrains from mentioning the exact office of the "star of clerks"—hereditary benefices among the higher clergy could be written of only indiscreetly.

Though it too dealt primarily with clerical celibacy, the Council of London, 1125, received ample notice in the *Historia*:

> At Easter, John of Crema, a Roman cardinal, came to England, and visited each of the bishoprics and abbeys, not without collecting large gifts, and at the nativity of Mary he solemnly celebrated a council at London. But because Moses, the scribe of God, wrote, in sacred history as much of the vices as of the virtues of even his own relations, of the crimes of Lot, Reuben's sin, the betrayal of Simeon and Levi, the inhumanity of Joseph's brothers, it is fitting that we, also, make a true selection of good and evil for history. If any Roman or prelate is annoyed, he would do well to keep quiet lest he seem to follow John of Crema's example. For in the council he dealt with the wives of priests very severely, saying that it was the greatest sin to rise from the side of a whore and go to create the body of Christ. Yet having created the body of Christ that same day, he was caught after Vespers with a whore. Something so notorious cannot be denied, and should not be concealed. From being held everywhere in the highest honor, he was thrown into the greatest shame. He hurried away, confounded and inglorious by God's judgment.[116]

By 1125, more than protective loyalty to the memory of his father (dead fifteen years) provoked Henry to that righteously salacious treatment of the papal legate; he had a wife and children of his own to support and protect. Knowledge of Henry's personal loyalties changes the John of Crema story from malicious gossip to the desperately ungenerous attack of a failing cause. The suggestion of the legate's greed and the rhetorical elevation of the subject through biblical analogy (an uncommon technique in the *Historia*) work to persuade the reader without exposing the author. The women from whom the clerks must separate are always politely called "wives" (*uxores*) by Henry, and are insulted only by the legate as "whores" (*meretrices*).[117] And, of course, the legate is caught with a whore. Another bit of significant diction is the consistent use of the word *priests* to indicate the men who must not marry, though Henry could hardly help knowing that the canons specified subdeacons and deacons as well. The divine judgment that Henry invokes as principal agent in exposing the legate's hypocrisy is intended, I think, as an implied judgment of the legate's reforms.

Though Henry excuses his scandal-mongering by calling the incident too "notorious" (*apertissima*) to be denied, it did not seem to come to the attention of the chronicler he most often consulted. The Peterborough redaction of the Anglo-Saxon Chronicle, used extensively in the *Historia*, merely notes that the legate, John of Crema, held a council "and there proclaimed the same laws which Archbishop Anselm had formerly proclaimed and many more—though it was of little use. And from there he went overseas soon after Michaelmas."[118] Further, as C. N. L. Brooke suggests, Gilbert Foliot had a different memory of John of Crema and would scarcely have praised him as an effective, peaceful reformer in a circulating letter to the bishops of England had his name become a byword for hypocrisy and vice.[119]

The account of the Council of London, 1129, is the final occasion in the *Historia* for indignation over the suppression of clerical marriage. The vigorous adoption of the cause by Henry I—holding clerical wives for ransom as it were—is related with a kind of gloomy disdain for foolish prelates and venal king alike:

In August Henry held a great council at London to prohibit wives to priests. [Here, the *Historia* lists the bishops present, including Bishop Alexander of Lincoln.] These men were the doves of the realm and the light of sanctity at this time. The king deceived them through the simplicity of Archbishop William. For they conceded to the king justice over clerical wives, but they had no foresight, since it afterwards became apparent what a shameful situation had occurred. The king took infinite sums from the priests to redeem their wives. Then, but it was no use, the bishops regretted their concession, when everyone saw how the prelates had been deceived and the people oppressed.[120]

Clearly, Henry had little more patience with the naive "doves" than with the opportunist king. For, as he glumly remarked, it was "no use" (sed frustra) for them to recognize their mistake after having made it. In fact, the depression of his tone suggests that he very probably recognized that, though slipshod enforcement of the canons and payment of bribes could preserve clerical families for a while, protest against the law of celibacy was "no use" any longer.

The Henry of the epistle to Walter might seem to be quite a different man from the one who told dirty gossip about the papal legate. But he was sore and irritable on the subject of clerical marriage, and it is easy enough for us to understand how absurd the notion of putting aside his family at the behest of a Roman whim must have seemed. He did not put aside his family or his benefice, or put down his pen until compelled by mortality. Weakness before the demands of belief has always been a perfectly orthodox Christian experience and one easy to ridicule. Dr. Johnson, profoundly religious and profoundly human, always spoke kindly of the man he knew who always removed his hat when passing a church, although he never stepped inside one; it showed his principles were sound though his conduct was faulty.

Yet, a command to relinquish the world quite literally by becoming a monk is not, finally, the most compelling facet of Henry's contempt for the world. The "contempt" which he found to be the true and repeated wisdom of history is not so much a mode of life as a state of mind. Henry calls on his reader, "whoever you are," to despise wealth, power, and pleasure, to acknowledge their fragility and ultimate hollowness, and in so doing, to turn the mind to the secure happiness that only God can give. *Contemptus mundi* is an act of recognition and humility: the mind acknowledges that the best we can achieve for ourselves are castles of sand and, humbled, turns toward the eternal mansion. This *contemptus mundi* demands of prosperous men a genuine self-contempt and an ironical view of the world, but it does not undervalue the joy of life. The world of human attachments and human achievement draws every man powerfully after it—but the wise man goes without illusion.

On Himself

Your verses, Poet Henry, are quite well-worked,
    And so is your house, and your field;
And well-cultivated are your marriage bed,
    And your orchard.
A garden so variously cultivated thrives.
    O, everything of yours is done well—except yourself.
If anything is lacking, tell me,
    Tell me what it is.[121]

II
WILLIAM OF NEWBURGH

Two
THE SCHOLARLY SPIRIT

Among medieval historians, William of Newburgh is an extraordinarily attractive writer to modern readers.[1] Across eight centuries of ineluctable time, his voice sounds reassuringly near and intelligible and his mind gratifyingly limpid to those who would like an acquaintance with men of his century. William's historical work offers the reader more than the cold promise of deciphering; it promises intimacy. Modern historians have spoken of William with an exuberance of praise that betrays quite beautifully the impression he gives of being a distant, honored, and familiar colleague. Kate Norgate, summing up William's accomplishments for the *Dictionary of National Biography*, writes: "Both in substance and in form William's book is the finest historical work left to us by an Englishman of the twelfth century, ... he deals with his materials in the true historical spirit. He has the true historian's instinct for sifting wheat from chaff." She quotes Edward Freeman, who called William "the father of historical criticsm," and adds that "he never stoops to gossip" (which is, happily, not precisely true).[2] Faults are dismissed with amused frankness: "His facts are not always exact, and his dates rarely so."[3] I have quoted these words of praise mainly to show how easy historians find talking about William in contemporary terms—and modern language does seem to fit him fairly well. Compared with Henry of Huntingdon, Matthew Paris, or even William of Malmesbury or Bede, William often sounds like that thing that can only be described, vaguely but correctly, as a "professional."

But of course, he was not. William was a regular canon, educated in Newburgh Priory, whose extensive learning was, even by late twelfth century standards, a little old-fashioned in its sole literary and devotional emphasis on the Bible, the Fathers, and classical poets. The cathedral schools, even during William's lifetime, were offering new reading and new approaches to the old. He was a man clearly of his time and experience, whose special qualities of mind, so apparent and

attractive to modern readers, involved no conflict with traditional monastic learning and the traditional methods and aims of
historical literature. The difference in William is a matter of
conscious refinement and caution. He does not by any means
reject the medieval practice of "reading" events to discover,
beyond them or through them, a higher Christian reality; but he
also paid scrupulous attention to secular events before venturing
an interpretation. He seems to have been conscious of history as
a genre of literature that makes special demands of the writer—
demands of close attention to the created world: nature, men,
and events. The tradition of historical writing in which William
worked demanded also that an historian attempt to be a higher
critic and judge who "reads" morally as he records; William's
thoughtful reserve before that responsibility gave his work
balance and reflective depth. His respect for the profundity and
obliquity of the divine mind made him unwilling to blot out the
complexity of human experience for the sake of an edifying (and
simplifying) lesson.

What makes him seem accessible to modern historians is his
unusual willingness to talk about testimony, plausibility, interpretation, and explanation—subjects that usually lie silent beneath the written surface of medieval books. He thought about
testimony (or evidence, as we would call it) in terms of veracity,
completeness, and reliability, measured himself against Bede and
Bede against other historians, and generally spoke more openly
about writing history than most men before and many after him.

The setting of William's monastic life must have encouraged
his acuity and freshness of thought, although in ways that elude
hard description. He was a canon in the Augustinian priory of
Newburgh in Yorkshire, which had been founded on land given
by Roger Mowbrey to the church of Saint Mary of Newburgh in
1145 and filled with canons from Bridlington, a large and
prosperous priory founded in 1113–1114.[4] William spent his
youth at Newburgh Priory, certainly receiving his education
there, probably never leaving.[5]

The Augustinian order expanded to great numbers of small
houses throughout twelfth-century England and achieved great
prestige. Its prolific record of intellectual accomplishment made
it clearly distinguished, and yet even its modern historian, J. C.
Dickinson, cannot quite describe that distinction without resort-

ing to comparison with the more strikingly individual traits of the Cistercians and Carthusians.[6] Even in the twelfth century, a most perspicacious observer of the regular life could not describe the Augustinians directly but had to point to what they were not. Gerald of Wales speaks of them, with uncustomary approval (and perhaps some conscious derogation of Cistercian pretensions): "More content than others with a middling and modest position, . . . though placed in the world, they live uncontaminated by it, not known as litigious or quarrelsome, they fear public scandal too much to be tempted by luxury or lust."[7] The Augustinians were indeed moderate and humane in their conventual life, a pattern they achieved, not by having relaxed their rule, but by firmly adhering to an ideal of balance grounded in the history of the Church as they understood it. They never encouraged extreme asceticism and generally maintained some degree of pastoral care. Throughout his study of the Austin canons, Dickinson stresses their brave fidelity to an ideal easy to deride in an age for which asceticism was glamorous. "Discerning minds . . . realized that the regular canonical ideal, far from being a spiritual second best, as the monks were apt to regard it, was an ideal worthy of the highest admiration, and in its distrust of the rather fussy puritanism of the time it certainly strikes a curiously modern note."[8]

The Augustinians were an order very attractive to learned men. They did not emphasize study but somehow created the right atmosphere for it.[9] R. W. Hunt, in his "English Learning in the Late Twelfth Century," notes the large number of writers who were Augustinian canons though he, like others, is at an admitted loss to explain why: "This predominance has hardly been brought out sufficiently; and it is very difficult to suggest reasons for it. The Augustinians are a very elusive order. They have no rule that is worthy of the name and their constitutions . . . are not very helpful. Yet we have this undoubted intellectual activity that springs up very gradually."[10] Sir Richard Southern has also noticed the quiet, elusive virtues of these canons: "It was an order of compromise—between the world and its rejection, between the splendors of Benedictinism and the trivialities of disorganized colleges of clergy. Its houses could be humble yet satisfy the founder's desire for independence."[11] An Augustinian priory did not make the brilliant

53

setting for William of Newburgh that some of the cathedral schools or large abbeys might have, but its own modest virtues were very real and, it is easily imagined, good for the mind.

Although one cannot generalize about other Augustinian houses from the situation at Newburgh, Dickinson comments on the strong influence of local circumstances on the priories because of their comparative poverty and lack of central organization.[12] Dickinson refers to financial and political circumstances, but the same influences can be seen in intellectual and spiritual life. Newburgh very clearly felt the attraction of the major Cistercian houses nearby, Byland and Rievaulx. Even in the mid-twelfth century, Yorkshire was in a state of recovery from the Conqueror's devastations, a recovery significantly advanced by the Cistercian monks, who pioneered in both agrarian and intellectual ways, having brought with them connections with their Continental motherhouses.[13] The Yorkshire Cistercians generally encouraged historical writing; William's *Historia rerum Anglicarum* was commissioned by and dedicated to Abbot Ernald of Rievaulx, his commentary on the "Song of Songs" requested by and dedicated to Abbot Roger of Byland.[14] He speaks to these abbots in his dedications with warmth and respectful friendship. Throughout the *Historia* there are references to frequent visits to Byland, and the foundation of the Northern houses of Fountains, Rievaulx, and Byland is each discussed at length. With no apparent conflict of loyalties, William appears a strongly "Cistercian" Augustinian—a possibility that probably was one of the strengths of his order.

Concerning William's identity and life, the evidence amounts to the usual twelfth-century paucity. William's life and the various critical opinions of it have been set forth with exemplary clarity by John Gorman, who edited William's commentary on the "Song of Songs." My discussion of the biographical data follows Gorman's exposition fairly closely. Gorman cites postscripts and an *incipit* to two of the three manuscript copies of William's *Explanatio sacri epithalamii*, which identify him as "William Parvus" and as "Master William Parvus, canon of Newburgh."[15] Richard Howlett, who did not see the *Explanatio* manuscripts, accepts the name William Parvus tentatively as "only a nickname" on Leland's assertion of having seen it, but admits that expressions such as "ego servorum Christi minimus" and "meae parvitati" in William's dedicatory epistle might play on his own name.[16]

William states in the *Historia* that he was born in the first year of Stephen's reign.[17] Howlett, the Rolls Series editor, fixes that year as 1136 by demonstrating that William followed Henry of Huntingdon's chronology for the reign of Stephen.[18] The year of his death is somewhat doubtful. The *Historia* ends abruptly in May of 1198 and was clearly left unfinished; for that reason and others, Howlett has established the date of death as about May 1198.[19] Norgate has revised that date to 1201.[20] Norgate's revision rests on the interpretation of a passage concerning Roger, abbot of Byland, from Book I of the *Historia*, which gives indirect evidence about the date of composition: "And God blessed them and brought them, under Father Roger, from mean poverty to great prosperity; we should marvel at the sincerity of the abbot, who is still alive at a great age, about fifty-seven years of his administration having passed (administrationis suae annis circiter quinquaginta et septim expletis.)"[21]

The passage indicates that at the time of writing, Abbot Roger was alive and had completed a fifty-seven-year term of office. Information about Roger's abbacy is given by his successor Abbot Philip, who wrote a chronicle of the founding of Byland in 1197 that is now available only in the *Monasticon Anglicanum*.[22] Howlett apparently did not take into account the information in Philip's chronicle. Abbot Philip states that Roger became abbot in 1142, ruled for somewhat over fifty-four years, and resigned in 1196; he lived on at Byland until his death three years later (1198–1199), about fifty-seven years after his election to office.[23] Since Roger was alive and in his last year when William was writing Book I of the *Historia*, the work must have been begun late in 1198. Gorman agrees with Norgate that William's apparent assertion that Roger's abbacy lasted fifty-seven years can be reconciled with Philip's statement that Roger resigned after fifty-four years and lived three years more by interpreting William's text to mean that fifty-seven years had passed since Roger's election.[24] Because of the time necessary for the composition of the rest of the *Historia*, Gorman concludes that William could have died no earlier than the summer of 1199.[25] Norgate, however, argues from internal evidence for a possible date of 1201, to which possibility Gorman accedes.[26]

Other than the facts that he was a canon at Newburgh and composed certain historical and theological books, William says little about himself.[27] He mentions certain "Gipse" springs in Yorkshire as being near his birthplace.[28] Because the stream from those springs enters the sea at Bridlington, all commentators agree with a note found by John Leland on a manuscript of the *Explanatio* that states, "William was born at Bridlington."[29] Bridlington Priory furnished the canons for the new Augustinian house of Newburgh in 1145. William states also that he was educated at Newburgh from his boyhood, "the church of Newburgh which nurtured me in Christ from my boyhood."[30] Since the canons from Bridlington stopped temporarily at Hood (later a cell of Newburgh) and moved to their permanent home at Newburgh only in 1150, William may have arrived there at about age fourteen.[31] Or, if he used Newburgh as a generic name including its cell, his monastic education may have begun five years earlier. In either case, it is certain that his early life and last years were spent at Newburgh. In 1907 H. E. Salter tried to expand William's biography with information from several charters of the 1180s and 1190s that he believed referred to the historian, but his thesis has not gained acceptance by subsequent scholars who have examined the material.[32]

Medieval historians with a sense of literary decorum did not talk about the creative impulse, the odd pleasures of writing, the substantial rewards of fame or advancement. Only the satiric poets mocked their more polite brothers by openly begging in verse. But there was a world of letters within or overlapping other more tangible worlds, and the patronage of men of taste shaped and moved that world. Authors did speak of and to their patrons, but we know vey little about how patrons and artists worked together, or to what degree the man of taste guided the man of letters into fashionable modes. Just as Henry of Huntingdon wrote for Alexander of Lincoln and acknowledged his explicit influence in a dedication, William of Newburgh wrote his two major books at the requests of influential men with decided literary preferences.[33] The letter in which William, "servorum Christi minimus," dedicated the *Historia rerum Anglicarum* to Ernald, abbot of Rievaulx, speaks to the patron both as spiritual father and literary critic. It seems that both William and Abbot Ernald agreed on the intellectual distinction between works of theology and of history and that, for the aged and ill canon, the history was also a spiritual discipline set by an indulgent master.

> To my revered father and lord Ernald, abbot of Rievaulx, his William, slightest servant of Christ.... I have undertaken literature at your holy behest, which has assigned to me the investigation and recording of the memorable things which have copiously filled our time and which deserve to be written down for the information and caution of posterity;... your pious prudence for your son has granted the merciful indulgence that the leisure (*otium*) of my illness be not idleness (*otiosum*).... Your cautious discretion has not insisted on a scrutiny of hidden things or mysteries, but has suggested a historical narrative proceeding through time, so that the light work might be recreation for the mind.[34]

Cistercian patronage also influenced the earlier book on the "Song of Songs" in honor of the Virgin, *Explanatio sacri epithalamii in matrem sponsi*. The *Explanatio* is an application of each verse of the "Song of Songs" to the life and spiritual nature of Mary. It begins and ends with letters (prologue and postscript) addressed to Abbot Roger of Byland. The prologue is a response to Roger's request for such a commentary and was written before composition of the book.

> Your frequent and sacred wishes, Father Roger, have projected for me, after a great deal of labor, the exposition of the sacred epithalamium for the glorious virgin Mary. How, either with respect to the Church, or with respect to the meritorious soul, that nuptial song should be understood has been explained by outstanding men in excellent works.... If your dignity desires that my slight abilities be tried, I will promptly and devotedly follow your order.[35]

Even more than in the case of the *Historia* and Ernald of Rievaulx, the patron and spiritual mentor is actively, creatively, "literary." He apparently conceived the idea of the work and gave the commission where it would be best fulfilled. Patronage and requests for literature very elegantly resolved for twelfth-century writers the tension (mostly conventional but partly genuine) between the self-effacing humility demanded by Christian propriety and the urge to excel and claim credit for one's own work. By acceding to the demands of an ecclesiastical patron, accomplishment became an act of obedience. It was both proper and humble to acknowledge that subservient relationship and thus gracefully sign one's book.

On the question of the uses or aims of historical writing William has interestingly little to say. History was not the most dignified of genres in the twelfth century; as William remarks, "Non altis scrutandis, mysticisque remandis," but it was popular and really needed no excuse. He makes only the most perfunctory comments on the importance of recording modern events. "Such a number of very memorable things have happened in our time that it would be quite culpable in modern men if they neglected to commit them to literature for eternal memory."[36] History, for William, had the assurance of past success and a ready audience.

His entire book assumes the intrinsic fascination of important men and great or strange events entirely apart from the possible moral worth to be derived from their stories. But that moral worth, the ultimate "reading" of history is not absent. Events are not clumsily pushed into exempla, but a lesson may be noted if it is especially striking or, sometimes, especially obscure. The bizarre career of Bishop Wimund who tried to turn a bishopric into an earldom only to end his life, castrated and blinded, a monk at Byland, offered a moral almost too patent. "Indeed, afterwards, I often saw him at our Byland, and learned about his most insolent career with its very fitting end. It should not be passed over in silence: future generations ought to know how in that man's life, He is glorified who resisted pride and sent grace to humility."[37] The slaughter and pillaging of the Jews occasioned by Richard I's coronation had to be interpreted as "a monument of supernal judgment on that perfidious and blasphemous people,"[38] though, as discussed on pages 226–27, William was troubled at the necessity of finding Christian meaning enmeshed in an event of such bloodiness and greed.

Generally described, the *Historia* is a fairly long narrative of political and ecclesiastical events in England and some related events abroad from 1066 to 1198, with a certain intensity of interest and fullness of detail about ecclesiastical matters. The structure of the book is an almost wholly straightforward chronological narrative, with occasional adjustment for events that were simultaneous or overlapping in time. The narrative is divided into five books of twenty-eight to forty-two chapters[39] (the last book was left unfinished), with larger segments of time telescoped into the early books. Book I covers eighty-eight years (1066–1154) in accord with William's stated plan of writing at length only where previous historians (he seems to refer to Henry of Huntingdon) had left off.

> Because I know that the progress of English history has been taken up by others down to the death of Henry I; having taken it up from the advent of the Normans, I will run through the time since then quickly; so that from the time of Stephen, successor to Henry, in whose first regnal year I William, least of Christ's servants, was born first to death in Adam, and reborn to life in the next life, I will begin, with God's aid, to write a fuller narrative.[40]

Book II covers only twenty years (1154–1174), Book III fourteen years (1175–1189), while Books IV and V take a leisurely course of five and four years, respectively (1189–1194 and 1194–1198). William adopts the most conventional points of division to separate the books—the beginning of reigns, or some major event to divide a reign into two books; the Becket affair and the reconciliation of Henry II with Henry III divides Henry II's long reign into Books II and III; Richard I's return from the East divides Book IV from Book V, which, had William lived, would probably have ended with Richard I's reign.

Unlike Henry of Huntingdon, William seems less concerned with delineating the higher forms of divine and literary reality and more content to examine events individually, to point out a Christian interpretation where he is able (most notably concerning the Crusades), and often to leave the ultimate "reading" to someone else. It is not that his stated critical and theological assumptions are very different from Henry's, but he feels greater trepidation about applying them.

Like all twelfth-century narrative writers, William did not attempt to cast his materials into anything like a unified structure, but the inherent order and clarity of his mind dominate the plotless, serial, digressive course taken by all contemporary history writing, and he was able to put down one thing after another with an effortless coherence quite sufficient for historical writing as then practiced. On occasion, he resorted to the simplest devices to relate events abroad to those at home, to restore chronological progression, or to pull in a wandering narrative.

> In the meantime, while such things were happening to or being done by our men in the east, England was languishing, bleeding and hurt, in intestine evils.[41]

> To return from Scotland: William of Saint Barbara, bishop of Durham, having died . . .[42]

> How the imperial expedition ended will be explained in another place.[43]

Unsurprisingly, the history is marked by a certain emphasis on events in Yorkshire: the town, the northern nobles, the archdiocese. He is eager to discuss the Yorkshire Cistercians and is concerned with royal policy toward monks generally and Cistercians in particular. Another aspect of the northern emphasis is William's interest in the Scottish royalty—carefully distinguished from the Scottish people.

As was discussed in connection with the date of William's death, the *Historia* appears to have been composed quickly: begun late in 1198 and finished—or rather stopped—sometime before 1201. The evidence assembled by Norgate also indicates, in agreement with Howlett, that the book is a first draft.[44] It was, however, copied soon after the author's death, as the manuscript upon which Howlett's edition is chiefly based is one belonging to Newburgh Priory and dated by Howlett, "to judge from the handwriting, not later than the year 1200."[45] The manuscript contains an alternative reading in one place: "This speaks plainly of an original in a cursive hand, and tells us also that the author could no longer be consulted as to what he had intended to write."[46]

The *Historia* is a very "bookish" book; it relies heavily on previous historical work supplemented by various documents, oral testimony, and a very little firsthand experience. William did not often copy what he had read but wrote his own prose from its information. He was working in the most widely accepted and approved mode of medieval scholarship, and custom did not demand that he cite the authors he used. Probably, learned readers of the time could recognize many of his literary sources. What a well-read man could not recognize—oral testimony—William describes and justifies.

He used Henry of Huntingdon's *Historia Anglorum* as the basis for Book I; Howlett has identified Jordan Fantosme, Richard the Canon's *Itinerarium Regis Ricardi*, and Symeon of Durham and argues for the use of a lost work on the Crusades by Anselm the Chaplain.[47] William also used the Old Testament as a source of historical precedent.[48] He refers to Augustine as an authority on angels and demons, to Gregory the Great on married clergy, cites the canons of the councils of Tours (1163) and of the Lateran (1179), and gives the texts of papal letters of Lucius and Gregory VIII. The historian Josephus is cited as authority for Jewish attitudes toward suicide. He also inserts the statutes for financing the Crusades, and the letter allegedly from the "Old Man of the Mountain." Isidore of Seville is called on indirectly for etymology.[49]

In addition to written authorities, William paid careful attention to the testimony of reliable men, and many of his most interesting chapters rest on this source. He disdains folklore and is contemptuous of Geoffrey of Monmouth for writing a book based on stories from the Britons, but he is more flexible than his critical principles would suggest when folk stories concur with his own belief or are part of childhood memory. On about two dozen separate occasions, scattered through all five books, William introduces into an account a few words to indicate the source and trustworthiness of his information, although he only once gives the name of his informant—Abbot Roger of Byland.[50] In most cases, he uses information from one person, but in five instances from several witnesses. He is frequently careful to distinguish between firsthand witnesses and others who only spoke with them: "from those who were there, or heard from those who were there."[51] Of the twenty-four citations, ten are specified as eyewitnesses. The reliability of the informants is usually indicated by the adjectives: venerable, worthy of faith, truthful, not ignoble.[52] Somewhat oddly, only four of the faithful witnesses are monks (Roger of Byland, a monk of Rievaulx, a prior, an old monk);[53] the rest are not designated by any profession except perhaps the few "not ignoble," who seem to be knights or better.

Only four times does William offer himself as an eyewitness: for information about Bishop Wimund, "whom I later saw many times at our Byland"; for the description of Scarborough Castle, "whose site I knew"; as witness to an astronomical prodigy, "a sign I saw with my own eyes along with certain others who were with me"; and for the last days of the hermit Godric, whom he visited.[54]

William has a number of competitors for Freeman's title, "Father of critical history"; Bede could easily adopt it—not to mention a variety of earlier Greek and Roman claimants. More modest but less disputable praise might credit William with inventing the bibliographical essay. The prologue to the *Historia*, following the dedication, introduces a few matters that William thinks should be mentioned before the main body of the history, "a few pertinent matters before embarking on the history."[55] It reads like a long, aggressive footnote. Since the prologue is the only place where William discusses other historians, it seems somewhat odd that he chose to speak of three—Gildas, Bede, and Geoffrey of Monmouth—whose books he never had occasion to consult for his own history, which begins with the Conquest.[56] Furthermore, the admiration he professes for Gildas and Bede is used as a kind of critical leverage to dislodge Geoffrey of Monmouth from his place in popular esteem. The sole purpose of the prologue is to discredit Geoffrey as an historian. The question of why William gave so much space and effort to an attack on an author whose work was mostly irrelevant to his own cannot be answered very well. He seems to be arguing with some other body of opinion—perhaps the "Geoffrey question" was a live topic in literary circles (something like an early Ossian debate), and William used the *Historia* to publish his views. The only other twelfth-century writer to express real doubt about Geoffrey was Gerald of Wales, but he also used Geoffrey's work as an historical source.[57] It might be that William's irate footnote *cum* essay reveals something of the nature of twelfth-century literary controversy.

William treats Gildas as a kind of scholarly discovery—a writer whose work is really much better than its age, obscurity, and peculiar style might indicate—and we are given one glimpse of medieval research when William remarks, "A few years ago I came across Gildas's book in the course of my reading; because his style sounds unpolished and tasteless now, few people bother about preserving or transcribing the book and so it is rarely found."[58] William gives credence to Gildas first, because Bede did ("inserting his [Gildas's] words into his own [Bede's] work")[59] and next, because Gildas derides his own nation, the Britons, and thus proves his impartiality: "His integrity is heavily documented because in disclosing the truth he did not spare his own people, scarcely finding anything good to say of them, he deplored many of their faults; nor did he, a Briton writing of Britons, fear to say (that he might not suppress the truth) that they were neither fierce in war nor faithful in peace."[60]

Bede, of course, is treated with more than respect; he is the standard against which all other historians must be measured: "It is improper even to doubt his sincerity, he is considered trustworthy in every instance."[61] He is the acknowledged expert on the British period: "Beginning with the earliest period he rapidly related the history of the Britons, the first inhabitants of our island, with subtle economy."[62] William's praise for Gildas and Bede directs the reader's attention to the history of the Britons and sets up the artillery against Geoffrey of Monmouth.

> On the other hand, a certain writer has emerged in our time who, to atone for the shame of the Britons, has concocted ridiculous things from their own myths, and raised them above the Macedonians and the Romans by his own impudent vanity.
>
> This person is called Geoffrey with the agnomen of Arthur because of the Arthur fables he made from ancient British tales and his own inventions, and which he translated into Latin and made the honest color of history pale.[63]

William's irritation with Geoffrey is totally humorless and his heavy-handed denunciations look rather silly next to the grace of his victim, but he took the Arthur stories very seriously and, like Victoria, was not amused. He assumed that Geoffrey's sole motive was to glorify (and falsify) the British past by raising their national folklore to the status of history and that he suppressed the story of Arthur's death from fear of them.[64] Modern scholars would certainly agree that Geoffrey drew on folklore and that at least one of his intentions might have been to provide his nation with a hero.[65]

A great deal of the energy firing William's denunciation came from his contempt for all Britons, ancient and modern. Bede, more than Gildas, had set the pattern for that opinion, picturing the Britons as weak, treacherous apostates who deserved the disasters they brought upon themselves. Normans and Anglo-Normans universally spoke of British descendants in Wales and Brittany in language derived from Bede.[66] They were perfidious, belligerent but unsteady, uncivilized, and suspicious. Although the word *Britones* referred, in the twelfth century, specifically to the Continental Bretons,[67] the same attitudes and adjectives seem to have been applied to all Celtic peoples, including the Scots and Irish.

William considers the ancient British, the Scots, Irish, and Welsh outright barbarians and the Continental Bretons not far advanced over them. He is obviously thinking of Bede when he recalls that, before the Albigensian incident in 1166, only the Britons had encouraged heresy in England. "England had always remained immune from this and other heretical plagues even when heresy was swarming through other parts of the world. When this island was called Britain because of its British inhabitants . . . it admitted the errors of Pelagius. . . . But since the English possessed this island, having expelled the Britons, so that it was called England, the poison of the heretical plague never flourished."[68] The Scots are barbarians, the Welsh, "known to be descendants of the Britons," are also, as well as being "unfaithful, avid for the blood of strangers, and prodigal of their own," and the Irish are barbarians, "uncivilized . . . ungoverned, and lazy" and superstitious in religion.[69] The Bretons are turbulent and they persist in the delusion that an Arthur will return: "They are said to have been waiting for a long time for the fabulous Arthur."[70] Geoffrey's book obviously struck at a chord of vaguely racial antipathy that was justified and substantiated by the authority of Gildas and Bede.

Perfectly in accord with Geoffrey's intention of improving the shabby history of his ignoble nation was his method; he told lies.

William's most characteristic term of opprobrium is "liar" (*fabulator*).[71] To prove that charge he compares Geoffrey's chronology and facts with Bede's and finds they will not fit together.[72] Then, for rhetorical emphasis, he brings some ponderous irony to mock Arthur's exploits and consequently to doubt his existence: "Next, lying with licentious profusion, he has joined against Arthur the greatest kings of the earth, namely of Rome, Greece, Africa, Spain, Parthia, Persia, Itruria, Libya, Egypt, Babylonia, Bithynia, Phrygia, Syria, Boeotia, and Crete; and he says they were all conquered by him in one battle."[73] William's critical methods are various and clever and all scholarly—he fights books with books: "Now, how could the old historians whose careful attention let nothing important escape being written down, who are known to have committed even commonplace things to memory, have passed over in silence . . . this incomparable man and his outstanding deeds?"[74]

William's contempt helped to "fix" Geoffrey of Monmouth's immortality (rather like Freeman and Round) because he was just too interesting to dismiss. The Britain matter, the writing of history itself, the fabulous Arthur, all attracted William's attention, but he was fascinated by Merlin. Demons, prophecy, and all manifestations of the supernatural were central to William's concern with the intelligibility of the world. With the irritable sensibilities of an expert, William found Geoffrey a gross and careless amateur in a field for specialists.

William regards Merlin as another of Geoffrey's fictions ("and he invented a certain Merlin born of a woman and fathered by a demon incubus"),[75] but it should not be concluded that he thought beings of half-demon parentage impossible, any more than that he denied the existence of heroic kings because he doubted Arthur. In the context of the entire *Historia*, William's disbelief in Merlin's very existence is something of an aberration, since he accepts many similar cases on less evidence. Merlin enjoyed a long Celtic tradition prior to Geoffrey,[76] and his prophecies (adaptably cryptic) were widely known. Ralph of Coggeshall, writing about John's loss of Normandy, suddenly remembers an apt instance: "And so in this year, according to the prophecy of Merlin, 'The sword was separated from the sceptre,' that is, the duchy of Normandy from the kingdom of

England."⁷⁷ Even Gerald of Wales, who considered Geoffrey's book a fraud, defends Merlin, though Gerald is understandably more sympathetic to Welsh tradition and denies the demonic side of the sorcerer. "But if a scrupulous reader asks by what spirit these prophecies were pronounced, I say it was not that of a Pythian and not of a demon; truly the knowledge of the future belongs only to God and so He gives knowledge of the future, or rather the spirit of such knowledge comes from above and is a gift of grace."⁷⁸

It appears that, in the twelfth century, demonology and prophecy, like medicine, were subjects that lent themselves to ready expertise. Gerald rests his defense of Merlin on the biblical ground that prophecy is a gift given only by God; William applies equally orthodox demonology to ridicule the prophecies.

> And he invented a certain Merlin born of a woman and fathered by a demon incubus, to whom he attributed, by virtue of his parentage, the most acute and profound knowledge of the future; though we are taught by true reason and sacred literature that demons, excluded from the light of God, can never foretell the future by contemplation: but that they infer (*colligere*) some future events by conjecture rather than contemplation, from signs which are better known to them than to us. In fact, although they are very subtle in their conjectures, they often make mistakes: but, among ignorant people, through the illusion of divination (which ability they never have) they arrogate to themselves knowledge of the future.⁷⁹

Since demons, whatever form they took—and they were capable of assuming various animal and human appearances— were the fallen angels, immediately allied to their chief Satan but ultimately controlled by God, they were an inevitable subject of theological discussion. There had been accumulated in the late Roman Church a body of opinion on the diabolic nature. Although he had predecessors, the most significant contribution was made by Augustine, whose anxiety to expose the pagan gods as demons and to bring scattered superstitions into some dogmatic order led him to write extensively on the subject of demons. His opinions, expressed chiefly in the *De civitate Dei* and in the treatise *De divinatione daemonum*, were the major authority for medieval demonology before Aquinas.[80]

Even if William did not here refer to Augustine specifically, which he does later in the *Historia*,[81] it would be evident that the "sacred literature" which teaches about demons is Augustinian. William says that demons cannot contemplate the future but can only make conjectures from certain signs that are more evident to them (being still semiangelic) than to men. Augustine, in the *De civitate Dei*, remarks: "Demons do not contemplate eternal causes in time or the cardinal points in divine wisdom, but they foresee more future things than do men by virtue of their greater experience of certain signs hidden from us."[82] He discusses the question at much greater length in the *De divinatione*. It suffices to quote one passage, "but they know the future beforehand by natural signs, signs which cannot be received by human senses, and so they make predictions."[83] Augustine also justifies William's refusal to rely on demonic prophecy, which, being only a higher form of reasoning, is fallible: "In certain of their predictions, demons often make mistakes." (William uses the exact words; see notes for the parallel Latin phrases.)[84]

Isidore of Seville, whose *Etymologiarum* William evidently consulted for the derivation of the word *castrum*,[85] is Augustinian in his demonology and certainly was included in William's studies: "They [demons] know many future things . . . knowledge of those things is better known to them than to human infirmity, partly by virtue of subtler senses, partly through the experience of very long lives, partly through divine revelation to angels."[86]

The discussion in the prologue of Gildas, Bede, and Geoffrey and his Arthur and Merlin, epitomizes William's major concerns as an historian: What is acceptable as a true or plausible account; how to deal with unlikely or quasi-divine phenomena; and how to detect fraud. He is concerned with creating a standard of consistency with acknowledged authority as a guard against intentional deceit and foolish credulity. The trying question of the intervention of superior forces into human life made William reflect on the difference between superstition and explanation and on when to believe and how to discuss suprarational events in a rational manner. It is precisely the most irrational, "prodigious" subjects that best expose the energetic clarity of the historian's mind.

Three
THE ECCLESIASTICAL WORLD

AN HISTORIAN CANNOT BE EXPECTED TO SPEAK DIRECTLY OR DEEPLY about his experience of the Christian life and yet, in a medieval writer, that experience was supposed to suffuse his work; medieval readers consistently spoke of Bede as holy, reverend, venerable, by which they meant, in part, that he wrote good history. The various tones of devotion were undoubtedly clearer to medieval ears than to ours, and must have made one of the subtler pleasures of reading in all genres; while a modern reader can only clumsily pursue the more furtive shadings of a medieval Christian mind through signs that must have been quickly and rightly noticed by contemporaries. There is no reason to doubt the expressed humility of William's dedicatory epistles, but the conventionality of both language and sentiment resists analysis. The *Historia* itself tells more. Precisely because William does not talk very much about virtue and vice, his moral preoccupations emerge best from stories told with a certain intensity of emphasis and with repetition of certain themes, such as the following anecdote, which is typical of this class of didactic stories:

> For Malcolm [young king of Scotland] was held back for God in blessed sweetness, so that from boyhood he cherished the fervor of supernal love, and through his whole life the whiteness of chastity, . . . among secular men whom he resembled only in dress, he was a monk . . . and seemed a terrestrial angel. There was no lack of people who were angered by the unaccustomed impulse and thought he should be rebuked or refused to allow him that mode of life. . . . At the onset of his puberty there were some sent by Satan who, when they could not induce him to lose his chastity, tempted him to the experience of carnal pleasure with criminal audacity and poisonous persuasions. He, however, desiring to follow the lamb . . . guarded his treasure of chastity in weak flesh as though it were in a frail vase. . . . His mother warned him that he should be a king and not a monk. . . . And constrained rather than conquered by the importunities of his mother,

he seemed to agree rather than dismay his parent. Happily, she conducted a beautiful and noble virgin, and not at all reluctant, to her son's bed. But he, ignited by the fire of charity rather than carnality, left the royal couch to the virgin and slept all night in his cloak on the floor. And so he was found in the morning by the chamberlain and with the testimony of the girl, both were declared virgins.... Let the venerators of signs say what they wish, and measure out merit to miracles.... I think that that miracle in a boy king, of chastity besieged but untaken, ought to be preferred not only to the illumination of the blind but even the raising of the dead.[1]

The anecdote of Malcolm the virgin king, "an angel though on earth,"[2] is one of several instances in which William speaks of sexual continence, whether celibacy or chaste marriage, with a special kind of enthusiasm. There is no single, sufficient, "medieval" interpretation of such a concern with sexuality; in any number of medieval writers it might illustrate nothing more than an unattractively peculiar misogynism. William's concern, however, was shaped by a particular cultural moment and from a particular set of influences—friends and ideas; it expresses his deep absorption in Cistercian life. R. L. Graeme Ritchie, in his study of "Normanized" Scotland, sensitively examined that anecdote about Malcolm IV (of which William seems the only source) and noted William's "strange use of the word *charitas*":[3] "ignited by the fire of charity rather than carnality."[4] In his defense of the tradition of Malcolm's virginity against the evidence of one charter that suggests he had a son, Ritchie summarizes some of the meaning *charitas* held for the Cistercians:

> It was because Malcolm "burned with the ardour of charity" that he emerged triumphant from the ordeal in William of Newburgh's narrative.... *Charitas* was the watchword of the Cistercian order.... Saint Bernard expounded the mysteries of *Charitas*, love of God, Christlike conduct, but it was left to his interpreter Aelred to clarify Cistercian doctrine.... William of Newburgh's strange use of the word *charitas*; his close connection with the three great Cistercian Abbeys of Yorkshire ... the decisive part taken by the Cistercians in the institution of the military orders,.... all help to explain how the ideal

of the Virgin Knight was, rightly or wrongly, attributed to Malcolm IV.[5]

It is not really surprising that a peculiarly Cistercian ardor should pervade William's history. His commentary on the "Song of Songs" for the Virgin Mary—a favorite Cistercian text and a favorite object of reverence—was written for his friend and spiritual guide, the Abbot of Byland, who himself had assisted his friend, Aelred of Rievaulx, on his deathbed.[6] It is more than likely that William would have read Aelred's *Speculum caritatis*.[7] The gravity of William's disapproval of any deflection of passion from its divine object and his evident feeling that the impulse to physical chastity is central to love of the divine perfectly accord with Aelred's teaching in the *Speculum:* "But in Christian love there is perfect chastity, and therefore there is no lust."[8]

William's fondness for the Scottish royalty may in part reflect Aelred's loyalties and the stories current at Rievaulx, and his enthusiasm for Malcolm may also mirror Aelred's feeling for a more famous virgin king, Edward,[9] whose spiritual descendant Malcolm felt himself to be.[10] Ritchie also saw Cistercian influence on Malcolm in the ideal of the virgin knight, as realized in the Templars;[11] the same influence might be seen in William's dismay over the presence of women in the camps of the crusading army or in his admiration of any degree of chaste behavior in kings. He extols David I of Scotland (in whose court Aelred grew up) for sincere piety and, especially, for chastity. "Now we have taken this testimony from persons worthy of faith who knew his [David I] life and acts.... After an honorable marriage and an undefiled nuptial bed from which one son was born to him ... he remained celibate for many years."[12] William was probably acquainted with Aelred's formal eulogy for David: "Just king, chaste king, humble king."[13] There is, however, no way of knowing exactly whose testimony William took, especially as he differs with Aelred on David's ability to control his "barbarous" people and states that David fell into various sins late in life, about which Aelred did not or preferred not to know.[14]

A story about Archbishop Thomas of York is so directly analogous to the one about Malcolm that it undermines the possible reality of both even while it stresses the importance of the subject for William. The Thomas anecdote presents another case in which a man vowed to celibacy is urged by his friends and advisers to relinquish his virginity for plausible but worldly reasons.

> I learned of a truly memorable thing about Thomas of York from a man of the highest veracity. . . . He was told by his doctor that intercourse with a woman was the only cure for his illness. His friends insisted that he do it, protesting that it could hardly be offensive to God since it was done solely for medical reasons and not from lust. He seemed to agree lest he grieve his friends. An attractive woman was placed in his room. Afterwards, when the doctor had inspected his urine it was revealed that Thomas only seemed to assent in order to placate his friends. His friends rebuked him and said that not obeying a doctor's orders was almost like killing oneself. "Be quiet," Thomas said, "I will not hear any more about it; I am not going to lose the immortal glory of chastity for the sake of the mortal flesh." And he died happily of that same disease.[15]

In a sense, both Malcolm and Thomas were urged to place "reasons of state" above a discipline they felt to be central to their love of God; and just as Malcolm disdained the "ignis carnis," so Thomas renounced even the "salutem carnis."[16] Both anecdotes were clearly written with great satisfaction—the precise circumstantial detail, the delusive "reasonableness" of the tempters bespeak a thoughtful composition.

The sexual license of the second crusading army seemed to William nearly sufficient to account for its failures. "There were so many offenses against Christian as well as military discipline, misfortunes abounded, and it should not be surprising because divine favor never smiles on such filth and pollution. Camps are so named from the castration of lust."[17] The Cistercian exemplar, the Virgin Knight, can plausibly be imagined in William's mind as the impetus to his anger with Eleanor of Aquitaine for, it almost seems, debauching the whole crusading army: "She refused to be left at home but determined to set out to the battles with him. Following that example, many nobles took their wives with them . . . in that Christian camp which should be chaste, a multitude of women swarmed."[18] For William, the unchasteness of a crusading knight was a gross deformation of his mission.[19]

In contrast to the chastity of archbishops, kings, and crusaders (however lapsed) demanded by doctrinal and historical precedent, and perhaps most revealing of the centralness of chastity to William's religious feeling are his accounts of the impulse to sexual denial as felt by simple and devout men. The story of the hermit Godric's early devotion to Christ is informed with the implicit idea that a higher love quite naturally excludes a lower. "For he [Godric] was an ignorant rustic, knowing nothing but Jesus Christ and his crucifixion. . . . By chance he learned that celibacy was pleasing to God and worthy of the highest merit and embraced it with devotion."[20] Another rustic, Ketell, felt a similar impulse toward celibacy upon receiving the divine gift of the ability to see demons: "He embraced celibacy and did not care about marriage."[21] The chastity that William so often refers to as a measure of purity is never merely an ascetic denial but the embrace of another love.

William's ironic finish to his story of the ordeal of the virgin Malcolm—concerning flashy "miracles" and his own mock-modest satisfaction with the genuine thing—indicates another strong reaction to contemporary religious life. His reverence for chastity as an authentic expression of divine love is equaled by his contempt for the meretricious. It is exactly the attitude one would expect (or hope for) from a man who regarded demons as a subject for close scholarly investigation and superstition as the mark of a fool. The brief flurry of veneration in 1190 for one very unlikely "martyr" is reported with characteristic fastidiousness in a chapter titled "What Happened to the Jews at Stanford and of a Certain Popular Superstition":

The Jews' houses were plundered and a great deal of money was taken. . . . One of the plunderers, named John, a very audacious youth from Hampton, deposited some of his booty with a certain man who secretly murdered him for the money and threw the corpse out of the city at night. When the body was found and recognized, the greedy murderer fled secretly. Soon, because of appearances in the dreams of an old person and some illusory signs, the simpletons accorded him the merit and glory of a martyr and held night vigils at his grave. . . . Prudent men laughed at it but they were clergy happy to profit by accommodating the superstition.[22]

The sorry business was eventually investigated by Bishop Hugh of Lincoln, who squelched the incipient cult with the threat of excommunication.

Mixed with William's intellectual fastidiousness is a leavening of plain snobbery. He is thoroughly suspicious of any spontaneous, popular veneration, and his use of the word *vulgus* seems to carry all its modern connotations as in the chapter title, "How the Crowd (*Vulgus*) Wanted to Honor That Man as Though He Were a Martyr, and How That Error Was Squelched,"[23] which refers to the execution of William Fitz Osbert and the London uprisings of 1196. The feeling that led the lesser citizens of London to venerate the—perhaps—demagogue, who focused their resentment of fiscal abuse, is totally lost on William, who sees only the idiocy and grossness in their nightly trips to scratch up the earth where Fitz Osbert's blood had dripped.[24]

But even if he is openly contemptuous of "vulgar" enthusiasm, he is no more tolerant of the more questionable "religious" impulses of a higher class. William had a good eye for the politically useful miracle, and he dismissed the reports of cures at the tomb of the traitorous young Henry III as the inventions of partisan "licentious liars."[25]

An interesting and rather touching variation in the sophisticated religious sensibility of this scholarly monk is his attraction to certain instances of the simplest, most naive sort of Christian life. Something very like a longing for simplicity is hinted at even in Thomas's and Malcolm's single-minded intentness on an essential purity and is more clearly expressed in William's interest in the hermit Godric. A chapter is devoted to Godric's life, "in which clearly can be seen how pleasing he was to God to the confusion of nobility and the ignoble things of this world."[26] Godric is described as "rusticanus et idiota"—simple and unlearned—with reverence, although elsewhere those same words emphasize the baseness of heretics and fools. Godric's chastity, as has been noted, was a spontaneous gift to his God and, therefore, very pure. He was a "very simple man,"[27] and William visited him on his deathbed, next to the altar of his own chapel, to hear him repeat over and over "the words familiar to him, that is 'Father, Son, and Holy Spirit.'. . . In his face could be seen a certain dignity and uncommon loveliness."[28]

William's susceptibility to a "natural," even sentimental, religion is emphasized by his placing the story of Ketell, "a rustic
person, but of singular innocence and simplicity,"[29] directly after
the chapter about Godric. Ketell's gift of seeing demons
probably impressed William with the value of having a pure
heart even though the mind was untaught. The very complexity
of a religious sensibility informed by the most refined spiritual
exposition of the age, the Cistercian *caritas* (and his own cool
mind), appears even sharper and stronger against its occasional
attraction to the simple and rustic spirit.

The papacy occupies very much the position in the *Historia
rerum Anglicarum* that it aspired to in late twelfth-century
England generally, that is, central to all ecclesiastical life. There
is no sense in William's book of papal business being "foreign
affairs"; his treatment of popes, legates, and the curia is marked
with a thoroughly accustomed sense of the natural involvement
of England with Rome. The pope is responsible for maintaining
order, coherence, and a kind of moral decorum in the Church;
he must furnish direction for the energies of the lay nobility
toward crusades for example, and away from internecine war.
The pope in the *Historia* is often seen in those roles, but above
all he is a judge—his curia is always a court of law and he is
always involved in "cases." By the late twelfth century, despite
royal challenges, clerical conservatism, and the resulting set-
backs and compromises, the right of the pope to the status of
universal ordinary[30] in ecclesiastical suits was completely accepted and his right to general influence over all Church life was
substantially admitted.[31] The *Historia* reflects the dominant
trend of its age.

William mentions by name every pope from Eugenius III to
Celestine III, with comment of varying fullness that depends on
how closely the events of their lives and reigns touched on his
own specific concerns for the Church. William could have had
only slight and faded memories of Eugenius's reign (being
seventeen when Eugenius died), and so his remarks carry the
clear imprint of Cistercian informants. Eugenius is spoken of
with great respect as much, it seems, for being a former monk of
Clairvaux and a friend of Abbot Bernard as for his pontifical
rank; the two are at least closely tied. He is the "pope of pious
memory"[32] even when deposing (the future) Saint William from

75

the archbishopric of York for reasons that William hints may have been insubstantial. The subsequent choice of Henry Murdac for the office is presented as rather obvious and self-justifying because, I think, it arose from the pleasant mixture of friendships shared in Cistercian discipline. "William being deposed, Henry, abbot of Fountains, undertook the archbishopric of York through the powerful influence of the venerable Eugenius; who had once been a friend and fellow student with him under father Bernard at Clairvaux and had good knowledge of his life and work."[33] Eugenius is also shown holding a council at Reims, "in his zeal for ecclesiastical discipline,"[34] at which the demon-aided heretic Éon de l'Étoile was tried. Though William gives a long, circumstantial account of Éon's career and trial, he does not mention any other business of that council, which included the trial of another, more respectable heretic, Gilbert de la Porrée, who was accused by Bernard himself. The last incident in William's highly selective account of Eugenius's career is his advancement of Nicholas Breakspear, later Hadrian IV, which demonstrates the pope's "pious and wise perspicacity"[35] as well as Nicholas's merit.

Eugenius's death, in 1153, seemed to William significantly close in time to that of Bernard and of Henry Murdac. "Three memorable men who were closest friends in their lifetime died about that time [1153] and in their death also were only separated by the smallest interval, that is, the Roman pope Eugenius, Bernard abbot of Clairvaux, and Henry archbishop of York."[36] In that juxtaposition of Cistercian monks, the papacy, and a pontifically chosen archbishop, William was pointing to a combination of genuine force in the twelfth-century Church. The same excitement over the rediscovery of apostolic purity that attended the exuberant growth of regular orders also encouraged the acceptance of a vigorous papacy. The Cistercians especially were the leaders of a renewed devotion to the spirituality and discipline of a nonfeudal and truly catholic Church.[37] Bernard's anxious concern for his spiritual son on the papal throne (expressed in letters of chiding, advice-giving, relentless love)[38] was also a concern for the highest prerogatives and duties of the papacy.[39]

William's account of Hadrian IV (Nicholas Breakspear) is again full but highly selective, since he concentrates entirely on

Hadrian's early life and ignores the pontificate,[40] and it is hard to decide whether this emphasis is the result of literary taste or of availability of information. Perhaps he thought that "everyone" would know enough of the official life. Nevertheless, William relates the English part of Hadrian's life and his years as an Augustinian canon, and his account has thus become a major source for the prepontifical life.[41] He was obviously impressed by Hadrian's having been English and a regular canon as well as by the glamour of early destitution and his discovery by the Cistercian Eugenius.[42] R. L. Poole has constructed a coherent (though hypothetical) account of Hadrian's early life from mainly English sources including William, who, "as an Austin canon, was careful to collect all the information he could find about a member of his order who had become famous."[43] Poole speculates that Hadrian had become an Austin canon at Merton before leaving England.[44] William, however, thought that the only monastic connection Hadrian had with England was to his father's abbey, Saint Albans, which had turned him away as a youth. The only reference to Hadrian's papal policy is one remark (perhaps glancingly ironic) about his great favor to Saint Albans[45]—but then, all monks took pointed interest in the privileges popes could grant monasteries.

The one other long account of a pope's career reflects both an event important in its own right and William's own sense of importance. Alexander III's struggle for recognition of his right to the papacy seemed to William a shocking disorder at the center of things—"the discordant cardinals split the Church in the papal election ... and ruptured the bonds of ecclesiastical peace throughout the terrestrial world"[46]—and gross misuse of political power on the part of Frederick I. William focuses on two councils: the rigged council at Pavia, which Alexander refused to countenance ("Alexander not cautiously but openly refused the prejudgment which had been prepared for him under the name of justice"),[47] and another (at an unnamed place) at which, he asserts, Alexander was recognized by the kings of France and England: "Having repudiated Octavian's (Victor IV's) party, they acknowledged Alexander's dominance."[48] The disputed matter of when and where Alexander was acknowledged by Henry II and Louis VII has been discussed by Mary Cheney, whose close questioning of the varying evidences suggests that William's account is, in fact, correct and that the council he describes was held at Beauvais.[49]

William does seem to want to slant his account just the few degrees necessary to make Henry II's support of the pope appear more disinterested and wholehearted than it was. Given the concise and logical selection of events (two conflicting councils) through which he relates the schism, he is not dissembling when he neglects to mention Henry's wavering allegiance before Beauvais.[50] But there is a certain disingenuousness in neglecting to mention Henry's diplomatic coup at Beauvais, where he bullied Alexander's legates into granting a dispensation for the immediate marriage of the children, Henry III and Margaret of France, and the transfer of her dowry of castles.[51] William mentions the marriage and Louis's anger at the loss of the strategic dowry, but he records these events as separate from the council.[52] Henry's adroit manipulation of the pope's weak and threatened position during the Becket affair also draws no comment.[53] Because of his strong feeling for the legitimacy of Alexander's election and his revulsion at the spectacle of the Church acrimoniously split, William's account stresses the basic accord of the Christian West against the emperor's isolated perversity and his almost miraculous reconciliation with Rome.[54]

Subsequent popes enter the *Historia* as more than names when pontifical business seems, to William, of special importance, such as when Lucius III or Gregory VIII sent letters to Christian princes urging a crusade, or when a humanly fallible pope makes a "mistake" like Celestine III's grant of a divorce to Philip Augustus or of a legateship to William Longchamp.[55] But wrong decisions do not weaken his loyalty to the papacy; William does not expect the pope to be a saint but rather, like Gregory VIII, "a good shepherd."[56]

The shepherd's flock more often than not is a flock of litigants. The papal curia is a place where factions fire up a balky system with influence and money into movement toward, sometimes, expensive irresolution.

> Before the year [1142] was over the archbishop of Canterbury and the bishop of Winchester collided and broke up the peace of the Church because the archbishop claimed ordinary jurisdiction over the bishop, and the bishop

claimed legatine power over Canterbury. They went to the Roman pope and brought a load of gold in proportion to such a weighty question, but neither won his case and both went home with empty purses.[57]

In this particular case, as in William's general treatment of the papacy and the English Church, there is a sophisticated, accommodating recognition of partially corrupt Roman ways that somehow serves to emphasize his acceptance of Rome's legitimate authority. William's knowing comments about an astute cardinal who is "a true Roman soul" or about "Roman greed"[58] are those of a man who approaches elaborate, quirky, authoritative institutions with a desire to learn his way around rather than to upset them. Thus, he tells of the deposed William of York going to Rome after Eugenius's death to try his luck with a new pope, and of the king of Denmark's vain attempt to get Celestine III to reverse his sister's humiliating divorce, and of the same Celestine's wise support of Richard I against the archbishop of Rouen, and he speculates that the archbishop of Canterbury and the bishop of Salisbury could have gotten a dispensation for the perjury of violating their oaths to Matilda.[59] Curial justice in the *Historia* is fallible and reversible but always essentially legitimate.

But if the court is unreliable, the law is not. The *Historia* contains two full transcripts of council decrees (Tours, 1163, and Lateran, 1179),[60] though William did not fill his book with documents. He twice refers to canon law: to underscore a rebuke to an uncelibate bishop, and to Richard I for holding tournaments.[61] Popes may be harried and misguided and their court a quicksand bog for money and time, but Rome in its full authority (and in its familiar sins) stands central to the *Historia* and to the *Historia*'s world.

Both William's most personal religious sensibilities and his broadest conception of the Church Universal as focused about the papacy were shaped by his profession, his Cistercian friends, and Cistercian ideas; and the Church in England, too, is presented to the reader through a monastic glass. The Church and the English Church take analogous forms—a large, busy outer world dominated by strong secular prelates enclosing an equally complex inner world filled with monks. Cathedrals and cloisters fill the urban and pastoral landscape of the *Historia* like countervailing fortresses against noble, bellicose, secular castles. The mass of humdrum clerks and little churches is almost invisible, except for a few of outstanding badness such as the clerks who profited from the cult of the "martyr" of Stanford. The bishops are ambiguous, powerful figures, seldom—indeed it sometimes seems, hardly ever—entirely praiseworthy, but always and aggressively "there." The monks, however unequal in ascetic fervor, are at the center of religious life, and when William wants to show noble lords, including bishops, in truest sin or penance, he places them in characteristic relation to monks. Thus, Roger of Salisbury constructs monasteries to atone for his castles; Henry II's abasement after Becket's death is enacted among the monks of Canterbury;[62] and both Richard I and Philip Augustus are impartially rated for their heavy taxation of religious orders:

> Men in religious orders who were accustomed to be free and immune from all secular exactions by pious indulgence of the former prince complained in vain about the great unwonted burdens. And among memorable kings, their most Christian fathers are known to have been outstanding patrons and protectors of monks; their sons, we are sorry to say, hardly took after their fathers in this respect.[63]

But the monastic tint given to the English ecclesiastical scene is not insipidly rose. With characteristic disinterest, William subjects his revered Cistercians to a didactic tale of the most embarrassing sort, which he says he heard from a truthful man.[64]

> I shall briefly relate a memorable anecdote concerning Saladin which I heard from a truthful man which points out how clever a proponent of his own sect was that insulter of our religion. There were presented before him two captured Cistercian monks. Understanding that they were a sort of Christian philosophers, he asked through an interpreter about their status or profession. They answered that they were monks following the rule of blessed father Benedict. Having inquired many things about their rule and hearing that they were celibates, he asked if they drank wine and ate flesh? They re-

sponded that they could always have a moderate amount of wine but could eat flesh only by necessity of illness. Then he placed them in lenient confinement guarded by two pretty women and sent a meal of flesh with water to drink to them. Having eaten the flesh and drunk the water . . . in sober companionship they evaded the solicitations of their guards through prayer. . . . Saladin ordered the flesh and water changed to fish and wine. . . . This clever man plotted to trick simplicity with art and arranged a slander of religion. Having drunk the wine they soon fell prey to the blandishments of the women—their unhappiness having led to excessive drinking. They scarcely followed the apostolic rule: "Take a little wine for the sake of your stomach." Enough for the stomach is not enough for drunkenness. . . . In the morning, with the wine digested and consciousness returned, they wept bitterly. . . . Saladin asked, "Why are you so sad?" "Because," they said, "we have sinned after drinking too much." "Your philosopher Benedict seems to be a foolish man in forbidding you flesh which is harmless and letting you drink wine which enervates the power of reason as you have so recently discovered.". . . And that inveterate enemy sent them back to their own homes after having insulted what he could not understand: and our way of life appeared ridiculous.[65]

That small laxnesses might lead to great falls was always a sensitive issue for monks, both for those who thought their small comforts harmless and for those who professed a stricter austerity—told by any other writer the story would be nothing but one more funny addition to the store of twelfth-century anti-monastic wit. It would be equally mistaken to overread one anecdote. Coming from William, a story about Cistercians (who should not have been so far away from their abbeys anyway) forgetting their rule, to the amusement of an infidel, demonstrates his freedom from blind partisanship or, rather, that he was so deeply devoted to the meaning of the *regula* that he would not spare anyone who travestied it. Even in a tale that would have delighted Gerald of Wales, the Cistercians' rule, or Benedict's, is "ours,"[66] and their shame is resented because it is shared.

In point of space and attention the Cistercians take precedence of all other religious in the *Historia*, specifically the major northern houses of Fountains, Rievaulx, and Byland, whose foundation histories are succinctly told—in that order and consecutively—early in the book, so that Cistercians seem in a way to preside over subsequent English history. In a simple way William wrote what he knew, and he was certainly a familiar visitor at Rievaulx and Byland; even Fountains was not very far from Newburgh. But just as his vignettes of the papacy fit into larger contemporary scenes, his emphasis on those few abbeys is at once personal and typical in a larger sense. It has become a truism, though still true, that the Cistercians made their greatest impact in the north partially because the relative lack of older houses left a free field[67] but also because there appears to have been an affinity of landscape and atmosphere with austerity and feeling that has inspired a mildly purple passage in even a recent, coolly economic appraisal of English Cistercian foundations.[68] In modern eyes as in William's the northern Cistercians sometimes seem to be the English Cistercians, though the houses were evenly distributed throughout the island.[69] The great northern abbeys seem to have been most reminiscent of early Citeaux and Clairvaux and, at the time of the *Historia*, had not yet come to mean only wool and greed and lawsuits.[70] To William at the end of the century, the Cistercians in the north look new and fervent.

The foundation histories of Fountains and Rievaulx are told together in one chapter, placed in the narrative sequence by the death at Pontefract of Archbishop Thurstan,[71] whose protection of the infant community of Fountains thus stands as his own eulogy and also neatly introduces the subject of Cistercians into the *Historia*.[72] A scholar who has worked through the obscurities of Fountain's foundation documents describes William's account as simply "inaccurate" though based on Cistercian materials.[73] William transmits in précis the idealized Cistercian tradition, free of acrimony and ambiguities, which is one of contagious spiritual longing breaking off from complacent tradition to win sympathy and, finally, a home. The monks of Saint Marys, York, whose "scrupulous consciences" could not tolerate the lax observances among the "Cluniacs or others like them," left to become "better and stronger" that is, Cistercians.[74] Thurstan, acting as both mother and father, protected them and provided them with a home called Fountains, "where then and now, as though from the fountain of salvation, many have drunk the waters springing into eternal life."[75]

The account of Fountains is typically Cistercian in its ideas and emphasis and could not have been composed by someone unfamiliar or unsympathetic with the ways Cistercians liked to think and talk about themselves, but its language does not resonate to particular Cistercian documents in the way the account of Reivaulx does. In dramatic essence, the story is one of collaboration between the holy Abbot Bernard and a pious nobleman, Walter Espec, to make an English desert quick with spiritual life. With delicate literary appropriateness, William speaks of the daughter house, created directly from Clairvaux, in the language of its own memorials; the place called Rievaulx at first "was a fearful place of solitary waste," but it was blessed and it multiplied. "As they worked like bees they were known by their fruits, that is, numerous holy colonies which, after the example of hives of bees, they sent out from themselves not only through English provinces but even scattered through barbarous nations."[76]

The phrase "in loco horroris et vastes solitudinis" (translated here as a fearful place of solitary waste) was the common way of describing Cistercian sites[77] and was used by various authors to describe Citeaux, Clairvaux, and subsequently, Fountains and other daughter houses.[78] William's use of those words for Rievaulx's site proves that he used some Cistercian document. William of Saint Thierry's *Vita prima* of Saint Bernard was widely read in and out of Cistercian circles; it was the model for two other *Vitas*,[79] and, as L. G. D. Baker has suggested, was probably the place where writers of foundation histories found the attractive phrase about fearful places. In William's case, one more verbal echo makes the *Vita prima* appear his probable source. William of Saint Thierry speaks of the propagation of Cistercian houses:

> The brothers were sought everywhere and were sent to distant cities and regions and even to barbarous nations (*ad barbaras nationes*).[80]

William of Newburgh speaks of Rievaulx sending out colonies:

> not only through English provinces but even scattered through barbarous nations (*in barbaras nationes*).[81]

The verbal echoes in two narratives that both express the idea of barren places made fruitful by holy monks suggest that William may have read the *Vita prima*,[82] and that suggestion in turn could support Baker's argument that the book was in circulation in England in spite of its absence from monastery catalogues.[83]

Works such as the *Exordium parvum*[84] and the later *Exordium magnum*, which told of the unsatisfied monks leaving Molesme (and provided the literary and spiritual model for the exodus from Saint Marys—at least in the retelling) could have been available to William. Similarly, Aelred's work *De bello standardi*,[85] which contains more information about Thurstan and Fountains and about Walter Espec and Rievaulx than is in William's brief accounts, might have been accessible. He was seldom given to exact verbal imitation, but his accounts are similar in organization and point of view to original Cistercian records.

Because he has told the early histories of "two of our outstanding monasteries,"[86] William thinks it fitting to add Byland and suggests with pride his intimacy with that house. "I ought to explain the origin of Byland also, which being nearby is well known to me; it stands one milliard from the church of Newburgh which nurtured me from boyhood."[87] Recalling what he had heard many times there,[88] he sketches in the eleventh-century Continental background of devout men with radical ideas for the regular life: Robert de Arbrissel founding Fontevraud, Bernard and Tiron, Vital and Savigny. Again taking his imagery of work and fruition from literary nature (like Rievaulx as a beehive) he sees the new orders as roots that spring up to bloom and scatter holy seeds,[89] one of which germinated into Byland whose migratory early years are indicated in a few words. The Abbot Roger, "a man of wonderful sincerity who is still alive"[90] (and to whom the commentary on the "Song of Songs" was dedicated) is credited with bringing the house to prosperity; Byland's (*née* Calder's) misfortunes at the hands of King David's army and its stormily unfilial relations with Furness are, charitably for all, omitted. The reluctant union of the English Savigniacs with the Cistercians becomes, in the *Historia*, "a unity bound by regular discipline and united souls."[91] Rievaulx, Fountains, and Byland are the "three lights of our province."[92]

Another northern historian, Bede, had also once spoken of holy lights shining in a dark England, but he was speaking of saints. Five centuries later, when William saw the light of sanctity shining in a country darkened by civil war, with significant difference, he saw luminous monasteries; the change was from the individual, unpredictable nature of saints to unified institutions of corporate saintliness. In a famous and accurate observation, William remarks that more monasteries were founded in Stephen's brief reign than in the previous hundred years[93]—a phenomenon noteworthy but not incomprehensible, since in those days when "the powerful men of the realm, or all who could, built fortresses either to protect themselves or to invade the territory of others" there was the most need for "fortresses for the King of Peace,"[94] and they were duly and divinely supplied. William's explanation is curiously similar to that of most modern historians, who simply exchange psychology for religion and consider that men founded monasteries when they felt they needed them most—for security in the face of chaos or as expiation in the midst of sin.[95] In his feeling for the centrality of monasticism to the Church and to the spiritual condition of the state, William is perfectly at one with his age, which recognized monks praying in their houses as true soldiers holding besieged castles.

Unlike the somewhat beleaguered and irritable Black Monks, William has a ready and eclectic sympathy for new orders. He maintains a delicate reticence about his own order and gives generous praise to others: the career of Gilbert of Sempringham, whose special gift was for the spiritual direction of women, is described with evident pleasure.[96]

Even monks he does not especially admire (note the remark about the lax Cluniacs and others like them) have his support against their own enemies who, again significantly for the late twelfth century, appear to be bishops. The scandalous contentions between Archbishop Baldwin and the monks of Canterbury and between Hugh of Nonant and the monks of Coventry—"foul contention between the shepherd and his own sheep"[97]—seem to him amazing as well as disgusting. The desire of a prelate to replace monks with secular canons appears incomprehensibly irreligious. These two episodes suggest the ambiguous position bishops occupy throughout the *Historia*.

In William's history bishops are great men moving naturally in the great affairs of the world, and he has almost nothing good to say about them. They are virtually never seen doing anything that pertains to episcopal office, unless quarreling among themselves over precedence can be considered a pastoral duty. He sees few signs of personal holiness among their order; hardly any are even as morally neutral as Richard of Canterbury (1173–1184), who was "half educated but laudably harmless,"[98] and many are corrupt with ambition and sensuality. The common spectacle of the bishop entangled in royal tax collecting, warfare, secular justice, and, inevitably, pursuing the rewards held out before the king's servants could provoke the usually dispassionate historian to bursts of sarcasm. He offers the caustic, witty idea of Walter of Coutances, former clerk, then vice-chancellor and general emissary for Henry II, torn between retaining his rich see of Lincoln or accepting transfer to Rouen with less income but more prestige:

> It is well known that as much as the church of Rouen excels Lincoln in dignity, it is that much inferior in wealth. That man who had wanted the see of Lincoln so much for its great wealth ... hesitated for a long time over whether to be more eminent or more rich and scrupulously deliberated with himself; however, ambition for a higher office triumphed over the love of money.[99]

The bishop's scrupulous inquiry into his mercenary heart is exactly the style of bitter parody that William uses to expose so many strange unpastoral shepherds to his readers (whom one irresistibly pictures as monks). But it is almost too easy to be overconvinced by firm, sharp comments about split service of the King of Heaven and the King of England: "For if a bishop wants equally to please the heavenly and terrestrial kings and divide himself between both offices, surely the King of Heaven who wants to be served with the whole heart, soul, and mind does not praise, love, or accept half a servant."[100] Statements like that are convincing because they are sincerely meant and well phrased, but they are too unshaded to express the full complexity or the vigor of episcopal roles in the *Historia*, which, along with William's reproachful judgments, also reveal his society very accurately.

The tradition of royal service among secular clerks was far too strong and William was far too realistic for the twelfth-century bishops in the *Historia* to figure simply as mammon-distracted pastors. They were, after all, the natural counselors of Christian kings. Even after Anselm's struggle to bring English election practices into line with Gregorian ideas, the king continued to choose most of his bishops or to approve candidates he did not directly select; Henry I gave bishoprics to his best servants and depended heavily on episcopal service and support in return for his patronage.[101] In any case, in addition to the impulse of a shrewd ruler to control and exploit a pool of useful ability was the fact that large episcopal estates were held in military tenure and the king naturally wanted close supervision of his tenants-in-chief. The increasing influence of the papacy and its ideas of reform, which accelerated during Stephen's reign, had to encounter Henry II's determination to hold his own against experiments in ecclesiastical independence and to recoup Stephen's losses. The Anglo-Norman episcopate worked in a complex tradition of royal and ecclesiastical service and their loyalties (and actions) were necessarily sometimes ambivalent, especially after Gregorian spokesmen had exposed that double loyalty as tense with irreconcilable interests. Even conservative English bishops of the middle and late twelfth century could not ignore a revivified and demanding Church Universal, but neither could they slough off centuries of accumulated secular responsibility. Even William does not really seem to expect that of them. Bishops pass through his landscape with terrific energy, embroiled in everything that made the governance of laymen and churchmen effective (or at least struggling to be effective), often at cross purposes with each other and sometimes with the king, always in movement with purpose.

It is, I think, a revealing corrective to William's caustic sketches of power-hungry, sumptuous bishops to notice that his balanced appreciation of Henry II upon his death includes a firm regret for Henry's practice of leaving sees vacant:

> He wanted to leave vacant episcopal sees unfilled for a long time so that he might hold on to their temporalities and divert them to his treasury rather than ecclesiastical purposes. The king is said to have offered the following excuse for this business, "Is it not better that this money be employed for the pressing needs of the realm rather than be used up in luxuries for bishops? For these days prelates hardly model themselves after the old ideals, but are remiss and lazy in their office, and embrace the world

with both arms." By saying these things, he branded an infamous reputation on our bishops in the course of contriving a vain and trivial defense for his own actions.[102]

Henry, in that anecdote, quite obviously and almost comically says about bishops what William does even more sharply, but the king's offhand sarcasm calls up in William a certain familial protectiveness; criticism and reform of churchmen, however grossly necessary, seem to him improper, coming from laymen. Even his admirably cool evaluation of the Becket affair, in which he blames both archbishop and king for wantonly destructive intransigence, has as its key argument the failure, not of archbishop or king, but of the English episcopate generally, who neglected to enforce the disciplinary regulations already available to them and thus called down upon the Church the interference of secular authority. If William would correct the prelates (or, rather, have them correct themselves), I think it would be toward a juster evaluation of the claims on their attention and authority and a less showy display of grandeur. He clearly does not expect a bishop to be saintly or monkish but, rather, to observe a certain decorum with regard to his office and a kind of moderate, unprovocative distance from the king.

As a man of his own time, William seems implicitly to acknowledge that bishops must inevitably be feudal lords and royal servants, but as a reformed canon he is equally sure of the finer moral state of his own profession. The only two bishops singled out for their personal religious eminence are Thomas II of York for his determined chastity (a particularly monastic virtue) and Thurstan of York for his sympathy with the Cistercians. In the *Historia*, the bishops act the contradictory roles of the Church in the world while the monks keep watch over Christianity. The moral distance between bishops and monks is immense. Any failure of sympathy between them is a bishop's moral failure, any open clash a shocking outrage.

It would be pointless to look to a man committed to the monastic life for any understanding of why bishops of monastic cathedrals often sought, eagerly and bitterly, to replace their monks with secular clerks (though it should not be forgotten that Cistercians were sometimes enthusiastic about the displacement of the Black Monks from cathedrals). William's portraits of Baldwin of Canterbury (1184–1190) and Hugh of Nonant (bishop of Coventry, 1185–1198) in full battle with their monastic chapters is at least part of the evidence that has marked out the last two decades of the twelfth century for "the growth of a sentiment hostile to the monastic order to which the previous age in this country can provide no parallel.[103] But it is also true that the same antimonastic feeling, especially among the higher secular clergy, was alive in the first half of the century. The aggressive monastic reformers of the late eleventh century, specifically, Lanfranc and Anselm in England, had provoked resentment among the secular clergy[104] (Henry of Huntingdon is a good example), and the secular clerks who became bishops of monastic cathedrals in the reign of Henry I were often on cool terms with their chapters.[105]

The increasing complexity and expense of episcopal administration through the century and the maintenance of a large *familia* made secular canons appear to many bishops the only reasonable staff for a cathedral and monks a peculiar provincial anachronism. Roger de Pont l'Éveque, third successor at York after Thurstan, was a man not at all enamored of monks. He saw only greedy monasteries sitting on vast accumulations of land and income in his see and frustrating his efforts to provide adequately for the diocesan clergy.[106] William takes the opportunity of Roger's death to rail at him for the connected sins of excessive attention to temporal goods and hatred of monks:

> He hated Christian philosophers, that is, monks, so much that it was said that he said that Thurstan, once archbishop of York in happy memory, never did anything so bad as when he built that mirror of Christian philosophy, the monastery of Fountains.... He said ecclesiastical benefices are better conferred even on sensual men than on religious ... and he effected a deterioration in the condition of all the religious in favor of secular clerks.[107]

William quite naturally takes time to chronicle the really fierce struggles between Archbishop Baldwin and the monks of Canterbury, and between Bishop Hugh and the monks of Coventry. As a former Cistercian monk, Baldwin was a vulnerable target; in studied amazement, William enumerates the steps of his ascending career as though they had to lead, mysteriously, to that final debased state of mind which prefers secular canons to monks. "It is amazing that that man, the venerable Baldwin, who from an archdeacon became a Cistercian monk, and soon an abbot, and from abbot of Ford became a bishop, and from suffragan metropolitan, . . . it is amazing, I say, that that kind of man of the religious life should want to propagate secular canons."[108] After giving a capsule summary of the events of the Canterbury struggle and admitting that in other ways Baldwin was a good and religious man, William wonders that he could be so perversely contrary to the tradition of English church reform, which was always to replace seculars with regulars.[109] Hugh of Nonant, with no mitigating Cistercian past, appears a pure malefactor for evicting the monks from Coventry,[110] all the more so because, at the time of writing, the "detestable work," which occurred in 1198, had not yet been reversed.[111] Implicated as Hugh's supporter and counselor is William Longchamp, bishop of Ely and royal chancellor.[112]

The implied connection between royal service and hostility to monks is not chance coincidence in one man, Longchamp. The same hardening of spirit that makes a bishop want to drive the monks from his church seems, in the *Historia*, to characterize men who too gladly work the king's will and too eagerly pursue his rewards. William's reflections on the conduct of men such as Walter of Coutances (bishop of Lincoln, 1183–1184), Hugh du Puiset (bishop of Durham, 1153–1195), and William Longchamp (bishop of Ely, 1189–1197) are very strong, very acid, and should, I think, be seen in the light of Bernard of Clairvaux's epistle *De moribus et officio episcoporum*[113] and, generally, his strong inclination to give unsolicited and probably unwanted advice to people like Alexander of Lincoln ("the Magnificent") on the vanity of the world's goods.[114] Bernard's assertion of the pastoral ideal as expressed in the epistle focuses about the abandonment of splendor and the rediscovery of essential Christian virtues (of a Cistercian cast) as the true honor of the episcopate. "You will be honored not for the refinement of your clothes, not for the elegance of your horses, not for great building, but for decorous manners, spiritual zeal, good works. How many are otherwise!"[115] Chastity, charity, and humility must be substituted for fine clothes, horses, and buildings: "The most potent and dignified ornaments of a prelate are chastity, charity, and humility."[116] The anecdote about Thomas of York refusing to be unchaste even on medical advice rests neatly in a

Cistercian frame of mind, in view of Bernard's proposal of chastity as the first episcopal virtue.

William presents several great ecclesiastical careers as exempla of greed, power-hunger, and the oil-and-water incongruity of combining royal and religious responsibilities in one man. Roger of Salisbury, of the famous fast-patter Mass, makes an easy target: "And when that young king [Henry I] said, 'Follow me,' he did not cling closer to him than Peter once did to the King of Heaven."[117] He blames Roger for making money from both his offices (bishop of Salisbury and royal chancellor, then justiciar) and then not giving it to the poor,[118] and he finds his misfortunes under Stephen a satisfactory conclusion, rhetorically and morally, to the life: "By the clear judgment of God, he dragged out the end of a life of splendor in wretchedness."[119]

Fulminations against Roger of Salisbury and others like him were set pieces on the topos of *vanitas mundi* for twelfth- and thirteenth-century chroniclers, and therefore must be read with caution; medieval rhetoric was strong by convention. Still, a number of William's comments are calm and precise and seem to indicate a thoughtful, not entirely stylized, reaction to men who serve two kings. When Hugh du Puiset, bishop of Durham, became a cojusticiar for Richard I in 1189, William noted that no bishop who was also a king's servant could give even half of himself to his diocese.[120] It is noted that, from the time he held public office, the Bishop of Durham lived entirely in the south of England. All his further ambitious projects and commensurate disappointments follow, in William's account, from that central wrong decision. The Bishop's purchase of the earldom of Northumbria with money William claims was intended for crusade equipment,[121] thus becoming the butt of Richard I's banal joke about old bishops and new earls,[122] is made to appear a bad joke in itself.

On his death in 1195 Hugh is given a long and bad character. He was greedy for money, greedily attached to the world, and unbecomingly reluctant to leave it. Not satisfied with a bishopric, he insisted on becoming an earl; he built castles on earth and neglected his heavenly edifice.[123] He gave up the crusade to be justiciar in England. Flouting the minimal demands of his order, he fathered and, what is worse, recognized and secured promotions for three bastards of three different mothers.[124] William quotes, rather unnecessarily, from a letter of Gregory I on the necessity of celibacy even in deacons.[125]

The historian's treatment of William Longchamp, bishop of Ely, who William thought was entrusted with the government of the realm in Richard I's absence,[126] is the best instance of fierce resentment provoked by a man who combined secular with ecclesiastical authority. William complains less of Longchamp's violation of episcopal character and more of his confiscation of the temporalities of York and his willingness to tax the religious orders, ignoring Richard's role in that taxation. He lingers over the story of Longchamp's downfall and exile, playing on bestiary imagery, in which Longchamp is first a rhinoceros, then reduced to a man and then to a woman—a glancing version of the story of the unicorn trapped by the maiden. Acknowledging Longchamp's strenuous efforts for the imprisoned Richard, William nonetheless reports that "England rejoiced in his death."[127]

The nature of William's complaints about civil-service bishops reveals that he felt that men who were too eager to serve the king's will would eventually be called upon to betray the essential loyalty to their own office and order. He sees the same process operating among the French bishops when the prelates of Beauvais and Chartres, "two pseudobishops," contrive Philip Augustus's divorce from the Danish princess, thereby abjectly pandering to Philip's sexual whims.

It cannot be assumed that William thought that bishops never tended their flocks, nor is it surprising that details of ordinary diocesan administration do not appear in a twelfth-century history. History was, in its written form, the "extra-ordinary," and so governing, castle-building, quarreling bishops take literary precedence over visiting, confirming, ordaining ones. Only twice are we allowed to see Hugh of Lincoln, distracted undoubtedly from more important business, dealing with the problems, at once bizarre and trivial, of eccentric rural Christendom.

The second, more compellingly literary, arena of the magnificent and contentious bishops of the *Historia* is ecclesiastical politics. William observes the internecine quarrels of the English Church with the disdainful yet partisan attention of a man whose idea of the Church transcends local boundaries but whose sympathies are determined by inside information and provincial loyalties.

What he thought was a careful and original investigation into the disputed election and rumored murder of Saint William of York[128] has been severely treated by modern historians, whose disapproval of William's methods and conclusions is terribly solemn.[129] Modern readers may be, I think, too easily disturbed by William's introduction of the medical interpretation of black teeth in corpses as crucial evidence—scientific arguments probably sounded as clever and fashionable to his contemporaries as to us. Although he does not solve for us the question of William Fitz Herbert's real character and the reasons for the opposition to him,[130] there is a great deal to be said for William's capacity for disinterest in the fact that he does not ally himself with the Cistercian attack on the archbishop but only comments, discreetly, "Pope Eugenius was implacably roused against him either by the truth or rumors."[131]

Of the recurring Canterbury–York disputes that span the century, he concentrates on those between Richard of Canterbury and Roger of York in 1175, and between Hubert Walter and Geoffrey Plantagenet in 1195. In spite of his strong loyalties to York, he maintains a cool distance and a kind of conscious refusal to understand the intransigence of the combatants.[132] The brawl over precedence at the legatine council at London in 1175, with the result that "the council was not celebrated but dispersed,"[133] is credited to the wrongheaded values of modern bishops. "The Apostolic rule, 'Alternate in the highest honors,' is so abrogated by the bishops in our times that, putting aside all pastoral cares, bishops litigate over precedence with as much obstinacy as futility."[134]

He discusses the general issues and history of the Canterbury–York struggle on the occasion of a particularly firm show of power by Hubert Walter as legate and archbishop. This exposition is placed very late in the *Historia* as though it were a general rule derived from history and applicable to the whole century. He cites Bede as authority for Gregory's suggested arrangement for the primacy (the York argument), sets against that argument Canterbury's historical rejoinder, and finally pronounces it all a "vain contention," in weary acknowledgment of the impossi-   *93* bility of any settlement. And, in reaction to another pointless episcopal squabble: "In our times, pastoral virtue has so diminished that among ecclesiastical pastors rare is the one who understands or seeks God, while almost all are after His possessions."[135]

But William's total view of the episcopate emerges finally as a kind of balanced realism; the explicit disapproval is moderated by the grander scene of the *Historia,* in which William places bishops at the center of all major secular and ecclesiastical affairs and makes them appear there so naturally and vigorously that even his distaste seems more a corrective than a condemnation.

Four

THE SECULAR WORLD

WILLIAM WAS NOT A WELL-TRAVELED MAN. NONETHELESS, HE HAD vivid, well-defined ideas about the Church in all of Western Christendom and could feel strongly and pronounce with conviction on popes, bishops, monks, and heretics with a European breadth of confidence. And he had sufficiently good reason for that confidence because his firm, detailed vision of dioceses he had never seen reflects, in its cosmopolitan sameness, the Church as it wanted to be and almost was. His ideas about the nations into which Christendom was arbitrarily divided are much less distinct, and that characteristic, too, has a certain cosmopolitan air even if it is also provincial in obvious ways. Except for England's nearest neighbors, the Scots, the Welsh, and the Irish, whose familiar presence had bred the inevitable effect, other nations appear in William's book with a certain vagueness—the result of the fact that he had never seen them and, really more importantly, that he was not given to the kind and degree of xenophobia that bloomed so brilliantly in, for example, Matthew Paris. All of which does emphatically not mean that he viewed foreign matters and ambitions with happy tolerance. No one who has ever lived with even the dimmest awareness of the existence of other nations than his own has not had opinions about them, usually disparaging. And if ideas more or less uninformed and deprecating constitute prejudices, then William was full of prejudices about foreign nations. But his ideas or prejudices were not fiery or implacable or filled with suspicion—the true xenophobe's emotions; they were merely the conventions of an age not yet nationalist but increasingly ready, perhaps, to locate certain human attributes within still fluid national boundaries. In any case, a certain antagonism must be allowed as natural because almost every other state enters William's English history as a hostile power led by a prince. Standing out in bold relief before the undistinguished mass of their countrymen are those rulers: kings of England, Scotland, France, emperors in Germany and Byzantium. William does not achieve full portraits of these men because he is generally quite as hostile to them as they were to his own kings—in all cases, considerably; he uses anecdotes and gossip to underscore the vicious characters of men who quarreled incessantly with Henry II, supported an antipope, disrupted Christian harmony on crusade, or held Richard I for ransom. But he is not completely blind to foreign virtue and has a discerning eye for royal vice at home. Princes are individual and distinct in a way that nations are not; unlike their subjects, they have a firm if two-dimensional outline.

The history is permeated by the vague implicit idea that some people are essentially "like us" and some are very different. The similarity of the first, at least as it appears through William, rests on the acceptance of an undefined but clearly recognizable code governing conduct, expressed in the languages of Christian morality and of feudal honor, often merged. What makes the others so alien is that their understanding of the dominant religious and secular codes is so peripheral or distorted or their adherence to them so weak that they seem hopelessly unpredictable and ungovernable. They are the barbarians. Even prejudice has its degrees, and human worlds lie between the stern disapproval William directs toward people who have violated their and his own sense of fitness and the condescending distaste he feels for people who are, in his eyes, merely simpleminded and erratically destructive. He judges both rulers and subjects by the same aristocratic Christian standard of behavior, but the prince does not necessarily embody or epitomize a national character; the ruler may be strikingly superior to his subjects, or certain of his countrymen—his own counselors—may be far nobler in character than he. It is, of course, assumed throughout that a nation, for William, includes only those members to whom Christian and chivalrous standards of conduct appropriately apply.

Unlike other nations that have some shadowy existence separate from their rulers, "the English" do not appear except insofar as the nation is represented by the king at war. William seems to be able to conceive of an unvariegated English interest only when it is directly opposed by another, French or German. Otherwise, he sees classes, orders, and stations too clearly for a larger, inclusive body to have much reality in his mind. He concentrates on the kings with an attention that is loyal but critical and cool as well. William was able to observe the entire course of Henry II's reign, and his summation of the royal character on the occasion of Henry's death is balanced and realistic.[1] In those two inevitable tests of a medieval man's moral character, lust and hunting, Henry was found very imperfect: "He exceeded the conjugal measure" though not by so much as his grandfather did, and he liked the hunt too much, but, unlike Henry I, he did not consider poaching—or "fericide" as William calls it—as serious a crime as homicide. He was more solicitous of the Jews than was proper because he profited from their moneylending and was generally "somewhat excessive" in the search for money but not, on the whole, unreasonably so. Henry's worst fault, committed for the sake of money, was refusing to fill vacant bishoprics, and William is reasonably indignant about that failing, especially about Henry's facetious excuse that he was saving the episcopal income from being spent on luxuries by his worldly bishops. But Henry did not burden churches or monasteries with taxes and he was markedly respectful of monks. William's best praise goes to Henry as chief enforcer of the law and keeper of domestic peace: the king was stern, fair-minded, reluctant to inflict the death penalty, and capable of maintaining order. William sees the sin of Henry's marriage (following the "illicit license" of Eleanor's divorce) resound in the public scene through that sin's retribution, the rebellion of the young king. Not unflawed in any part but great in the whole, William's Henry is, like Solomon, the "pacific king."

That part of the reign of Richard I that William recorded was filled with high adventure, personal glamour abroad, and chaos at home. Richard provoked great personal admiration as a crusader, outraged anger with his captors, and furious annoyance with the collection of his ransom. Aside from these general attitudes, made evident throughout his history of Richard's reign, William does not offer any particular observations on his qualities as a prince. He was angered when the general exemption of the Cistercians from taxation was ignored during the ransom collection, and even more so when Richard himself politely despoiled the Cistercians again of their wool after his return.[2] But William died before Richard; the last words of his

unfinished book are half-amused disapproval of Richard's stubbornness in continuing to build a fort at Andely in spite of a
terrible portent of raining blood: "If an angel from heaven had
tried to persuade him to stop, it would have been anathema."[3]
Richard appears as a noble Christian knight, but far from a
perfect one.

The French are the familiar enemy. Practically nothing is said
about them in general because practically everything can be
assumed to be known by an English reader. Their success in war
and quick belligerence are reflected in William's resentful descriptions of them as men whose frequent victories are always
tinged with dishonor: "The French who are by nature fierce and
arrogant at once, especially when they seem to have the
advantage in numbers and the equipment of war, disdain
warnings, thinking they can have no effect on their enterprise."[4]
The French knights were trained at illegal tournaments—a
practice imitated by Richard I.[5] William complains a bit too
much about a broken truce on the feast of Saint Lawrence in
1174[6]—war ethics were not then as sensitive as he pretends. The
French, that is, the knightly classes and their prince, figure as the
distorted mirror image of the English. When the French king is
unusually pious, as was Louis VII, his piety contributes to a
weakness of mind that makes him easily influenced by less
scrupulous men; as William has it, Louis was "a little more
simple than is fitting for a prince," and he seriously com-
promised his personal reputation by supporting the rebellious
Prince Henry.[7] The ambitious, daring Philip Augustus offered a
more provocative moving target for an English critic, and
William wrote about him in a tone of perpetual indignation. As
soon as Richard left on crusade, Philip tried to get absolved from
his oath promising not to attack Richard's lands during the holy
war. He set fire to a church. His marital complications—and
William always found sexual lapses difficult to excuse or
forget—were shocking. Philip tried to obtain a Danish invasion
of England as the dowry with his Danish bride, and when the
Danes refused, repudiated her after the wedding night. "Various
causes were assigned to this shameful levity. Some said it was
because she had bad breath, others that he repudiated her
because of some hidden deformity or that he discovered she was
not a virgin."[8] Everyone likes gossip. William presents Philip as

a monster of impiety and lubricity, all compounded when he married a second time. (Perhaps he made as much as he could of Philip's marital irregularities to counter the common gossip about his own prince's homosexuality.) The French were too powerful and too belligerent to be viewed with composure or justice, but, on one occasion, William let slip a telling little reference to the English and French rulers as "our kings."

The Germans are not assigned any national characteristics at all, although the emperor's counselors are occasionally given speeches containing perfectly conventional and even laudable sentiments. The Holy Roman Emperor, though a large and threatening figure, has only a political and no personal existence. Fredrick I's refusal to accept Alexander III as pope for eighteen years allows William to describe him as "the disrupter of ecclesiastical peace" and to hint that his troubles in Italy were punishment for fomenting schism—a punishment completed by his inglorious death in a river in Asia Minor.[9] Henry VI's astonishing feat of holding a Christian king for ransom thoroughly justified outrage: "Roman Emperor, for shame! For the sake of money he closed his eyes to all honesty and justice and decency. He was ignorant of imperial propriety; he did not blush to be another Saladin."[10] The emperors, however infuriating their actions, are castigated as bad Christians, shameful knights, and ignoble princes, but never as barbarians.

Closer to home, where the peculiarities and bad manners of one's neighbors glare in intolerably sharp focus, the quality of "foreignness" increases proportionately. When the Cistercians came to England, "they dispersed not only through English provinces but even into barbarous nations,"[11] which is William's way of indicating Wales and Scotland. I have already, in connection with the prologue's attack on Geoffrey of Monmouth, described William's distaste for "Britons" who anciently, according to the clearest evidence from Bede, brought down the curse of conquest on themselves, and latterly inspired a fraudulent, self-aggrandizing, and lamentably popular history and, in the form of their Continental descendants, continue to make trouble as often as possible. The Scots (in spite of their noble ruling family), the Irish, and the Welsh alike are poor and lazy in agriculture, ignoble and nasty in war, and crudely superstitious in what religion they profess to practice. The overseas Bretons idiotically persist in believing that a fabulous Arthur will return to them. The characteristics of these people are explained in detail with something of the tone that, in the recent past, was used to describe savages, though it must be felt that some of William's savage tone was the result of his personal literary quarrel with Geoffrey of Monmouth's reputation. Only the very Normanized royalty of Scotland is exempted from the slough of barbarism. But when William speaks of King David or of that miracle of chastity, Malcolm, he is careful to mark them off at a considerable distance from their uncivilized subjects.

Somewhere between the barbarian neighbors and the civilized foes are people about whom William has, or chooses to divulge, little information, whose political and military impact on England is fairly unimportant or indirect. These include the Norwegians and Danes, who were familiar as part of England's population, especially in the north,[12] and the Byzantine "Greeks." The Norwegians and Danes are seen as half-barbarian, and the Greeks as half-civilized. When Nicholas Breakspear was sent on papal service to Norway and Denmark, he went "among the most warlike peoples, the Danes and Norwegians . . . in barbarous nations."[13] But that description was probably exaggerated a bit, in compliment to Nicholas, because when William imagines the debate at the Danish court over the dowry Philip Augustus demanded with his bride, honor and England prevail. The Norwegians do not come off quite as well in William's account of the rebellion of Sverre,[14] though he seems to find them exciting. The Norwegians' confidence that their first anointed king would be safe from assassins because all their previous unanointed kings had died violently is regarded as a bit of touching simplemindedness: "a certain Christian simplicity."[15] The Greeks are conceded more in the way of sophistication, but the sad effects of the meeting of Catholic West and Orthodox East are mirrored in William's language when he speaks of perfidious and soft Greeks, "more faithful to Saladin than to Christ."[16]

Admittedly, William's judgments of people and their rulers are inconsistent: the stigma of "barbarian" is rather cavalierly applied; Philip's sexual imbroglios are treated far more severely than Henry II's; political moves by both rulers are seen only as sexual vice; the Scottish kings are idolized; and the Byzantines are unfairly vilified. When in command of enough realistic information, however, he appraises the qualities of his own prince coolly and rationally. His judgment of Henry II shows that William did not really expect a prince to be a crowned monk and that he could appreciate the benefits of strong, consistent government. Under the circumstances of an almost constant, if sporadic, state of war, he probably could not be expected to appreciate the virtues of hostile princes, and his social short-sightedness that made him see only courtiers and warriors was at least then universal.

"In the month of June when kings customarily go to war . . ."[17] begins chapter 28 of Book II, and that resigned little phrase tells much of William's attitude toward the major activity of medieval rulers. Provocation, justification, where and when, all ultimately stand second behind the one primal, unchangeable fact: war is what kings do. Some moral dissent may be expected—and usually is forthcoming—from monks, and William is no exception. Consciousness of aristocratic birth and connections often was more deeply rooted in the monasteries than religious principles, but William manages to shade his own visceral acceptance of perpetual armed quarrels with irony.

> Therefore the evil of dissension between the kings [Henry II and Philip Augustus] involved many people. For each nation was so jealous on behalf of their own prince that they roused up and made preparations against one another as though each man were out to seek his own gain or glory or avenge his own injury. And multitudes of armed men gathered together . . . excited to the most ferocious state for the astonishing madness of spilling their own blood for the glory or rather pride of their king. For what could be more insane than to be zealous for pointless glory, and not even your own but another's? And what is more iniquitous or more pitiful than that so many Christian knights should perish for one man's profit or naked pride? . . . With the troops arranged for battle a short time before engaging, behold!—The voice of the herald announces to both armies a truce for several days. Certainly that voice sounds more happily in all ears than

101

the voice of the trumpet sounding the battle cry. And
the people who a little before were roaring angrily . . . by
the grace of God, go home with unbloodied swords.[18]

It would be going too far to read that wonderfully unchivalrous
sketch of an abortive (and quite typical) medieval battle as a
dramatic rendering of Christian pacifism. The passage is boldly
antichivalrous or antifeudal in its mockery of the glory of
warfare and of a knight's obligation to fight for his liege lord
("astonishing madness"), and, from a later point of view, it
refuses to acknowledge a "national" interest or obligation involved in royal ambitions. The quarrels of kings are private, and
their victories aggrandize only themselves at the cost of the lives
of their muddleheaded followers, who are excited by angers and
ambitions that have nothing to do with them and whose only
realistic impulse is a little sensible fear at the sight of another
army. But William overstates his own views in this passage; his
distaste for the idiocies and carnage of the battlefield is ultimately grounded in the premise of perpetual war. He usually
takes sides with his own king and never suggests seriously that
the king's men should refuse to fight in his service; he is resigned
to the whole of royal warfare without approving any one
particular of it.

The suffering of those innocent people with no interest at all in
aristocratic bloodshed, whose land and lives furnished the chief
battleground and spoils of locustlike medieval warfare, did not
entirely escape William's attention, though neither he nor any
other medieval chronicler lingered over the simple wretchedness
of war, as distinct from the sin or glory of it. This time, he is
speaking of Richard I and Philip Augustus in 1195: "It was
winter . . . but neither the severity nor the solemnity of the
season had any force against the evil lust for destruction, and the
Christian population was ground down by rapine, death and
fire. . . . And finally the third year of the terrible famine that
was afflicting almost all Europe entered with more severity than
the two preceding."[19] And the next year, the next quarrel: "And
so peace was despaired of, for the one could not be persuaded to
resign until it was recovered into his jurisdiction. As loudly as
proud princes roar at one another, so do the miserable people
(*plebs*) groan. For whenever kings rage, innocent people suffer."[20] So long as the fighting is overseas, war is seen as a series of

private quarrels among a class of persons whose very nature is to be passionate, touchy, and cruel; the writer's point of view is distant and wry.

A typical meeting of medieval armies did not end in battle but in a temporary respite hastily negotiated before the final trumpet call, often concerted between the drawn-up ranks of opposing troops. One class of men, whom William calls *viri pacifici*, counselors to kings and therefore great magnates, bishops, career statesmen of various sorts, invariably are present on the battlefield, patiently shuttling from side to side like Aesopian owls trying to bargain with pit terriers. These are the men who persuade their lords to some agreement or at least a space of quiet, and their services allow the kings to back out of bad situations and thus to preserve their armies and their pride in one piece. In an oddly effective choreography, William's irrational, bellicose princes travel always circled by these nameless peaceful men who act as the nation's repositories of common sense. The role of the prince as negotiator and peacemaker is reduced almost out of existence. For example, watch Henry II and Louis VII in 1160: "At last the immense armies had gathered . . . and each prince with his multitude stood his ground because it seemed too dangerous to proceed and yet shameful to retreat, and because the outcome of battle appeared questionable each prince and his army was rather more willing to avoid than engage in battle. Therefore pacific men took advantage of this hesitation to disseminate. peace . . . and persuaded without much difficulty."[21] There is quite evident pleasure in the telling of these deflated military exploits. But "peace" was only another tactic of war, and princes would violate any current truce when they felt ready to fight and then agree to another when they were tired. "And so the kings [Richard and Philip] were now as avid for peace as they were weary of the labors of war."[22] And presently, one knows, it would all be in reverse.

Although he is more sensitive than many to the cruelties of war, William is disgusted most by the sin of war among Christians when the Holy Land lay captured or besieged by infidels. In one line of bitter contrast (in 1149): "Meanwhile, while such things were being done near or by our armies in the East, England wasted away bloody and wounded from internal maladies."[23] There were Saracens in Spain, but Christian princes remained intent on "killing and consuming one another one by one."[24] When, in 1195, another crusade was proposed and many took the cross at Worms, "our kings"[25] stayed home to fight one another. William's views on common, territorial warfare are colored heavily by the fact that there were two major, disastrous crusades during his lifetime, and he found the crusading ideal impelling and noble. Christian princes did not have to be *viri pacifici*, but as Christian knights he expected them to divert their ferocious energies to a proper object. The contrast between the high importance of securing the Holy Land to Christian control and the endless bloody frivolity of war at home shocked him, and this reaction explains the contemptuous irony of many of his observations on war and princes.

William was an enormously interested though not an original or unusually well-informed chronicler of events in the Holy Land. His information is important only for the few events in England preliminary to the Third Crusade; otherwise he summarizes and recasts very secondhand materials, the *Itinerarium Regis Ricardi* being his most important source. He is interesting when he reflects—which he does at greater length than many writers—on the causes and proper interpretation of the two solemn disasters in the Holy Land during his lifetime.

William was not moved to chronicle the successive failures of the Second Crusade at any length; an English king was not involved, and Henry of Huntingdon, whom he follows closely for those years, is terse on the subject. William introduces a Christian history of Edessa, perhaps inspired by Eusebius, to explain its great symbolic importance and appropriateness as an object for a crusade.[26] As for the crusade's fate, both William and Henry found a supernatural explanation in the sins of the crusaders during the expedition.[27] William, however, makes some small but typical alterations in Henry's explanation, "Their incontinence rose to the sight of God, for they committed fornication openly and even adultery which is most displeasing to God, and went on to rapine and every form of crime."[28] William is of a similar opinion, but he places a little more emphasis on the subject of unchastity and military camps: "However, in our army, there were so many violations of Christian as well as camp discipline that it is not surprising that divine favor would not smile at all on such polluted and unclean beings. For the word camp (*castra*) is derived from the phrase, the castration of lust (*castratio luxuriae*). But no one was chaste in that camp of ours where the lusts of everyone were foaming with licentious freedom."[29] His characteristically strong feeling about unchastity, combined with implacable disapproval of Eleanor of Aquitaine's divorce, bring him close to assigning to her almost sole responsibility for the ruin of the Second Crusade: "She refused to be left at home and insisted on going with him to battle. Her example was followed by many other noble wives ... with the result that that Christian camp which ought to be chaste swarmed with a multitude of women. And so our army was made a scandal."[30] War at home is brute force in the service of ambition and irritated pride, and all at the mercy of unpredictable fortune; but war in the Holy Land is a series of moral movements across spiritually charged ground.

By the time William was an adolescent, the Second Crusade was part of the past; the Third Crusade was the event that occupied his mature attention and a full twenty-seven chapters of his book. While his description follows in summary fashion the *Itinerarium Regis Ricardi*,[31] he follows his own inclinations as usual in expanding the reflections on spiritual significance far beyond anything Richard the Canon wrote.[32] After telling of the Patriarch's visit to England and something about Saladin, William introduces the major events of the Third Crusade with his own spiritual guide to the history of Jerusalem.[33] At this point (Book III, chap. 15) there begin to be clear verbal parallels with the *Itinerarium* (Book I, chap. I), but William's excursus on what he calls the "prerogative of the Land of Jerusalem" is not a part of his source. The Holy City, scene of the Passion and Resurrection of the Lord, was currently being punished by God—given into the hands of the most foul Saladin. "No one should doubt that the cause of this miserable and well-known banishment was the unusual inundation of sin. And indeed from the beginning the Divinity tolerated sin more patiently in every land under the heavens than in that land which was graced with so many and such great works of God."[34] The holiness of the Holy Land resides in its spiritual history and its enduring sensitivity to profanation: All sin is there punished promptly. It is not, as William, irresistibly moved to a realistic appraisal, admits, an especially valuable place by mundane standards: If

God had wanted to endow His chosen people with some good agricultural land, He could have given them India.[35] (It is clear that William, like many monks a shrewd farmer, had been unable to keep from wondering why the Holy Land was reputed to be so poor.) The special prerogative of the land was an active intolerance of sinful inhabitants and the ability to evict them. The Canaanites and the Amonites were evicted, not because they were worse than other peoples, but because they had sinned in a holy place. And so on through its history until, at the present time, "It tolerates that most unclean people the Hagarenes until at some unknown time in the future these too will be devoured according to God's will."[36]

William sets an epic stage, but the drama is all anticlimax. The motives of the soldiers were a sad mix, with many English nobles taking the cross in 1188 only to ingratiate themselves with Henry II.[37] In the Holy Land the Christian princes spent most of their time in quarrels with one another, Philip Augustus leaving halfway through the expedition and Richard's few victories accomplishing, in the end, nothing. "Truly, of those who were pilgrims for Christ following the Christian army in the Holy Land, not a quarter returned home."[38] He clung to the notion of an ultimately beneficent, if temporarily mysterious, divine judgment directing the fate of Jerusalem and its fainéant liberators. The popular conception of the crusade indulgence had developed quickly; even after the First Crusade, chroniclers considered that the crusaders had enjoyed an immediate entry into heaven, without penance, after death.[39] At the time of the Second Crusade, Bernard of Clairvaux compared a crusader with a prudent merchant who exchanges service in the Holy Land for eternal salvation.[40] William says of the victims of the Third Crusade: "There is no doubt that those who left their fatherland and all carnal necessity for such great labors, dangers, and ruin for Christ ... are numbered among those of whom it is said, 'Blessed are those who die in the Lord' for it is considered better to die not only in the Lord but for the Lord."[41] And he goes further to discover triumphantly the occult reasons of God's judgment on the crusade in the fact that the decimation of the Christian armies populated the heavenly Jerusalem and inspired the living to repentance: "While He handed over the inhabitants of His terrestrial Jerusalem to the hands of their enemies because of their sins, He subtly was seeking a richer reward for His celestial Jerusalem."[42]

But even William's highest spiritual insights are leavened with caustic reality, and two chapters later he returns to the same subject to criticize the crusaders for rushing to battle unprepared and against too great odds, thus tempting God by arrogantly relying too much on His aid. They should have done more for themselves, in William's opinion.[43] His thoughts on the crusades are a little contradictory and unresolved; a passive, resigned Christianity was not easy for him.

But even far from the special battlefields of the Holy Land, knights were not always brutish, vainglorious, and secretly eager to go home. William did not view with contempt or disdain those members of society who were trained to fight on horseback, and, whatever his occasional impatience with tiresome, indecisive skirmishes, he could appreciate a bold and chivalrous deed. He perfectly understood the rules or, put more realistically, the traditional vision of noble and chivalrous behavior and could respond enthusiastically to an exploit daringly achieved. One particular event or "deed" could have come directly from an epic: the capture of William, king of Scotland, by some Yorkshire noblemen in 1174. The heroes of this exploit of arms were Robert de Stuteville, Ranulf de Glanville, Bernard de Baliol, and William de Vesci.

> The Yorkshire nobles, quite naturally angry because the Scots were encroaching on English borders, gathered at Newcastle on Tyne with a strong army of horsemen. Because of the urgency of the matter, they were not able to collect many foot soldiers.... When they discussed together what ought to be done, the more prudent proposed ... that it was not safe or useful to the king of England to progress any farther lest they seem to expose their small force to be devoured like a loaf of bread by the infinite multitude of barbarians.... To this the impetuous ones replied that the base enemy should be attacked and they ought not to despair of victory ... and finally their opinion prevailed.... As they traveled, the fog was so dense that they could scarcely see their way. Then the prudent men said that the way was very dangerous and certain disaster threatened them unless they turned back. At this, Bernard of Baliol, a noble and great-

hearted man said, "Let anyone go back if he wants to, as for me, I will go ahead even if no one follows and I will not brand myself with eternal disgrace." And so they went on.[44]

They encountered the Scottish king near Alnwick Castle with a few knights, and the king at first confused the English with his own returning hunting party and thus rashly exposed himself and his men; then, seeing their standard, he decided to fight.

Rousing them [his knights] to arms by his words and example, he said, "This will show who knows how to be a knight." And he rushed into the enemy . . . and was captured by our men when his horse was killed under him, and almost his whole troop was captured as well. Those who were able to escape, disdaining flight when the king was captured, willingly gave themselves up to the enemy. Even some nobles who were not there but a short distance away because they did not know what had been happening, returned rapidly and did not fall but threw themselves into the enemy hands for the honor of sharing their lord's danger.[45]

I think that this story should act as a mild antidote to the Christian antichivalric view that William, when he had the unrelieved suffering Holy Land in mind, usually takes of warfare. In this case, local pride and, probably, the mental habits of his social class produced a fine portrait of a perfect (and perfectly secular) noble exploit. The plan was daring. William, who usually favors the opinions of men he describes as "prudent," here sides with the impetuous knights for whom unequal odds enhance the glory of the deed. He admires Bernard of Baliol's bold resolution to march on alone if no one would come with him. The battle itself, as described, is thoroughly satisfying to secular medieval tastes. Every knight charges in fearlessly and no one is killed—with the exception of one horse. The victors have the glory of defeating and capturing a king, and the vanquished, especially all those Scottish knights who galloped over to surrender with their lord, have the glory of impeccably noble, chivalrous conduct. In all, an honorable encounter reflecting credit on all sides. No "low" foot soldiers are mentioned in the fight, neither English nor Scottish "barbarians," none of whom could add much glamour to this paradigm knightly deed.

Another exploit of a sort, also provoked by sensibilities sensitive to degrees of nobility and honor, gets a very different report. This event began near Béziers in 1167 during an expedition formed by William Trencavel, viscount of Béziers and ally of Henry II, to aid a kinsman. William heard many reliable reports of it.[46]

A large number of young men from the subject [to William Trencavel] cities of Béziers and Carcassonne, practiced in arms and eager, hurried to join the army. It happened that a certain man from Béziers, relying on the presence of a number of his fellow citizens, impertinently insulted a certain noble and well-known knight by taking away his war horse (which is called a destrier) and making it carry baggage. The knight, with the support of all the equestrian order, complained to his lord, describing the insult as perhaps not very injurious but extremely shameful. The leader, wishing to placate his knights who were threatening to leave the army if the Béziers citizens went unpunished, handed over the author of the insult to the knights. Having inflicted a light but rather shameful punishment on him, they sent him away as dishonored.[47]

The citizens of Béziers, feeling the dishonor as a general affront, demanded some reparation, and William Trencavel, desperate to keep his army together, agreed to a meeting of both sides at the cathedral of Béziers. Here follows a dramatic scene in which the dishonored citizen and his friend enter the church with concealed weapons; he delivers a desperate speech beginning, "Behold an unhappy man, weary of life because I must live with dishonor." Trencavel reasonably promises to stand by any decision reached by the assembled citizens and nobles, but the man is impatient of deliberations and, declaiming that only blood can wipe out his shame, murders Trencavel and his noble entourage before the horrified archbishop. The city was placed under interdict and under siege as well, and eventually the matter was thought settled when the citizens agreed to accept Trencavel's son as their lord. This young man, goaded into a tardy revenge by the taunts of some noble friend, borrowed troops from the king of Aragon (traditional enemy of Béziers), tricked the citizens into allowing the soldiers into the city, and then ordered a general slaughter. William's final remarks are complacent: "And so that cursed populace, by the just ordinance of God, took the fitting price of their perfidy and cruelty. Moreover, the ministers of vengeance, as reward for their work, are said to have accepted habitation in the city—now that expiation had been made by the slaughter of its perfidious citizens."[48]

A different kind of story from the Yorkshire field of glory—mean, trivial, and sordid—but similar distinctions of honor and dishonor are present though in grotesque form and with disgusting consequences. It is interesting how even in the late twelfth century the war horse still carried a surprising burden of social distinction. The general panache of the Yorkshire exploit was greatly enhanced by its being solely an encounter of mounted knights; one feels, reading of the Béziers quarrel, that William himself is quite sensitive to an insult to a noble horse. It was the knight's destrier, not his sumpter, that was taken; and he never indicates that he considers it a foolish or meaningless provocation. Though William suggests no reason for the Béziers citizen's rude affront, the atmosphere of the story is one of generalized, irritable animosity between the citizens and the knights, and consciousness on both sides of injured dignity and revenge. The insulted destrier was probably not the real beginning of the story. William is so unequivocally a partisan of the knights that he refuses to specify the revenge they took against the Béziers man, passing over the matter by saying that it was light but shameful. It must have been grossly humiliating. And although the citizen uses the language of chivalrous honor, his speech about the impossibility of life after the disgrace he had suffered is made bankrupt and hypocritical because he ends his fine oration by stabbing his lord to death in the cathedral.

William's satisfaction in the terrible revenge taken on the citizens of Béziers (by mercenaries whom he calls divine agents) is ugly but not incomprehensible if one remembers that Trencavel's murderers had committed the last violation of the feudal bond by killing their lord and thus, according to a code that had then more emotional than political or military reality, became outlaws deserving no pity. The terrible incongruity is that here the town of Béziers is regarded as a collective outlawed vassal, while the anonymous knights and William Trencavel are not representative ciphers but individual men. The whole anecdote is played out against a field of complicated, shifting, and essentially unrealistic notions about the kinds of behavior appropriate to various classes of men. The pervading, underlying note of the story is that townsmen simply do not belong on military expeditions, equipped like noble knights, and that it is insolent in them to have war horses and to talk of honor and revenge. They murder their lord and desecrate a church in the name of a form of secular pride that (William makes his reader feel) is not for them to claim or defend. In contrast, the Yorkshire exploit is a frieze of dignified and graceful postures against a heraldic shield, and one is almost moved to grief for the death of the Scottish king's noble charger.

In general, an unspecified code of feudal, chivalric behavior with some deference to religion is the tacit standard for William's judgment of conduct in the lay, secular world which, he usually assumes, is aristocratic and agrarian. He seems unsure about towns. He does not wholly despise them nor wholly ignore them; he even expresses pride in London's wealth, but on many occasions he does not seem to know exactly what can or should be expected of the cities' inhabitants. The case is simpler when noble persons violate their own code, as when Richard, the "noble king," was put in chains, "contrary to the honor of a king," by the "most infamous" duke of Austria.[49] Towns often appear in William's book as vigorous and active in their own right, as when the citizens of Rouen fought the French army off their scaling ladders in 1174, or the citizens of the "renowned city of Nantes" chose Henry II's son Geoffrey as their lord.[50] He is, in fact, rather sympathetic with Milan's revolt against Frederick I but chiefly because of the emperor's schismatic adherence to an antipope.[51] But towns figure as centers of a new kind of unpredictable and erratic violence—different, one feels in reading William, in quality if not intensity from the violence of the countryside.

Of course, William was right about the towns—they were violent in a new way, and new kinds of violence always appear more destructive and more fearfully repulsive than traditional kinds. William's account of the brief, hectic uprising in London led by William Fitz Osbert, "Longbeard," in 1196 is vitriolic to a degree matched only by his approval of the Béziers massacre.[52] No reader of William of Newburgh could expect him to understand or sympathize with the spirit of aggressive independence during the reign, *in absentia*, of Richard I when London wrested concessions from William Longchamp—the spirit Gwyn Williams has described as the background to the popular anti-oligarchic uprising led by Fitz Osbert.[53] Still, William Stubbs considered that Hovedon thought the provocation of the poorer citizens who were inequitably burdened in taxation by their richer, influential neighbors was a genuine grievance.[54] Later, Matthew Paris, that hater of taxes, saw Fitz Osbert as a martyr for the cause of the poor.[55] The combination of urban mob violence against established governing powers and the, to us, pathetic attempts after Fitz Osbert's death to treat him as a martyr grated intolerably on a mind with a strong sense of order and even stronger disdain for vulgar, popular piety. William devotes, for him, a large space to the 1196 uprising, telling it in two chapters titled "Concerning a Conspiracy in London Created by a Certain William, and how he Suffered the Penalty of his Insolence" (Book V, chap. 20), and "How the Vulgar Wanted to Honor that Man as Though He Were a Martyr, and How that Error was Exterminated" (Book V, chap. 21).

William assigns the whole of the uprising to the personal spite and ambitions of Fitz Osbert, who had the gift of shrewdness and "was uncommonly eloquent."[56] He passes over the general grievance of the large body of poorer citizens quickly though accurately—"that at every royal edict [asking for money], the rich used their power to impose the whole burden on the poor, sparing their own fortunes"[57]—treating it as merely the pretext for Fitz Osbert's self-seeking plot. It might well have been both. It is not that William displays special sympathy for the rich and powerful of London. He deplores rousing the lesser people to violence against their position in life with false hopes as Fitz Osbert did, "inflaming the poor and middling people with a love of excessive freedom and happiness,"[58] as a heinous assault on public order. (Under the circumstances, one must agree that it was a cruel deception.) William's fierce anger is reserved for Fitz Osbert alone until, after his execution, the "stupid populace," the "fools 'whose number,' as Solomon said, 'is infinite' and the herd of curious",[59] tried to worship Fitz Osbert as a martyr and crept out at night to scratch up the soil where his blood had dripped. That error was promptly discouraged. William had a remarkably short temper with what he considered crass religious superstition.

Both the fracas at Béziers and the uprising in London were, in William's versions, the work of upstart, wrongheaded, violent urban men who had no respect for the inevitable patterns of an orderly society. In both cases, private rage, vengeful or envious, led to public crime and guilt. William does not object to the existence of cities themselves; he just seems to regard them somewhat nervously. He never finds an equivalent urban ideal for the noble Christian knight or for the simple, saintly rustic. The fact that towns and citizens are far more absent from his book than from his actual world indicates mainly, I think, that he lacked a ready vocabulary that could have fit them more harmoniously into his already slightly anachronistic agrarian world of nobles and peasants.

Five
ANOTHER WORLD

THE GREAT SUBJECTS OF WILLIAM'S HISTORY—THE CHURCH, AFFAIRS of state, great and sometimes holy men—all testify to his fine reluctance to sink all the complexity of human life for the sake of a plausible literary or even Christian scheme. His seriousness and candor achieve something that cannot be diminished by mere factual inaccuracy. His treatment of the Becket tangle alone will always be a quiet triumph of the disinterested mind over partisan rattle. But implacably seated in the middle of everything that makes William a sober and high-minded Christian historian in modern eyes is the fact that he does give so much space and obvious effort to very peculiar things. He prefaces his book with the first major assault on Geoffrey of Monmouth and Merlin and then proceeds, in all high seriousness, to Ethiopian demons and talking skulls and vampires; it looks like the stuff of banal satire, especially if one chooses to remember his repeated and, from a scoffer's point of view, unfortunate remarks about superstitious fools. But William's numerous, painstaking descriptions of supernatural events—if studied with the same seriousness with which they were composed—reveal more about rational analysis and realistic observation in the twelfth century than even his own careful discussions of mundane "reality." Unlike Walter Map or Gerald of Wales, he was not willing to retell every prodigious story he heard so long as it was amusing, and his self-confessed hesitations in the face of certain bizarre but well-attested events give us a mirror of active thought perhaps wholly unequaled by his contemporaries for candor and immediacy.

There are in William's book some twenty-five supernatural occurrences, most of them fairly elaborate descriptions of demons and their activities. He includes a few common portents: two that he accepted on Henry of Huntingdon's authority, and various celestial aberrations that occurred in his own time, but the England that William observes is not under a constant fall of ominous comets, nor does he seem to think (as some chroniclers can be accused of doing) that God and the Devil had nothing better to do than dabble in English politics. Most characteristically, he never reports an obviously natural or accidental occurrence as though it were supernatural, and he never attributes personal miracles to saintly men—a strong, pure faith and perfect chastity seemed to him quite sufficiently miraculous. He was by nature disinclined to accept casually every exotic story that traveled the excitable currents of monastic gossip, but his attention was compelled by events that seemed to reveal direct, preternatural interference in human life if those events were surrounded by the insistent testimony of respectable persons. He offers these prodigious events to his readers with questions, hesitations, and doubt—with, in short, all the confessions of a critical and honest mind.

In every case a "prodigy"—that is, an occurrence that cannot be accounted for by natural causes and explained fully by human reason—suggested two questions to William: Did it, in fact, happen? If so, what did it mean? In deciding whether a particular event was credible enough to be included in his book, William employed the best critical methods that were available to him, methods that can be defined as critical "in the sense that the user, after reflection and study, was satisfied as to their reliability,"[1] as has recently and very aptly been phrased. The introduction to the first major prodigy occurring in William's history reveals his attitude toward the whole class of such events:

> An unheard-of prodigy which is known to have happened in England during the reign of Stephen should not be ignored. Indeed, I hesitated over this matter for a long time though it was asserted by many people; it seemed ridiculous to me to accept on faith something with no explanation or one completely hidden. Finally, I was so overwhelmed by the amount and quality of the testimony that I am compelled to believe and marvel at what I cannot reach or unravel with a human mind.[2]

The theme of the passage is doubt; the resolution is testimony. Given the universal conviction demanded by traditional Christian orthodoxy of the reality of supernatural beings (angels, demons, spirits of the dead) and of their ability to interfere in earthly life, the fact that any particular incident might be bizarrely incongruous with the natural, expected order of things could not, by itself, prove it impossible. Even if we ignore popular beliefs, as a contemporary could not, the clear biblical precedents in the Genesis story of the fallen angels, Pharaoh's magicians, the exorcisms performed by Jesus, to cite only a very few,[3] and numerous discussions by the Fathers forced any educated man to assume that the temporal order was helplessly vulnerable to invasion by heavenly forces though, of course, he did not have to credit every report of such an event. However, the Bible and the Fathers only gave assurance that supernatural events could happen; they offered no clear patterns or other criteria according to which the credibility of any particular example could be judged. While rains of blood, comets, and rods that turned to snakes had become familiar, no limitations were set down by the authoritative writers on the subject. To complicate matters further for a medieval scholar, the immaterial or subtle substance and shifting forms of heavenly agents would have made the search for objectively verifiable evidence pointless even if he had attempted that kind of investigation. In fact, as all modern students know too well and too unsympathetically, twelfth-century curiosity about prodigies never turned to much factual or natural evidence but, rather, concentrated on the testimony of the people who claimed to be witnesses or to have spoken with them. As William says, "These and similar things appeared unbelievable, if they had not been asserted by witnesses worthy of credence."[4]

We do not have to become embroiled in the impossible question of "what really did happen" to concede that at least some of that testimony might have been persuasive enough in its consistent detail, general plausibility, and in the intelligence and moral rectitude of the speaker to inspire belief. Even if the witness had been, in our "reality," overly susceptible, imaginative, or nearsighted, there is no reason why a story told well and in sincere good faith (especially when supported by corroborating testimony, as these events often were) should not have convinced an intelligent man in a world not yet governed by laws of physics. Any twelfth-century man who denied the existence of supernatural creatures and the possibility of miracles had to be a fool, a madman, or arrogantly frivolous. Recognizing that in the twelfth century the evaluation of testimony rather than laws of probability was central to the problem of authenticating prodigies is not the same as saying that they (unlike us), with their undeveloped or erratic reasoning powers, believed everything they were told. Ralph of Coggeshall remarks in the preface to a vision he believed to be authentic that there were so many people going about these days claiming to have had visions that genuine ones were being dismissed as lies along with the rest.[5] Belief was never the same as credulity. For every prodigy that inspired enough respect to be written down, there were undoubtedly hundreds that dissolved in the laughter of skeptics.

The medieval *saeculum*, free from physical laws not yet discovered, was subject to a richer and more startling variety of possible events than ours. There was, in the minds of men, no reason why an authentic experience—that is, one clearly apprehended and honestly described—should not be equivalent to an authentic event so long as the witness offered a method of at least detecting outright fraud and possibly arriving at the truth. As usual, the heart of the matter has been remarked by Dr. Johnson, a consistent traditional Christian, in his distinction between what he called "physical and moral truth": "Moral truth is when you tell a thing sincerely and precisely as it appears to you."[6] Johnson's "moral truth" is acceptable testimony from a medieval point of view—sufficient, for a society that had little reason to see any distinction between them, to establish "physical truth." Eighteenth century ideas had changed from those of the twelfth in many obvious ways, but the basic assumptions of traditional Christianity had not yet disappeared from many educated minds. That clearest mind of a self-consciously reasoning age, the one that gave the eternal command that we clear our minds of cant, quite simply admitted the influence of evil spirits, saying, "Nobody who believes the New Testament can deny it,"[7] and, speaking of belief in ghosts, concluded, "All argument is against it; but all belief is for it."[8] In the twelfth century, when not only all belief favored the supernatural but also all argument, the pursuit of moral truth was the clear and certain mark of a critical intelligence.

There is no reason to assume that William relinquished his doubts of the prodigy in the reign of Stephen easily or rapidly; by his own admission, the kind of testimony offered to him made disbelief seem more unreasonable than belief. On another occasion (I am, doubtless annoyingly, withholding the descriptive details because they are too interesting and distract from the underlying question of evidence. They will come later.), he assures the reader that his information of a certain event came "first from a person born in the locality, afterwards from the venerable archdeacon of the area, Stephen," who was involved in the incident. Elsewhere we are told that reports came from a monk; from "an aged monk who was famous and influential in that area"; from "certain people of noble birth who were there"; from "men venerable and worthy of credence who claimed to have heard it from the bishop of Le Mans himself."[9] These capsule descriptions attest mainly to the moral weight of the informants, a certain public reputation for authority and trustworthiness, though there is also a persistent attention to their ability to observe firsthand. We do not have to be similarly impressed by this array of ecclesiastical and social credentials to be convinced of the honesty of William's efforts to reach the truth. The ecclesiastical informants whom William clearly sought out and trusted most were, after all, his colleagues and "specialists," as men whose education and daily responsibilities gave them special knowledge of the supernatural.

As a preventative to the possible impression that William was incapable of appreciating the more ordinary productions of God and Nature, there is his striking firsthand description of Scarborough Castle in its physical setting:

> A huge rock, almost inaccessible on account of precipices on all sides, drives back the sea which surrounds it, except for a narrow ascent on the west. On its summit is a beautiful grassy plain, more than sixty acres in area, with a spring of fresh water issuing from a rock. At the entrance, which is difficult of access, there is a royal castle, and below the incline begins the town, which spreads to the south and north but faces west, defended on this side by its own wall, on the east by the castle rock, while both sides are washed by the sea.[10]

Because of its careful and appreciative observation of nature, this description has been recently cited as an example of the increasing powers of realistic observation in twelfth-century English writers.[11] The description of Scarborough Castle, it should be remembered, is not the only instance that can be cited of William's ability to observe, reason, and judge completely within the confines of natural and human possibility. He describes the influence of Wales's geography on the national character (fierce confidence, supported by the safety from invading armies that is provided by wooded mountains and valleys) and of its economy on relations with England (lack of arable land, which spurs frequent border encroachments). He uses medical knowledge to discredit the alleged evidence supporting the rumors of poison in the death of Archbishop William of York.[12] Even the Third Crusade, on which divine attendance and influence were confidently expected, does not distract William from the value of plain common sense. Speaking of the ignominious defeat suffered by the Christian armies in Syria in 1192, he suggests, in a pragmatic revision of certain clearly applicable Old Testament examples, that while His will could make the smallest troop invincible, attempting battle ill prepared and against great odds as the crusaders had done was only tempting God and ensuring defeat, "for God wants Christians to confide themselves in Him so long as they do not forget to act with prudence and foresight."[13] His judgment of men and affairs is clear-sighted and experienced, not least when he speculates that William of Canterbury and Roger of Salisbury decided to perjure themselves and crown Stephen because they assumed they could get a papal dispensation later.[14] The celestial presence, divine or diabolic, in William's history adds a moral dimension without pushing events out of their natural courses or inhibiting free and—often fallen—will. Thus, a war-angered God inflicts famine and plague on England and Gaul (1196), but the reckless princes disregard the obvious signs and continue to wage war. We are often taught to recognize men acting as the unwitting instruments of a higher will, but they are also allowed sufficient intentions of their own.[15]

If the political and grandly scaled ecclesiastical affairs of the *Historia* are eyed with a sober shrewdness, that same quality permits only the best-attested examples of the supernatural to intrude into the same realm with eminently material kings and bishops and diplomats. But even with all critical precautions taken, the problem remained for the serious observer of a sometimes astonishing world that a prodigy supported by the most impeccable testimony and described in fullest circumstantial detail did not yet, unlike a battle or an episcopal election, satisfy an historian's instincts. Admittedly, not all medieval historians were serious or reflective, and the inevitable bizarreness of miracles easily lent itself to (or was shaped by, if one must be psychological) thrill-seeking, guilt-assuaging, and prurient impulses;[16] William, however, was compelled always to take the one difficult step further and ask what it all meant. While he talks about supremely unusual things in the language of surprised and affronted rationality, about "such very unaccustomed," "stupefying," "prodigious," "unbelievable" things, closely conjoined words of intelligibility like "explanation" or "reason" (*ratio*) and "signifies," or even, "the Divinity wished to signify" reassure us of a genuine belief in a rational universe— that beneath the apparent chaos of experience there is always meaning. But only for those who can find it.

"Let anyone say what he wants, and reason about these things as he is able; as for me, it does no harm to describe a prodigious and miraculous event,"[17] is William's final remark on the prodigy he accepted but could not "unravel." And elsewhere: "Anyone may interpret this miraculous sign as he wants, I learned of it simply to be the narrator and not the interpreter of a portent, for I do not know what the Divinity wished to signify by it."[18] The admirable, though perhaps for William, sad, fact is that for all his anxious concern to find the *ratio* somewhere, he so seldom allowed himself the comfort of a conclusion. Henry of Huntingdon, who did not take these matters nearly so seriously, connected heaven and earth gracefully enough, as reflected in those parts of his book William adopted from Henry: "[The site of Battle Abbey] exuded blood ... and so clearly by that evidence it was said that the voice of so much Christian blood even to that day called to God from the earth which had opened its mouth and taken in that same blood by the hands of brothers, that is, Christians."[19] And he retells the miracle Henry claimed to have seen: "the walls of the church he invaded [Ramsey Abbey in 1143] and of the adjoining cloister sweated blood; by which as was made clear afterwards, was signified the savagery of his crime, and the imminent judgment on that savagery."[20] William could never bring himself to such easy connections; his freehanded offer to allow the nameless "anyones" to interpret his simple reports is probably an ironic protest against the facile significances that "anyone" all too easily invented.

Only two miracles were vouchsafed directly to him, one being a reddening of the sky in 1192 or 1193, which, though he took it for a prodigy, was the aurora borealis; but he labored in his conscientious scholarly manner toward a rationally acceptable explanation for the prodigies that so many others witnessed. Moving beyond the speculative meaning of each individual prodigy, he tried—and here it genuinely helps us to use the word "scientific"[21]—to discover principles that could make all such occurrences intelligible.

The intractableness of the material William had to investigate can be told only by relenting of a perhaps boring chasteness and revealing the odd events that increasingly excited twelfth-century attention.[22] Early in his book, William relates four major events, each "strange and prodigious." The first, the one over which he hesitated because it had no rational explanation and which he finally accepted in deference to testimony, concerned the inexplicable emergence from a ditch in East Anglia of two children, a boy and a girl, both totally green in color.[23] They were seen by field workers who, with enviable aplomb in the face of the miraculous, were more curious than alarmed by the green children and fed and cared for them. "Eventually, the nature of our food prevailing, they changed little by little to our color and looked like us; they also learned our language."[24] Prudent opinion demanded that they be baptized. They told fascinating stories of their homeland, a Christian place where Saint Martin was held in special veneration and where the sun did not rise and so scarcely illuminated the land; their last memory was of watching their father's sheep and they had no idea of how they had been precipitated to England. The boy died quite young, but the girl grew up, "not in the smallest way different from women of our own race,"[25] and married at a village called "Lennam." William's final remark about this touchingly homely prodigy, the more curious for its very banality, has already been quoted: "Let anyone say what he wants, and reason about these things as he is able; as for me, it does no harm to describe a prodigious and miraculous event."

He immediately proceeds to three more prodigies, not for the sake of sensation, but for their "hidden explanation": "Other things equally strange and prodigious happened in our time a few of which I shall describe. I am telling marvels of this sort not so much for their curiosity value but because they have a hidden explanation."[26]

A huge rock split open at a stone quarry proved to have an internal cavity, "but with no breathing holes,"[27] containing two live dogs of a recognizable breed but with fierce faces, a bad smell, and no hair. One of them died; "they say that Henry, bishop of Winchester kept the other, which had a huge appetite, several days for his own amusement."[28] Another quarry yielded a strange rock, "a double rock, that is, one formed by two rocks joined together in a subtle manner," which was brought to the bishop (unnamed) who ordered it broken open. It contained a toad wearing a golden collar. Everyone watching was stupefied with astonishment except the bishop, who had the pieces sealed back together and the thing thrown into the quarry and buried, "in perpetuity."[29] The third of this series was told to William "by a boy" and occurred not far from his own birthplace, near a village on a spring called "Gipse" (whose channels and flow he pauses to describe carefully).[30] A rustic from the village on the Gipse spring was returning late and drunk from a convivial visit with a friend when he heard singing voices from a familiar earth mound. Investigating, he found an open doorway and, inside, men and women feasting in a large, lighted room. One of them noticed him and hospitably offered a drink, which he accepted but stealthily poured out. He then ran away with the cup, was chased by the enraged feasters, but escaped home with his prize. "Eventually this chalice of an unknown material, strange color, and unusual form, was given to the senior Henry, king of England, for a great price, and next was given to David, king of Scotland, the brother of the queen ... and only a few years ago as I learned from a true report, it was given up by King William of Scotland to Henry the Second who saw it and wanted it."[31]

I again want to admit quite fully and frankly that I consider the process of worrying over the suggestive details of these wonderfully pointless miracles in an effort to find natural or psychological explanations of what "really," if anything, happened, to be useless to the study of William of Newburgh or, for that matter, of the Middle Ages. Being convinced that the twelfth-century scholar did make use of the best critical methods available to him—and that is where the real point of discrimination lies—I simply, and at the risk of being accused of a different kind of credulity, accept whatever he accepted as the subject at hand. The questions that surround those persons who claimed to have seen the green children and toads with golden collars are quite different and, I think, impossibly difficult. Henry of Huntingdon says quite clearly that he saw blood flow from the walls of Ramsey Abbey. Aside from the silliness of flatly contradicting him, there is not terribly much an historian can say, though psychohistorians may well disagree. William of Newburgh's acceptance of Henry's assertion because miracles were not forbidden to his world by science or religion and because of contemporary educated opinion's respect for Henry, brings us thankfully back that one crucial remove to reflections and refractions in the human mirror, that is, to history. And there we can speak sensibly, saying, for example, that William accepted the story of the midnight revel because the solidity of the stolen cup, passed among curious royal hands, lent its own indubitable weight to the inebriated testimony.

Whatever the authority on which he accepted them, William strenuously tried to see these miraculous appearances as random examples bound together by one intelligible, though *occultus*, *ratio* to which alone he directed his efforts. William's natural science did not—really could not—profit from techniques of observation and experiment, but his studies deserve the name of science because he was consciously searching for rational connections between unique events and the permanent structure of the universe. These kinds of rational connections are what modern scientists call laws, and William might well have agreed to that term. The difference lies in how he went about finding them. The recourse to authority is not an escape from realistic observation but a means away from flaccid credulousness and toward the rational domination of experience, at least in the case of the immaterial world. Taking as his working hypothesis the idea that the dogs, the toad, the midnight feast were effected by supernatural agency, he studied the most appropriate authorities and summarized the results of his research.

These things and others like them seem incredible unless they are proved to have occurred by the testimony of credible persons. If, however, as is written, the Magi were able by means of incantations and certain Egyptian secrets, in every case through the operations of evil angels, to turn rods into serpents and water into blood and newly produce frogs, as Augustine says, we still do not call the farmer the creator of the crop. For it is one thing to make and control a creature in a cardinal manner in accordance with the deepest and highest causes, which only God the Creator does, and it is another to apply some secondary operation by means of the powers and faculties allotted by Him so that from time to time and in various ways a created being appears—something which not only evil angels but evil men are able to do. And therefore I say that if evil angels acting through the Magi, by the permission of God, were able to do those things, it is not amazing that they are able by means of that power of the angelic nature (which we are now investigating), if they are permitted by a superior power, to produce, sometimes by trickery and illusion as in the case of the noctural feast in the earth mound, sometimes even in actuality as those dogs or the toad with the golden collar or the chalice, by which acts men are kept in a harmful stupor. The evil angels freely do those things, when they are permitted, by which men are perniciously deceived. However, the explanation of those green children, who are said to have emerged from the earth, is very hidden and the weakness of our sense is not sufficient to trace it.[32]

It is clear from William's exposition (*précis* is the more accurate term for the amount of information he conveys in a compressed space) that the Bible supplies precedent and example, but Augustine is the master of theory. As in his theoretical discussion of the powers and limits of demonic divination with which he attacked Merlin's alleged prophetic gifts, brief verbal echoes, really too short to be called quotation, allow us to identify the works of Augustine he had consulted. After alluding to Exodus, he cites his authority: "As Augustine says, we still do not call them the creators of the serpents or of the frogs, just as we do not call the farmer the creator of the crop (ut ait Augustinus, creatores draconum vel ranarum non dicimus, sicut nec agricolas segetum)." Augustine seems to have liked the simile of the farmer and the crop, since he used it several times to illustrate the difference between original creation, which belongs only to God, and the kinds of intermediary efforts (magic or natural) whose similarity of effect (something being produced that was not there before) is merely specious. Therefore, God, not Adam, was the creator of Eve, "quia nec agricolas creatores segetum."³³ And in the chapter of the *De Trinitate* titled, "Solus Deus creat etiam illa quae magicis artibus transformatur," we are again taught that the Magi were able to make serpents and frogs in a secondary manner by means of certain seminal properties hidden in all corporeal things, and we should no more call them true creators than we would call parents the creators of their child, "nec agricolas creatores frugum."³⁴ In his exposition of the Heptateuch, commenting again on the transformation miracles performed by the Magi in Exodus, Augustine repeats the crucial lessons that the Magi were aided by evil angels and that not even the angels were creators of serpents and frogs, "sicut nec agricolas segetum . . .; deus vero solus unus creator est."³⁵ Though William's preference for paraphrase over extensive quotation makes exact identification difficult, the context of the agricola phrase in the commentary on the Heptateuch (demonic production of small animals), a slightly better verbal similarity (*segetum* rather than *frugum*), with the appropriate nature of Augustine's discussion there, to William's uses point to the *Quaestiones in Heptateuchum* as the ultimate, though perhaps not sole or even directly consulted, source of his information.

Augustine was certainly not the only patristic writer to think and write extensively on demons, on the problems of their origin and continued existence, their relation to God and Satan, their inherent nature, and their powers over corporeal objects and humans; Justin Martyr, Irenaeus, Tertullian, Origen, Eusebius, Jerome, Gregory the Great, and Isidore³⁶ gave the subject an elaborated tradition, convincing complexity of information, theoretical boundaries, and respectability. But Augustine, second in medieval libraries only to the Bible, dominated the early Middle Ages on this subject as on others by the complex, unified, and wonderfully applicable brilliance of his ideas and the sheer force of his reputation. A careful student of demon literature remarks that "Augustine treats the doctrine of the Devil and of demons upon so large a scale that it would almost be possible to construct a complete demonology from his pages."[37] Simple information from an informed source still does not prevent feelings of foolish surprise when, with a mind newly aware of demons, a desultory turning of pages through the *De civitate Dei*—to choose only the obvious—brings demons everywhere to view. Perhaps we think it a mark of respect not to remember Augustine as a demonologist, but scholars in the Middle Ages (at least until demons seemed to them to ally with witches in panic-inspiring numbers) were impressed and grateful for lucidity and system in a doubtful, frightening region. Augustine's demonology is, with the exception of one whole treatise on divination by demons, scattered through many of his works,[38] and various early medieval scholars excerpted and combined appropriate passages to place them in the new structure of their own work for the convenience of later scholars who in turn could insert those passages into still newer compendiums. Along the way, Augustine frequently mutated to "Augustinian."

Recognizable fragments of Augustine's *De divinatione daemonum* and of his discussion of demonic "creation" involving the agricola simile from the *Quaestiones in Heptateuchum* appear, joined together, in varying states of truncation and with the addition of other related passages, in Rabanus Maurus's *De magicus artibus*, Burchard of Worm's *Decretorum liber*, Ivo of Chartres's *Decretum*, and Gratian's *Decretum*[39] (Gratian does not include any part of the *De divinatione daemonum*). All of these redactions appear to be scissors-and-paste creations—pieced together from excerpts identifiable, and some suggestive but not quite identifiable, as Augustine's—and any or all could have been seen by William who, I think, most probably would have consulted a useful topic collection rather than flounder through whatever miscellaneous (and unindexed) volumes of Augustine his monastery owned. The fact that the brief Augustine quotations found in his history are all to be found in these redactions suggests that, like most scholars, he depended on others. While Rabanus Maurus simply quotes long passages from Augustine without any ascription, Burchard of Worms in Book X, "De incantoribus et auguribus," identifies the passages as the work of Augustine (in one case as from the *De civitate Dei* and in others vaguely as "ex dictis ejusdem"). Both the quoted passages and the ascriptions in Ivo's *Decretum* are identical to

Burchard's and thus appear to have been copied from him. The lack of ascriptions makes Rabanus appear to be the less probable source for William; because the great popularity of Burchard's book outlived its supersession by Ivo and Gratian,[40] I think it a likely source of William's Augustinian demonology, though I by no means wish to imply that he read no further in Augustine's works.

Whatever he was able to find in the bookpress at Newburgh and perhaps at Rievaulx or Byland, William's theoretical demonology was classic and correct according to theological, not folk, authority. He scrupulously observes the distinction, observed throughout the New Testament, between the dark legions of demons (*daemones*) and their chief, the Devil or Satan (*diabolus* or *Sathana*). But the terms *daemones* and *mali angeli* are used interchangeably, suggesting that the origin of those creatures lay in the rebellion of Satan and his allies who, expelled from heaven, persist as angels with diminished powers and perverted minds. According to Isidore's definition of *daemon*, "Before their transgression they had celestial bodies. After the fall they were turned to an airy quality, and not the air of the purer spaces, but they were only allowed to possess a dark fog which is like a prison to them until the day of judgment. These are the prevaricating angels whose prince is the Devil."[41] Banished from the heavens of the blessed to some lower realm between heaven and earth, and diminished and coarsened in all their faculties, the rebel angels and their prince still retain powers beyond all human possibility. In his attack on Geoffrey of Monmouth and Merlin, William exposed the limitations of demonic divination, following Augustine's treatise on the subject, perhaps in the lengthy excerpts in Burchard's book. "Shut off from the light of God,"[42] demons cannot contemplate the future, but their finer senses gather information too subtle for human perceptions and enable them to make clever conjectures. They often make mistakes. More to the point of the present discussion is the demonic ability for which William, adhering strictly to Augustine's lessons, is at such pains to find a good verb; only God can be said to "create," but demons can do something very similar, variously described as "convertere," "producere," "admovere . . . sic exeat quod creatur," "valeant exhibere."[43] The idea is clearer than the explanation.

The uses to which demons put their considerable if not unlimited powers are always of active malevolence to men—a point that Augustine felt necessary to argue at length in the *De civitate Dei* and the *De divinatione daemonum* but that needed no elaboration by the twelfth century, when the willingness to see demons behind every misfortune had developed with, if anything, unorthodox alacrity. The peculiar difficulty posed for the very orthodox William by the demonic whims he had to explain was that they did not, on the surface at least, seem to do anyone any harm. Report, after all, had it that the bishop of Winchester was simply amused by his demonic dog. Perhaps the bishop was frivolous. William's solemn determination to see bizarre facts explained by immutable universal principles brings him to wonderful refinements: "by which acts (the dogs, toad, chalice) men are kept in a harmful stupor. The evil angels freely do those things, when they are permitted, by which men are perniciously deceived." The evil the demons have inflicted upon men is here purely intellectual; they have, with a few measly toads and dogs, reduced men to a state of "harmful stupor" and pernicious deception—intellectual humiliation being a sufficient evil in William's opinion. The green children, baptized and ingenuous, cannot be assigned to any reasonable category of demonic malice, and William, unwilling to distort fact or theory, admits that explanation of their appearance remains hidden from him.

The final, central principle of Augustinian demonology, suggested by William, is that demons, albeit evil and effective, are not free. They can produce startling effects "when they are permitted";[44] the evil angels, acting through the Magi, "by the permission of God were able to do those things."[45] In the passage used by Rabanus, Burchard, and Ivo (just above the line William quotes) Augustine explains: "No one should believe that he is able to effect anything by means of the magic arts without the permission of God who either Himself does, by His just judgment, all the things that are effected or allows them to be done by His permission."[46] Far from equality with God, the entire force of evil acts only by His suffrance, although for reasons beyond human understanding. The ultimate divine control of evil is a fact that William, like Augustine, underscores whenever apt and that must have been reassuring intellectually and emotionally.

If he was not entirely and unnaturally immune to the little excitements of hearing and telling demon stories, William's larger controlling purpose was not to provoke his readers to titillated fear. His theme is rationality and faith. If it is true, as recently stated, that during the twelfth century "the refinements of theology limiting the powers of Satan were lost on the people, who dwelt in awe and terror of the Lord of all evil," it is also true that at least one writer was trying to remind his readers that evil is not without limits.[47] Demons are orthodox members of the Christian universe, and their mysteries yield before careful study just as they themselves yield before true faith. Whatever extravagance they perform, they cannot befuddle a correctly informed mind or pervert the faith of one who knows how grossly inferior they are in the hierarchy of celestial beings.

The basic principles of demonology are established early in the *Historia* (Book I, chap. 28) and serve as a rational control over the succeeding stories of supernatural prodigies. Brief discussions of three of those stories will show William's consistent efforts to bring things diverse and apparently irrational into some intelligible congruity with faith and reason.

Following the life of Saint Godric, whom William admired for his rustic simplicity and purity, is an account, based on the testimony of "truthful men," of another "rustic man but whose singular innocence and simplicity was rewarded by a gift from God."[48] His name was Ketell, and he was especially interesting to William because God had given him the power to see and converse with demons. One day he was thrown from his horse, and when he stood up he saw two "little Ethiopians"[49] sitting in the road, laughing. "He understood that these were demons who were not permitted to do him any more harm than that and were rejoicing to have hurt him even a little. He received a gift from God such that from that day henceforth demons were visible to him, and however much they wanted to hide, they could not hide from him."[50] In response to this somewhat unnerving distinction Ketell devoted his mind to prayer, his body to celibacy, and his services to Adam, a clerk of Farnham in Yorkshire. Ketell's special sensitivity (reminiscent of the superior faculties of demons and angels) brought him adventures and a great deal of practical demonology. He watched as demons drove off to hell with a cartload of captured, sinful souls; his guardian angel saved him from the same fate when demons crept up on him when he was asleep; he observed the ape-demons sitting on the heads of drinkers in the taverns, spitting into the beer.

The irresistible thing to William must have been precisely the naïveté of it all; in the illiterate, pious Ketell he seemed to have found a source of unlearned, untampered experience of demons that completely bore out his own book-learning. (To William's credit in our eyes and probably his own disappointment, he never had any direct experience with demons.) This uniformity of folk knowledge with patristic teaching on the subject of demons may suggest something to us about the continuity and force of Christian education,[51] but William could logically only observe that modern experience demonstrated the usefulness of ancient authority, rather like a scientist reaffirming new data on an already established theory. Thus, Ketell discovered for himself exactly what any cloistered scholar could have told him about demons: that they are hierarchically arranged, in something of a parody of the orders of good angels, from some that are "large, strong, and clever" down to the "small and contemptible, impotent in strength and weak in their senses,"[52] that all of them delight in inflicting harm on men, that they act only by permission of God, and that the most casual, even blasphemous, utterance of the name of the Lord scatters them in instant confusion. These twelfth-century rustic demons are old-fashioned in nature and behavior and easily thwarted.

Much more threatening than demons busy with pastoral mischief, and probably higher in the demonic hierarchy, were the ones that dared to attempt the true faith. William's account of the Breton heretic, Éon de l'Étoile (Eudo or Eun in William's text), is valued as the fullest extant, reliably based on contemporary witness:[53] "We heard these things from certain persons who were in his [Éon's] band," and "I heard from a certain venerable man who was there while these things [Éon's trial] were happening."[54] The emphasis is not on the heresy so much as on the demonic forces behind it,[55] and demonology works to rationalize the otherwise, to William, irrational phenomenon of popular heresy. William's particular mark is visible in the ingenious way the extravagances of popular credulity are accepted and yet confined in a rational, theoretical pattern; again, a small triumph of the peculiarly Christian ability to sophisticate the simple and to effect the "abolition of the internal frontiers between the learned and the vulgar."[56] Éon or Eun, "in the language of Gaul,"[57] seems to have been a layman whose smattering of badly declined Latin led him to confuse his own name with the "Eum qui venturus est judicare vivos et mortuos."[58] He convinced others of his divinity and organized his followers into a roving band of looters who preyed on churches and monasteries. Accounts, exaggerated by fear and local famine, of the luxurious state of Éon and his band slipped easily into belief that there were demonic provisioners for his camp, forest-hidden and splendid.[59] Éon was eventually caught and tried before Pope Eugenius III at the Council of Rheims in 1148, where his wild speeches, perhaps with intention, convinced the judges he was simply mad[60] and he was sentenced to prison, where he died in a short time. William shapes the facts and marvels of Éon's career into an exemplum of the terrible fearfulness but ultimate impotence of the Devil—the distilled lesson of Augustinian demonology.

Éon himself is presented as a mere dupe, so illiterate and witless and "so demented by demon's tricks,"[61] he thought he heard his name in the liturgy. The perversion of the faith of the "simple souls" Éon attracted and the devastation of the churches and monasteries he plundered is entirely the Devil's desire (this is one of the few times William invokes the name of the *diabolus* himself), and Éon is Satan's instrument. Demonic powers of pseudocreation surrounded him with false splendors to lure the uncautious to perdition: "He appeared surrounded with great glory, equipped like a king, and his followers felt the effects of his solitude, dressed gorgeously and feasting splendidly, they seemed to live in the greatest joy.... They did things in an illusory way with the aid of demons."[62] The demonic food at the banquets was especially pernicious, "not true and solid but airy food," causing violent indigestion and heretical belief in anyone who tasted it.[63] The drunken, wary peasant who wandered into the midnight feast in Yorkshire knew he must pour out the wine before he stole the demons' cup. In these details William is expanding on strict tradition and filling out the bare theory of demonic "creation" with folklore about the properties of demon food. He refers, as does Isidore, to the demons as "airy spirits" and extrapolates to call their food "not solid but airy."[64] But the demons could produce more than cuisine, and one anecdote tells the story of a weak-willed squire who could not resist the gift of a falcoln from Éon. "Throw away," his knight said, "what you are carrying immediately, for that is not a bird as it appears but a demon thus transformed."[65] The squire refused, and his demon–falcon carried him away in its talons. Shape-shifting was a classic demon trait.

But, as Augustine insists and William reminds us, the Devil acts by the permission of God, and what God permits He can also refuse. "Finally that demon-deceived man, when the demons were no longer permitted to use him for their rage (for they can do no more than they are allowed according to the superior power and just judgment of God), was easily caught by the archbishop of Rheims." No longer a minister of Satan but only a madman, when Éon declaimed at his trial, "Ego sum Eun, qui venturus est judicare vivos et mortuos," the judges only laughed.

Most human contact with demons is presented as involuntary and unwanted. Twelfth-century England was not the lurid scene of devil worship and witchcraft either in actuality or popular imagination that other parts of Europe became somewhat later, and William, true to his own and the best spirit of his age, never shows any concern with finding, accusing, or punishing anyone who invokes demons. He knows, and probably quite correctly, that persons do exist who deliberately attempt to profit by demonic powers of divination, but even there his reaction is restrained and didactic; he demonstrates simply that such traffic is not only wrong but, given the nature of demons, ultimately useless and worse. No demon will ever bring anything but harm to men. Augustine frequently explained the severe limitations in demonic powers of divination[66] and somewhat less often, though the idea is implicit in his demonology, explicitly taught that demons would prophesy only to deceive or injure:

> We understand this about the lying spirit by whom Achab (III Reg. xxii, 20–23) was deceived.... God is the omnipotent and just distributor of punishment and reward

according to merit, not only to His good and blessed ministers to be used for their proper works, but even to evil ministers to be used for works appropriate to them. For they through perverted cupidity want to do harm; they are allowed to do just as much as He decides, who disposes all things in measure, weight, and number."[67]

Demons are relatively free to use their knowledge of the future for any nefarious purpose.

Commerce with demons for the purpose of discovering the future is, in William's anecdotes, an individual act of moral presumption that contains its own punishment. A typical example is the case of a certain Stephen, minister of Anjou for Henry II, who feared for the security of his position after Richard I's release from captivity, especially because certain encroachments had been made during the king's absence. He consulted a diviner and was allowed, for a price, to ask three questions of a skull, which told him, first, that he would never see King Richard, second, that he would hold his position until his death, and third, that he would die "in pluma."[68] (The denouement is admittedly obvious, but demons were not always up to the best standard of nastiness with originality.) After taking elaborate precautions involving his bed, Stephen died, of course, in a castle called Pluma, betrayed by the "deceit of a demon."[69] Basically similar stories are told of Pope Silvester II and of Alberic of Northumbria.[70] William clearly assumes that divination is a service easily available for a fee and that demons are quite willing to cooperate with diviners after their fashion. His stories are directed only to the arrogant fools who would connive with evil to cheat destiny.

The Devil and his demons are of respectable, ancient, Christian family; they acknowledge the Lord in every act of bleak malice. Their very orthodoxy leaves only a limited field for the rational investigator: research into correct established theory followed by sorting and classifying new observations under appropriate categories. If William's demonology is not very creative, he was working over a thoroughly tilled field. One eventually acquires, with William's guidance, a sense of certainty that some intelligible explanation can be discovered for every phenomenon in his world, provided one is willing to join sympathetically in deductive modes of thought. He clearly believed that principles, long ago discovered and recorded, will still explain a great variety of otherwise inexplicable things if only men would make the effort to study the appropriate authorities and be clever enough to see the connections between ancient dictum and modern fact. For all its obvious limitations, the cleverness able to make such an arrangement of theory with particular cases created the kind of systematic knowledge properly called science (not, of course, experimental science). It arranges the world and predicts.

Few twelfth-century men of learning lingered among the puzzles of inductive science—the investigation of things unrecorded and unexplained by any authority—but William allows us to watch him struggle through such a test when the repeated, consistent, experience of sober contemporaries had convinced him of something about which the ancients were unnervingly silent.

> Certainly the fact that the cadaver of a dead person, having gotten out of its grave, should be borne about by I know not what spirit to terrorize or injure the living, and be returned to that grave which spontaneously opens for it, would not be received easily in good faith unless there were many examples from our own time and the testimony were abundant. It is plainly amazing that such things happen, when there is nothing similar to be found in books of the ancients whose great zeal was always to commit everything memorable to writing. Since they neglected to record nothing of even moderate interest, how could they have suppressed something so bewildering and horrible if it had occurred in their time? However, if I wanted to write of every occurrence of this sort that could be discovered to have happened in our time, the work would be too elaborate and burdensome.[71]

William was the recipient or very likely the eager collector of a great deal of information about creatures that we more or less identify under the name of "vampire." Still far from the unctuous evil in perpetual evening dress made familiar (and still wonderful reading) by Bram Stoker, William's vampires are, just as one might expect, monsters in their formative years who are uncertain of purpose, clumsy in execution, rustic in manner. Nonetheless, the animated corpses that climbed out of their graves to terrorize villagers in the north of England at the end of the twelfth century are among the authentic ancestors of the Transylvanian aristocrat who planted his coffin in the cellar of an English country house. William knew no special name for the things and simply described them at length; I think the convenience of using the term that eventually became the common designation does not involve much anachronism. The word vampyre was introduced to English literature in 1734 in the journal of an English traveler who was making the grand tour in Germany. He admitted that "such a notion will, probably, be looked upon as fabulous and exploded, by many people in England," but was himself impressed by the antiquity of the legend as well as by the fact that the director of the gymnasium at Essen, "a person of great erudition," had published his doctoral dissertation on Servian vampires in 1732. After all, the traveler concludes, "the Supreme Being may make wicked spirits his instruments of punishment here, as well as plauges, wars, famines, & c. and, that he actually has done so, is sufficiently apparent from Scripture."[72]

Vampires must be distinguished from demons, spirits of the dead or ghosts, possessed persons, incubi, succubi, and werewolves. What we may call the classic vampire is defined nicely in the *Oxford English Dictionary:* "a preternatural being of a malignant nature (in the original and usual form of belief, a reanimated corpse), supposed to seek nourishment, or do harm, by sucking blood of sleeping persons."[73] (Count Dracula with his vampire harem, shape-shifting, and elaborate ritual behavior is a baroque rather than a classic specimen.) Although the sucking of blood is the automatic first connotation of the word *vampire* (as in *vampire bat*), what distinguishes the vampire from the array of common medieval supernatural beings is its gross corporeality after death. Angels are spiritual beings; evil angels or demons are degraded to an attenuated form of "airy" matter (hence their shape-shifting into animals and the sexual forms of incubi and succubi); werewolves, with an etymological origin similar to wergeld, are live men who become wolves. Only the vampire is a human corpse animated in an unnatural and evil way. Elements of the classic legend also include a sinful life, emergence from the grave to frighten and harm the living—especially close kindred (though not necessarily blood-sucking), a body uncorrupt and bloated in appearance when exhumed, and the necessity for ritual destruction of the corpse by impalement or cremation. William had no available means of knowing that vampires were neither new nor particularly English. The name *vampire* is Slavic in origin and the echt vampire of literature resided chiefly in eastern Europe, where the tradition was most ghastly; but corpses repeatedly climbed from their graves in early Scandinavia (perhaps the source of the English vampires) and in classical and Hellenistic Greece, where the existence of vampires would be openly acknowledged by the Orthodox Church.[74] Vampires rarely appeared in the medieval West.[75] Vampires are much more pagan than Christian in their heavy grip on the fleshly body, but the idea of possession by the Devil offered a plausible explanation for reanimation, once the monster became Christian. For western European and especially English vampires, William cannot be faulted for scholarship; the old books, ancient or medieval, that he consulted in vain would not have described vampires and modern scholars cite William himself as the first literary source.[76]

Walter Map should perhaps have that nominal honor by a few years because he included two brief vampire stories in the *De nugis curialium*,[77] but he was a recorder of amusing tales and not inclined to go burrowing through libraries looking for precedents to dubious information. His approach may strike us as more appropriate than William's—deep seriousness about matters the passage of time has made funny is not a dignified historical posture. But considering the severe difficulties surrounding the acceptance of any unprecedented novelty by a learned man at that time, William's decision to confront the vampires with his own mind, unaided by authority, was a braver, bolder course than most forms of denial could have been. If he now stands convicted of credulity, it is the price he pays for a curious mind.

I shall refer to the four vampires of the *Historia* (they are grouped together under the year 1197), according to provenance, as the Buckingham vampire, the Berwick vampire, the vampire of Melrose Abbey, and the vampire of Castle Anantis. The quotation given above, in which William admits to having found no precedent for the recent terrible events in northern England, is the preface to the story of the vampire of Melrose Abbey. In life the man was a priest, chaplain to a noblewoman and so addicted to hunting he was contemptuously called Hundeprest.[78] He was buried at Melrose Abbey but often at night emerged from the grave to wander howling about the bedchamber of his former lady; the holy lives of the monks protected them from such annoyance. The lady's past generosity to the abbey made her suffering the more pitiable to the Melrose monk she consulted, and he offered to hold vigil by the grave in company with one brother and two young men. The night went by, nothing appeared, and the monk's three companions went off to warm themselves by a fire. "Therefore when the monk remained by himself in that place, the Devil thought it was a good time to find out if he could break the man's courage and so he roused up his own vessel that had seemed quieter than usual for a time."[79] Seeing and hearing the monster advance on him, the monk started to run, then recovered himself and bravely struck the vampire with an ax. It shrieked and ran back to the grave, chased by the ax-wielding monk; the grave opened spontaneously and closed over it. "When they dug the thing from the earth, they saw the great wound it had received and a great quantity of blood that flowed from the wound filled the grave. They burned it outside the monastery and scattered the ashes."[80] William heard all this from a monk.

The Hundeprest was Satan's vessel; tradition, following the implications of the New Testament, taught that demons took possession of unwilling victims, but the Devil's own influence was exerted over the wicked and the guilty.[81] The animated corpse was susceptible to bodily injury and pain and, as the opened grave revealed, was unusually full of blood for a long-buried corpse. (The four vampires William describes are all eventually found to be turgid with blood, but none are accused of acquiring it from sleeping victims.) Not all vampire-infested societies accepted the dramatic and horrid Slavic remedy of a stake driven through the heart; cremation was the usual Greek ritual.[82]

Even cremation was so repugnant to western Christian sensibilities that some authorities would not countenance it in any circumstance. The Buckingham vampire sexually assaulted his living wife the night following his burial, then terrified his brothers and neighbors and the domestic animals until the entire village went in fear and sleeplessness from nightly vigils and the vampire was beginning to show himself during the day.[83] The villagers turned quite naturally to the Church—and here William lets us see a detail of daily pastoral administration as the clergy must have known it—and brought their plight before Stephen, archdeacon of Buckingham, who later told everything to William. The archdeacon sent a written report to the bishop of Lincoln, then the Carthusian Hugh (whom we have seen before in William's book, denouncing a false cult).[84]

> The bishop was astonished, and discussed the matter at length with his people. There were some who told him that such things often happened in England and explained with the aid of many examples that the people could not have peace unless the body of the wretched man were disinterred and cremated. But that seemed entirely too improper and indecent to the venerable priest and so he drafted an absolution with his own hand with directions to the archdeacon to determine accurately the state of the corpse. He ordered that the grave was to be opened and the absolution placed on the breast and the grave to be closed again.[85]

The bishop's instructions were followed and the vampire never wandered again. One can see in Hugh of Lincoln's actions both refinement and common sense beyond the ordinary, but there is no reason to credit him with a duplicitous and sophisticated use of mass psychology. He had surrounded himself with a carefully chosen *familia* and undoubtedly trusted their sincerity and sense.

William does not pretend to understand why vampires were appearing in England; he describes their characteristics and stresses the practical matter of an expeditious remedy. The cases of both the Berwick vampire and the vampire of Castle Anantis involved the further horror of contagious disease. A secondary trait often ascribed to vampires was the spread of disease through corruption of the air[86]—a theory of contagion long held by men who had no belief in vampires. After the Berwick vampire had raged for several days, a meeting was held:

> The question of what had to be done was discussed among the great and humble alike, the more simple people thinking that if by chance anything went wrong they would be even more assaulted by the monster later on.

The more prudent ones cautiously considered that if the remedy were delayed the air would become corrupted from the pestiferous cadaver wandering around and many would become ill and die as was made clear by many examples of similar cases.[87]

William clearly agrees with the "prudent ones" on the necessity of quick measures to protect the health of the community. The efficacy of cremation is, for him, a simple matter of experience, "because while the thing remained uncremated the populace had no rest. But once it was burned the people had quiet."[88] From such evidence medieval men drew their conclusions and we draw ours; the conclusions are contradictory but about equally consistent with the evidence.

William's vampire stories have sometimes the tone of a sanitary commission report. Delays before exterminating the vampire of Castle Anantis (who had died as a result of injuries suffered in a fall from a ceiling beam, where he had been lying concealed to spy on his wife and her lover) resulted in the almost complete extinction of a village by disease.[89] Fortunately, two bold young men were too impatient to wait for the deliberations of a solemn assembly of "wise men of religion," and they executed the vampire themselves, thus halting the epidemic. William approved.

Early English vampires may well have confined their attentions to isolated northern villages where excitement was rare and perhaps welcome, but the pious monks, the experienced archdeacon, and the incomparably sensible bishop of Lincoln accepted the vampires, it appears, as completely as the susceptible villagers with whom the stories originated. Quite a number of persons in the Middle Ages disinterred saintly bodies and believed they found them in much the same uncorrupt, lifelike condition that distinguished the remains of the vampire. The uncorrupt corpse was a fairly common phenomenon, though the similarity between saints and vampires is confusing. The consistency of vampire stories and the apparently widespread knowledge of how to destroy them show that the vampire had a more ancient English history than literature records. William selects a few of the stories he had acquired (he refers often to the many examples known) and arranges them to illustrate the consistency in appearance and behavior from one vampire to another and thus creates a category for them. He repeatedly insists that they are a form of demonic possession and thus suggests a Christian explanation. He is especially concerned to teach the necessity of immediate cremation to prevent disease. Given a subject of implicit and unreasoning horror, he made a brave effort to bring it under control for the sake of learned minds and simple lives alike.

This discussion of demons, diviners, and vampires must conclude with the mystery of the lime pit at Malton Priory in 1197.[90] The canons of Malton had prepared a shallow pit for burning lime, and one day, after sunset, one of the brothers fell in and called, "I am killed," and then there was silence. Another climbed in after him and never came out; a third went after and was pulled out, barely alive, and did not recover for several days. The next day the bodies were recovered safely and showed no bruises. Everyone was appalled and amazed. William heard these things from eyewitnesses, and adds:

> It happened a few years ago in an East Anglian village while three workmen were cleaning out an old well and dug deeply into the earth to find a better supply of water, that they died suddenly. When this occurred, the inhabitants filled the well with rubbish and decided the place would be an eternal grave for the dead men. But that event was not astounding because the explanation can probably be given. Perhaps the bottom of the well had a hidden vein of quicksilver or some other noxious substance which, as it is believed, was opened by the diggers.[91]

William's explanation is sufficient comment on his abilities and sense. Unlike Adelard of Bath, who promised to use observation for natural science and then never ventures beyond chastest theory, William modestly searches his authorities, but is able to speculate unaided when they fail him—about vampires and underground gases and whatever else the dazzling variety of twelfth-century "reality" offered for his contemplation. I can only conclude that the realistic observer of the twelfth century had a good deal more to observe than we.

III
RICHARD OF DEVIZES

Six

THE TEMPORAL WORLD

THE *Cronicon Richardi Divisensis de tempore Regis Richardi Primi*[1] is a sophisticated, original work of history. It begins with the coronation of Richard I in 1189 and ends when the crusading king decided to leave the Holy Land in 1192. The book covers these four years in the brief space of eighteen manuscript (*r* & *v*),[2] or eighty-four printed pages in the most recent edition. The author Richard, who identifies himself as "of Devizes"—a small town a few miles from Winchester—was a monk at Saint Swithun's, the cathedral abbey of Winchester. Other than the fact that he wrote the *Cronicon* and part of the Winchester Annals,[3] there exists no information about him. Internal evidence proves that the *Cronicon* was composed before 1198, and its editor thinks that it probably was finished before 1194.[4] Stylistic evidence strongly suggests that the 1196–1202 portion of the Winchester Annals is an original composition by Richard of Devizes; if so, he was writing at least until 1202. Unfortunately, there is nothing to suggest a birthdate. The *Cronicon* is completely original in that it seems to draw upon no other known written sources and is not mentioned by any contemporary writer; it has survived in only two manuscript copies.[5] The book was very likely read by the man to whom it is dedicated, Robert, a prior of Saint Swithun's who became a Carthusian monk, and by a small circle of Richard's friends.

The two manuscripts containing the *Cronicon* are described fully in the informative introduction to Appleby's excellent edition and translation; the evidence for his contention that one manuscript is an author's draft and the other a fair copy in another hand of that draft is quite convincing.[6] The nature of the author's draft—text accompanied by marginalia in increasing amounts until margin overwhelms text—demanded great editorial ingenuity, and Appleby's solutions to the problem of creating a consecutive text without misrepresenting the original are sensible and clear.[7] We do have, therefore, everything that Richard of Devizes wrote for his history, but we can never know his exact intentions with regard to selection and arrangement for the finished book. The sequence of events in the *Cronicon* is frequently abrupt; dramatic changes of time, place, and subject occur without warning or transition, yet the writer is clearly so intelligent and "literary" that one must think that he preferred such a technique—plunging over and over *in medias res* for the sake of excitement.

The subject matter of the *Cronicon* is chiefly the Third Crusade and the political situation in England during the king's absence. Richard's account of the Third Crusade is oddly truncated, factually unreliable,[8] and very interesting for its revelation of English attitudes toward the French and some of the author's particular characteristics of mind. The story of Count John's machinations in England, where he hoped his unmarried (until 1191) and heirless brother would not return, and the efforts of the unpopular chancellor William Longchamp to preserve his lord's kingdom are told in dramatic and accurate detail.[9] The career of Longchamp especially, from bishop, chancellor, and legate to impotent exile is the subject of greatest dramatic intensity in the book, and the character of Longchamp is the most carefully delineated. Professor Appleby and I differ in our opinions of Richard's appraisal of Longchamp and John; happily, the *Cronicon* contains all the material necessary for the reader to form his own. In addition to the main subjects of politics and war, the *Cronicon* contains numerous anecdotes and remarks on subjects that Richard and, presumably, his audience, found interesting: monks and monastic life, the respective merits of English power and wealth, and an account of the accusation of ritual murder brought against the Jews of Winchester in 1192.

As a stylist, Richard cannot be described quickly or adequately; he was a master of tone and nuance and has to be read—all the more so because he was a satirist. Although, among his classical sources, Richard does not quote Sallust, the *Cronicon* neatly bears out some recent remarks made by Beryl Smalley on Sallust's pervasive influence on medieval historical writing: influence toward the monograph instead of universal scale, brevity, pithiness, use of proverbial sayings, and the "imitable and imitated trait . . . analysis of motive, informed by cynical pessimism."[10] Many medieval historians were influenced, directly or indirectly, in these directions, but in comparison with his predecessors and contemporaries, Richard simply sounds different from all of them. That difference is one of voice; more consistently and more easily than any other historian, Richard adopted the persona traditionally the property of the poet of satire. Many critical observations on twelfth-century satire hold true for Richard as well as for poets such as Hugh Primas: the use of a "middle style" that incorporates elements of both popular speech and the elevated style, the implicit authority of the speaker, and his assumption of the audience's respect, attention, and consent for controversial or critical ideas that he assumes are shared.[11] The relative succinctness of the *Cronicon*, its subject matter, and its anecdotal style are precisely the elements of a satirist–historian.

Richard was a man of classical education and he displays it throughout his work. Among classical authors, Richard's taste is for satirists and epic poets: Horace, Juvenal, Ovid, and Lucan, Virgil, Persius, and Statius. His natural gift for satire, refined by study of the masters, gives the *Cronicon* its characteristic tone, and, in a casual way, the book has also a loosely epic effect. It has a central heroic figure in King Richard, engaged in a noble exploit—the Third Crusade; a traitorous brother; and a kingdom at stake. The parallel themes of the noble campaign of Richard for the Holy Land and the base campaign of John to usurp his brother's realm are constantly juxtaposed for dramatic tension. The effect of copious use of classical quotation in describing events in England is to raise the struggle between Longchamp and John to the heroic proportions of Richard I and Saladin. Regardless of the fact that the existing author's draft of the *Cronicon* is most imperfect with regard to structure and sequence, Richard's natural gifts for anecdote and for quick, strong effects could easily have led him to juxtapose English and foreign episodes for dramatic contrast without any of the usual transitions to shift the scene. Specific matters of Richard's narrative art are discussed at greater length in chapter 8.[12] The epic qualities are admittedly much weaker than the satiric, since Richard was much more strongly drawn to the colloquial language, smaller events, and sharp, comic observation of satire. Epic writers must inflate the proportions of event and character to heroic size; Richard's impulse was always to deflate.

Richard of Devizes was a man of conservative opinions expressed with audacious wit. A proud member of one of the richest houses of an old, complacent, and wealth-smothered order, he brought to the defense of England's monks whose poverty was an abstraction and of England's bishops whose pastoral cares were political, his best gifts: an aggressive mind of glittering surface and little reflective depth, a flip, nervous wit, an ironic eye for the absurd. These seductively attractive gifts show to their best advantage when Richard shows himself at his worst. Serious Christians as well as Jews could be offended by his deliberately artificial treatment of the ritual murder accusation brought against the Winchester Jews in 1192, yet nowhere is he so witty as on that terrible subject. As a monk, Richard is rigidly partisan, quick to defend all that was lax or indulgent in Benedictine houses, and closed to the appeal of spiritual adventure that led some of his most sensitive and heroic contemporaries to create or enter newer orders, but he is marvelously funny about Carthusians. Much of his urbanity and wit depended on his ability to treat lightly subjects that usually moved his contemporaries to solemn or angry feeling. It gives his observations the excitement of being faintly shocking at the expense of being shallow.

Richard's preference for placing daring cleverness at the service of conventional ideas is equally apparent in his manipulation of purely literary forms. The dedication to his chronicle is a perfect study in the art of manipulating a formal or conventional pattern in such a way as to make it a mockery of itself while never departing too far from the limits of acceptable expression. A salutation of almost unexceptional politeness (excepting perhaps the sly conditional "if"): "To his venerable father and always his master, Robert, formerly prior of Winchester: his servant Richard, called 'of Devizes': if what he has begun is good, may he persevere in it,"[13] introduces a dedication that parodies all the conventions of literary patronage in ecclesiastical circles. The superior patron who is both intellectual and spiritual mentor, the humble author, obedient and eager to comply with his patron's request but doubtful of his own ability and timidly aghast at so responsible a charge, the work itself transformed into a spiritual exercise begun in self-effacing obedience and published with trepidation[14]—all the usual postures are there at the beginning of Richard's book but deliberately made so transparently artificial as to be self-deflating.

(Consider that William of Newburgh managed to infuse the same conventional forms with plausible fresh sincerity.)

It is worth examining the dedication closely because it is significant in both form and content; it establishes the tone and attitudes of the author, the ironic voice, the contempt for behavior or ideas that are extreme, and Richard's characteristic use of the disingenuously naive persona for satirical purpose. The occasion for Richard's book and its dedication was the removal of Saint Swithun's prior, Robert, to the Carthusian monastery of Witham. According to the *Cronicon*, Robert had requested a history book from his friend and former spiritual son. The fact that his own superior could sacrifice a distinguished position at the center of all that was most cultivated, elegant, and dignified in English Benedictine life for the alleged spiritual benefits of a grubby isolated cell gave a biting, defensive edginess to Richard's account of his own pilgrimage to visit Robert at Witham—the theme of the dedication. Having the sort of cynical and self-indulgent mind that always finds hypocrisy in every act of which it is incapable, Richard had no self-doubts or spiritual unease to restrain his attack on the tiny, upstart order whose rule and life insulted the august traditions of his own.

God granted Richard's prayer to visit his former prior and to see for himself "by how much a Carthusian cell is loftier and nearer Heaven than is the cloister at Winchester."[15] Assuming an air of naive wonder and blaming his subsequent disillusionment on two anonymous companions who "threw cold water on my enthusiasm. (I will not say they pointed out my mistakes.)," he relates some of the marvels he found at Witham.

> In your community I saw something that I would not see anywhere else, something that I could not believe.... According to your rule, in each of your cells there is only one door, which you are allowed to open as you like, but through which you may not go out, except in such a way that one foot always stays short of the threshold and inside the cell. A brother may go out with one foot wherever he wants to, provided that the other foot stays inside the cell. There must be some great and profound mystery about a door that stands open and yet no-one is allowed to come in or go out through it. I wonder at another thing: you are abounding in all temporal goods,

since you have nothing and yet possess everything; you
are more merciful and kinder than all other men, since
you have perfect charity towards each other: and yet
you cut your charity to strangers in half, by giving them
a blessing without a meal. I wonder at yet a third thing:
you are men living by yourselves, secluded and alone,
away from the world; and yet you know everything that
is done in the world as soon as it takes place, and sometimes you know about it in advance, even before it is
done.[16]

He focuses his satire on three aspects of their respective rules
that show the Carthusians and Benedictines in pointed contrast:
stability, hospitality, and removal from the world. The
solemnity of the *profundum sacramentum* connected with the
comic vision of monks straddling the thresholds of their cells
points merely to the absurd behavior of Carthusians by themselves. The next idea of "perfect charity" for one another,
contrasted with the lack of sympathy for hungry guests, is more
stinging because it implies hoarding of the temporal goods,
deliberate neglect of an ancient monastic obligation, and thus,
very imperfect charity. The third comparison suggested by
Richard in his guise of ingenuous wonder is one step more
damning. The men who live most secluded from the world
somehow know the most about it; Richard implicitly accuses
them of a fascination with what they pretend to despise. He
writes with the confidence of one who thinks he has uncovered
hypocrisy in the ostentatious *contemptus mundi* of men who
have far more contacts with worldly people and far more
influence on worldly events than they would like to have
known. In a rapid crescendo of *faux naif* observations, he
sketches the Carthusians as pretentious, self-deceiving men,
whether alone, with passing travelers, or in relation to the
greater world. They are arrogant in their exaggerated claims to
spiritual purity, setting themselves rules that violate the spirit of
monasticism and that even they cannot observe very well. The
Benedictines, in implicit contrast, with their more lenient personal freedom, lavish hospitality, and unashamed involvement
with lay society, stand behind Richard's satire as the true center
of monastic life.

Because he is acute enough to recognize that the most telling
differences between Benedictines and Carthusians originate in

their attitudes toward and relations with the world, Richard expands his exposé of the weakness he thinks he has discovered. "And do not think that I am saying this to reflect on your rule of silence, which is more than Pythagorean. I dare say that men of such gravity and of such an arduous way of life are able to prophesy concerning the madness of the world, better than merely gossiping."[17] Even Robert's request for a chronicle, presumably to read in his new "cloistered heaven" lends itself to insinuations of hypocrisy:

> However, although the all-knowing God is with, as it is thought, and in you, and although you know everything, not by men or through men, but in Him alone; you wished as you said, that this exercise of mine might be a solace to you, a marking, as it were, of the beginning of the new morphosis, when the world moves, changing square things into round, especially after your transmigration to a cloistered heaven, and that I should write a chronicle for you, so that, with its fickleness more fully before your eyes, the world might seem vile to you and so that these letters might bring back the memory of your friend to you again.[18]

A man who communicates directly with God should scarcely require a book about corrupt, vain human affairs, and the fact that he admits to the desire for such a trivial production is itself suspicious. In spite of the evident affection that makes itself felt through Richard's jibes, the *Cronicon*, a book about the world, written for a man who has fled from it and offered as a sentimental tribute to an earthly friendship (now also disdained), is a double-edged gift; its very existence is made to appear the result of the contradictions, blindness, and pride inherent in Robert's new order and, considering the dedication, a constant reminder of them. One cannot help thinking that the strong and wounded feelings of a cast-off friend gave the dedication its satirical bite.

Richard's antipathy to the Carthusians was not a purely occasional reaction. In the Winchester Annals for 1198 he tells the story of another Benedictine official, Walter the prior of Bath, who became a Carthusian. In his case, the chronicler had the satisfaction of reporting a proper end to the mistaken enthusiasm:

149

Walter, the prior of Bath, a man of great learning and piety, ended his life in Christ at Werewellam. From the sub-prior of Hyde he had been made prior of Bath on account of his good reputation for piety. After he had guided his monks into perfect observance of the monastic rule, he considered to himself,

"quam frivola gloria mundi,

Quam rerum fugitivus honor, quam nomen inane,"

and he who had been promoted, preferred to give himself over rather than preside over others; he went to the Carthusians. When a certain monk from Hyde went to see him there, he saw him greatly intent on the pots and vegetables, a man who shortly before had been intent on saving souls.... He returned to his senses after not many days like this, understanding, as much through prayer as through the precept of great men, how much more holy it is to save many souls than to save one alone. He returned to his office of prior and was vigorous in it until his death.[19]

The story in the Annals repeats the defensive pattern of the *Cronicon*, which replies to Carthusian charges against Benedictine life as corrupt, world-centered, and spiritually empty with accusations of meaningless austerity and selfish neglect of others. Richard's old-guard Benedictine loyalties could yield no sympathy at all for the experimenters; he adopted the comfortable practice of seeing Carthusians as hypocritical poseurs or sincere fools. His closed, unbending reaction is a measure of the effect that anti-Benedictine feeling in the late twelfth century had had on England's richest monks. The very existence of one tiny monastery of recluses seems to have been felt an insult and a threat.

The dedication proper ends with Richard's exaggerated, effusive gratitude at the prospect of being the recipient of the prayers of a holy Carthusian: "Oh, how happy I should be if that holy soul, if that angel of the Lord, if that deified man, already counted amongst the number of the gods, should deign to remember me, who am hardly a man, in his prayers before the great God!"[20]

If one cannot avoid the embarrassing consciousness of what Richard might say about the plodding explication of his quick, aphoristic wit, it is because he is so unusually distinct and assertive a personality for a medieval writer. It is, in fact, enough to say that he *is* a personality. Within a page or two he contrives to makes perfectly clear who he is and what he thinks and that he will not submit to conventional propriety when it threatens his sense of dignity and worth. The traditional persona of the satirist poet, which was one of confident, self-assertive personality possessed of implicit moral authority, was a more congenial voice for Richard than that of the modest, self-effacing author.[21] He parodies the conventional relationship of patron and author, making his own humility a cover for aggressive criticism until, by the end of the dedication, it appears that Richard has exchanged a work of art for nothing but a prayer from a man who is himself much in need of prayers.

Selective description, comic exaggeration, and a sarcastic tone worked to double effect for the medieval reader in both the attack on the Carthusians and the sly reversal of the customary relationship of author and patron. For the modern reader, they have the additional interest of implicit information about the *Cronicon*'s intended audience. The manuscript tradition indicates a limited publication; the book was, perhaps, scarcely known outside the Winchester circle. The dedication strengthens that idea by suggesting that the writer was confident of the sympathy of his audience (or of all but one). But if Richard wrote, as one might reasonably expect, in the hope that his intended readers would understand and appreciate his book, they would have had to be more than Benedictine loyalists. They should have been men of sufficient classical education to appreciate the *Cronicon* as a refined pastiche of classical allusion; and they must not have been disturbed by the relative lack of biblical quotation and the entire absence of a Christian interpretation of history. Richard wrote for readers who had a power of classical recall quite similar to the faculty for biblical reminiscence that resulted from the *lectio divina* as practiced in twelfth-century monasteries.[22] That is, without necessarily having extensive knowledge or much understanding, they had read at least selections from a number of classical authors and had read them often enough to recognize an allusion and probably the author— perhaps not the context. The cultivation of verbal memory was an integral part of traditional monastic education.[23] The immersion of one's mind in the divine page was a spiritual exercise, and

151

although the pagans did not merit the same attention, men trained in the memorizing techniques of the *lectio divina* could hardly have refrained from applying the same methods to both. The interweavings of classical quotation in the *Cronicon*, such as Longchamp's replies to his accusers beginning with apt lines from Virgil and Juvenal, or the comic description of London incorporating Horace's lines on Rome,[24] give the impression of a useful cultivated memory, not a reference library. The author assumes the same of his audience.

It is also assumed that the *Cronicon*'s readers will appreciate the predominantly secular point of view (though much of the book's substance concerns the Church) as part of the classical atmosphere although that is only a partial explanation of Richard's secular outlook. Like the subverted dedication, the intricate patchwork of quotation demonstrates Richard's talent for manipulating received materials to interesting effect and may even suggest a refined if somewhat etiolated taste among his literary circle for very self-conscious style. But however elegantly educated, Richard seems to have made no attempt similar to William of Malmesbury's to penetrate the intentions and methods of pagan writers in order to assimilate them to the Christian revelation.[25] He seems content to arrange a glittering pastiche of classical learning over his implacable prejudices and narrow interests and remains strictly fixed in his own time and situation. By virtue of his complacent satisfaction with himself and his world, he is a mirror of both; modesty never caused him to hide his own voice behind the classical masters, or spiritual disgust to turn his attention to the incorporeal realities.

Compared with any other twelfth-century historian, Richard saw and described a surprisingly concrete world. It is not only that he virtually ignores the supernatural and that his few notices of portents are mocking,[26] but that he devotes pointed, careful attention to details of mundane existence that did not usually capture the attention of educated twelfth-century ecclesiastics, whatever their opinion of portents.

The *Cronicon* is a book filled with numbers. Whether or not his sources for those numbers were accurate, Richard clearly liked being able to give precise—or at any rate precise-sounding—quantities of things, men, and payments. There is a great difference between the way other medieval historians liked to inflate the greatness of an army with some imaginative number of impressive thousands and the way Richard offers us the hard reality of things with a figure. Bishop Godfrey of Winchester regains two lost manors for his church through the agency of the courts and a circumspect gift to the king of three thousand pounds of silver.[27] The first of King Richard's ships had "three extra rudders, thirteen anchors, 30 oars, 2 sails, and three sets of all sorts of ropes, and, in addition to this, two of whatever a ship might need, except the mast and the skiff."[28] That same ship carries forty war horses, armor for forty knights and foot-soldiers, fifteen sailors, and a year's food supply for all. In Sicily, Richard demanded the return of his sister Joan and her dowry from the king, and Henry II's legacy from King William, which consisted of "a golden table 12 feet long, a silken tent, a hundred first-class galleys with everything necessary for them for two years, sixty thousand quarters of wheat, 60,000 of barley, 60,000 of wine, twenty-four golden cups, and 24 golden plates."[29] King Richard's fleet contained "156 ships, 24 busses, and 39 galleys: the total of the vessels was 219."[30] In numerous other places Richard gives detailed information, such as how many men fought in battles and how many cured pig-carcasses, measures of wheat, and pounds of silver the king gave to Henry of Champagne to turn traitor to Philip Augustus.[31] He notes that the 10,000 count of the rabble watching Longchamp and John meeting outside London was only an estimate. He thinks easily in quantitative terms, like a merchant, and though his figures are sometimes suspiciously round and symmetrical (24 cups and 24 plates), they are not rhetorical devices in his prose nor are the numbers symbolic or biblical allusions; they give a sense of the specific, unique reality of corporeal things and a sense that everything has its price. In his preoccupation with the exact cost and size of things, he is perfectly in sympathy with the English proverb he quotes as a scoffing remark on the fools who bought Richard I's false bargains of honors and liberties: "A scholar who would learn to become a merchant buys for a shilling and sells for three halfpence."[32] Richard often seems more a merchant than a scholar.

If one approaches Richard from the earlier twelfth century, seeing him as one in a—by then—long tradition of ecclesiastic historians, he stands out sharply. The assumptions and focuses one has come to expect in twelfth-century writing about human affairs are missing and instead, there are unexpected interests, preoccupations, and a disconcerting sense of the earth-bound. The sharp, mercantile understanding of profit and loss, the sense that measurements encompass a complete and satisfactory reality seem to have replaced the allegorizing impulse, the distrust of everything mortal and transient, and the eager attentiveness to the signs of divine intervention.

If, through the force of his personality and prose style, Richard makes one sharply conscious of changes, they are not changes that, seen from another perspective, are idiosyncratic or personal. Reading the *Cronicon*, along with a selection of documents that reveal some of the characteristic tone and values of the next generation or two, it seems perfectly in place. Compared with later writers, Richard's prejudices and values appear commonplace and plausible, and conform to all the expectations one might have of a thirteenth-century Benedictine writer. Richard, who was probably born sometime about the middle of the twelfth century, often sounds like a characteristic product of the thirteenth. Certainly the Benedictines, who were forced to defend wealth and worldliness throughout a century when some men were trying to escape them and many were, at least, admiring the effort, tended to produce men who were more comfortable in an increasingly commercial and corporeal world.

To consider a rather obvious comparison, Matthew Paris, writing history in the large, wealthy Benedictine Abbey of Saint Albans a half century after Richard, exhibits the same narrow parochial loyalties and dim spirituality seen earlier in Richard. His most recent biographer and critic comments that Matthew's chronicle "betrays, on the part of its author, a rather mercenary outlook on life. Sums of money are mentioned on every possible occasion,"[33] and that he observed the vacillations of English trade and was aware of the effects of war and natural disaster on it.[34] To extend the comparison somewhat further, Matthew has also been noticed for his "patriotic feelings as a Benedictine"[35] and more particularly as a monk of Saint Albans. That warm combination of self-interest and loyalty has been described as creating an "outlook on life . . . in a large measure based on his own material interests as a monk, and on those of the small aristocratic community of which he was proud to be a member."[36] It follows predictably that he disapproved of all other religious orders and regarded the new challenge of Dominican and Franciscan friars with the same bitterness that Richard felt for Carthusians.[37] Not quite so predictable is the intriguing fact that Matthew, like Richard, impresses the modern reader with the same assertive confidence of personality: "Among English writers, Matthew stands out in front of the curtain of medieval anonymity as a real person, and in his *Chronica Majora* his outlook on life, prejudices, and interests, as well as his personality, are all revealed in a manner unusual among chroniclers of his age."[38]

It seems, at first, strange that an intense conservatism in men whose profession demanded self-abnegation into a corporate (if not spiritual) identity should have encouraged the rare expansion of human personality even in a literary genre traditionally noted for its modest authorial persona. Both Richard and Matthew had, however, freed themselves from the self-denying discipline of a deeply felt monastic vocation, if they had ever experienced one. Other men of their respective generations turned away from the rigidity and the enveloping corporate life of Benedictine monasticism for the greater personal adventure of the new orders. The impulse of individual expression in Richard and Matthew turned to the newer fascination with the natural world so increasingly evident from the twelfth century onwards. There was nothing in a world that could be measured and bought and sold that demanded the repression of human idiosyncrasy; in the created world, man holds the highest place, his intellect is sufficient for its objects, and his opinions and feelings, therefore, worth expressing. Jocelin of Brakelond is another good example of the kind of clever, narrow, practical man— attractive on a restricted and very "human" scale—that seems characteristic of the late twelfth- and thirteenth-century Benedictine world of farming, finance, and politics. He, too, wrote a chronicle laced together with sums of money and numbers of things.

To compare any of these chroniclers with the poetic seriousness of a Hugh of Saint Victor or with the high scientific curiosity and spiritual purpose of Grosseteste is to approach too near the absurd, but not to see that they, in their grubbier ways, were taken up in the same impulse toward the created world is equally unjust. They had lost the sensitivity and personal depth that monks acquired whose lives were begun and ended in spiritual desire, and having no revulsion from the world, they simply became part of it—of the earth, earthy.

The resemblance between Richard (or Jocelin and other late twelfth-century Benedictines) and Matthew Paris should not be taken to indicate an insular, rigidified tradition of monastic historical writing. Somewhat paradoxically, their shared paro-chialism and mundaneness suggest not only the close of one vital tradition of spiritual and intellectual life, but also the advent of a new one. Various writers and documents typical of the thir-teenth century clearly and pointedly reveal developments still inchoate in Richard. To return to my first example, the numbers that function so precisely and importantly in Richard's book are indicative of a changing state of mind toward the conditions of human life and the things of the earth. A significant if startling parallel can be seen between that earthiest of thirteenth-century works, Walter of Henley's treatise on estate management and farming (written in the last quarter of the century)[39] and Richard's elegant book. The treatise is cast in the form of a father's advice to his son.[40] One of the crucial tenets of that advice is to save part of each year's income against bad times and thus avoid money lenders, "Or els you may buy and selle, as some men (that make themselves out to be merchants) doe, which buy for a shilling and selle againe for ten pence."[41] The same point of view informs Richard's proverb about the con-temptible scholar–merchant who buys for a shilling and sells for three halfpence.

The development of a shrewd, practical mind, directed to the efficient management of the world's business, does not neces-sarily involve an attenuated spiritual life; Grosseteste, after all, wrote on estate management for ecclesiastical and lay lords, and Walter of Henley had become a Dominican friar by the time he composed his treatise on farming.[42] We know nothing of Wal-ter's spiritual life, however, and Grosseteste would have been exceptional in any age; the perfunctory Christianity of Matthew Paris and Richard was more typical of men whose gaze was drawn out of themselves but away from heaven. Even the

Cistercians, by the end of the twelfth century, had turned their wilderness into crowded worlds of sophisticated farming, high finance, and litigation, and while a modern student may sympathize with William of Newburgh in seeing them still as "fountains of eternal life," elaborate economic arrangements and prosperity eventually did distort their original purposes. On ancient, great estates such as that of the bishopric of Winchester, one of the wealthiest of the English sees, efficiency had never posed questions of conscience. Winchester was the first bishopric to introduce, at the end of the twelfth century, the systematic method of accounting and auditing developed in the Royal Exchequer. Its bishop from 1174 to 1188 was Richard of Ilchester, a leading Exchequer official who remained in royal service during his episcopate. Inevitably, because of the trained intelligence of the men running them and because of the need for good and continuous management on episcopal estates, which reverted periodically to the king, bishoprics (monastic and secular) were early and fully at the front of a general movement in English society toward a rationalized management and, more generally, an optimistic, manipulative view of the material world.[43] Men like Richard and Matthew Paris and Jocelin of Brakelond were conservative and "modern" at once when they concentrated their loyalties on the secular prosperity of monastic corporations.

The man who looks at a flock of sheep and proceeds to count them is very different from the one (perhaps a William of Newburgh or an Aelred) who is moved by the same sight to reflect on the Shepherd or the sacrificial lamb. A few generations seemed to mark out that mental distance in educated medieval society. Richard was one of those who count the flock.

Richard's interest in the cost and quantity of things can also, if obviously, be described as "mercantile," with all the attendant connotations of trade, merchants, markets, and, especially, towns. In spite of his pronounced conservative, aristocratic bias, the calculating tenor of his mind seems markedly bourgeois and reflects the experience and assumptions of an urban man. His close interest in exact value and profit and loss is more consistent with the marketplace than with a feudal lord's grandeur and *largitas* (even when accompanied by constant anxiety over funds). His wit is also of the town, "urbane" in every sense—a satirical, knowing view of things, based on the wide observation and various experience long associated with city life. From a literary point of view, this aspect of Richard's style can be connected quite directly with his classical reading. In terms of his own life, to be a monk in a cathedral abbey in an important town meant a life so thoroughly immersed in the business, politics, gossip, and, even then, rapid pace of city life that notions like a monk's death to the world and his seclusion were, under the circumstances, charming anachronisms.

Richard's feeling for towns involved an ambivalence between aristocratic distrust and contempt, and his very urban personality and attitudes. He regarded the grant of a commune or, rather, "conspiracy,"[44] to London in 1191 with strong disapproval:

> Now London first realized that the king was absent from the realm by this conspiracy granted to it, which neither King Richard himself nor his predecessor and father, Henry, would have allowed to be done for a million silver marks. How many evils indeed arise from the conspiracy may be gathered from its very definition, which is this: a commune is the tumult of the people, the terror of the realm, and tepidity of the priesthood.[45]

His nervousness at the prospect of towns moving away from their traditional overlords is typical of his class and order, but the million silver marks that he invokes as a measure of the repulsiveness of communes sounds like a townsman's reckoning. Since most communes were won at the expense of episcopal power, his distaste for them is unsurprising. In Richard's alliterative definition, a commune is the unruly desire of some universal urban class called the "people" (*plebs*), but a little farther on in the *Cronicon,* speaking of the crowd gathered to watch Longchamp meet his accusers outside London, he carefully distinguishes between "a circle of citizens" (*quiritum*—in his classicized term) who stood nearest the great lords and the common spectators (*populus spectans*) who looked on from a distance.[46]

In his hierarchy of loyalties, the town of Winchester stands second only to his order and house. The characteristically wry, double-edged style of Richard's compliments does not disguise his real conviction of the superior sophistication, manners, and acumen prevailing in Winchester. Praising the town for resisting the example of London and not rioting against its Jewish population after the coronation of Richard I, he comments, "Winchester alone spared its worms. They were a prudent and far-sighted people and a city that always behaved in a civilized manner. They never did anything over-hastily, for fear they might repent of it later, and they looked to the end of things rather than to the beginnings."[47]

If he sometimes jibes a little too much at London and sounds a little defensive about Winchester's merits, that has always been the inevitable tone of those who praise cities whose first characteristic is that they are *not* Rome or Rome's equivalent. Elsewhere, he tacitly admits London's first place in the realm when he quotes Richard I's jest, "If I could have found a buyer I would have sold London itself,"[48] as proof of the reckless, duplicitous bargains the king was willing to make to raise money for a crusade. But in Winchester, where people are accustomed to look "to the end of things," he sees the qualities that make city life so attractive and, eventually, indispensible to the true urban personality. Rational calculations and the ability to repress hasty satisfactions for the sake of greater, delayed benefits characterized burghers long before the rise of Protestantism. "Civilized" behavior invariably includes, for Richard, the signal ability to govern behavior with prudence. Punctiliousness in repaying debts is another point of particularly urban honor on which Richard insists—his highest proof of the personal merit of Bishop Godfrey of Winchester is that the bishop quickly repaid in full the money he had to borrow from his chapter.

All of Richard's urban tastes and attitudes are contained in his tour guide to the English towns, a tongue-in-cheek combination of satirical jokes and a few seriously held prejudices—engagingly like Jane Austen's *History of England* by a self-described "partial, prejudiced, and ignorant historian."[49] It is not only the best comic composition of the book but also an excellent guide to the most parochial and cosmopolitan attitudes of a twelfth-century city man. The description of the cities is cast in the form of advice from a French Jew to a Christian boy about to travel to England, and although the Jew, in Richard's story, is insidiously plotting the death of the boy in ritual sacrifice, he figures as the authentic voice of worldly urban experience (Jews were, as

159

Richard knew, the most consistently urban of medieval popula-
tions) and expresses views about English towns consistent with
Richard's own remarks elsewhere in the *Cronicon*. It is a
measure of Richard's sophistication and, perhaps, cynicism that
he uses the persona of a French Jew to appraise English towns,
although he despised both the French and the Jews. The combination of foreignness and non-Christian religion in the speaker
offers, however, a contemporary parallel to Richard's favorite
literary voice, the Roman pagan. And the French Jew, when he
speaks of London, recalls Horace on Rome, and perhaps Juvenal, in that funny pride city people take in their town's best
vices. "When you reach England, if you come to London, pass
through it quickly, for I do not at all like that city. All sorts of
men crowd together there from every country under the
heavens. Each race brings its own vices and its own customs to
the city. No-one lives in it without falling into some sort of
crime."[50]

Richard's Jew ascribes to the Christian city the same intriguing
array of vice that Horace (probably more justifiably) credited to
Rome—incorporating into his description some quotation from
the First Satire. Compare Horace, *Satires*, i, 2,

> Ambubaiarum collegia, pharmacopolae,
> Mendici, mimae, balatrones, hos genus omne.

with Richard's list of London's inhabitants:

> Histriones, scurre, glabriones, garamantes, palpones, pu-
> siones, molles, mascularii, ambubaie, famacapole, cris-
> sarie, phitonisse, uultuarie, noctiuage, magi, mimi, mendici,
> balatrones. Hoc genus omne totas reppleuere domos.

If London is Rome with every possible object of fascination and
disgust, every other English town is nothing at all. Each major
town is dismissed for its smallness, poverty, vile climate,
boorish population, or dangerous neighbors, and outside the
towns everything is worse.[51] Only Winchester is worth praise.

> That city is a school for those who want to live and
> fare well. There they breed men; there you can have
> plenty of bread and wine for nothing. Monks are there
> of such mercifulness and gentleness, clerks of such wisdom
> and frankness, citizens of such courteousness and good

faith, women of such beauty and modesty, that for a little I would go there myself and be a Christian among such Christians. I send you to that city, the city of cities, the mother of all and better than all others. There is one vice there and one alone, which is by custom greatly indulged in. I would say, with all due respect to the learned men and to the Jews, that the people of Winchester lie like sentries. Indeed, nowhere else under heaven are so many false rumours made up so easily as there; otherwise they are truthful in all things.[52]

His praise is typically equivocal, but the satire is playful. If Winchester's prevailing fault is telling lies, it is at least the vice of quickness and cleverness rather than ordinary boorishness, and it is not at all inconsistent with that same citizenry's calculating prudence. Winchester, by Richard's standards, is a civilized place. He even approves of its peaceful tolerance of its Jewish population ("in those parts the Jerusalem of the Jews") not from any particular sympathy with Jews, but because riots are uncivilized. London may be larger and richer, but it suffers the crudeness of violent mobs.

With attitudes learned half from classical literature, half from experience, Richard understands cities as places where transient, unassimilable elements exist by the side of traditional authority in tolerant peace. He is completely urban in his insistence on cleverness, restraint of violence, and farsighted planning as the marks of civilized—that is, city—behavior. In spite of his narrow and provincial loyalty to his hometown and the conservatism that makes him suspicious of independent town government, he expresses the eternal feeling of urban people, lost for many years in Europe but reborn in the twelfth century, that "in my opinion there is nowhere for you to live except in a city."[53]

Richard's ease in thinking in quantitative terms and his interest in city life are facets of his mind that reveal or illustrate those larger aspects of late twelfth-century society that point toward change. But he was not a man sympathetic to change where he was aware of it, and his conscious loyalties invariably defend whatever is traditional, dignified, and rich. His attitudes and feelings about the Black Monks disclose that part of his mind which is conservative, inflexible, admirably loyal but also sentimental and self-interested.

The *Cronicon* is a succinct work for its time, but it frequently digresses from its major theme of King Richard's crusade and the fate of his unguarded kingdom. When Richard strays from his theme, it is often to intersperse his book with stories about Black Monks (on about seventeen different occasions). His monks are always embattled—perhaps no longer Saint Benedict's *milites Christi* in arms against the devil, but engaged with a modern set of enemies just as powerful and, in Richard's eyes, almost as evil: hostile bishops, prebendary clerks, royal servants, and overambitious brothers. The Benedictines, as Richard shows them, are on one side of a partisan cause whose corporate autonomy and rights can be maintained only through constant, even aggressive, vigilance. They are threatened, not only by outbreaks of the rivalry between regular and secular clergy, but, more outrageously, by traitorous brothers who would subvert or override conventual autonomy in their ambitious scrambles toward high monastic office. In addition, there was the insulting presence of reform orders that found the great Benedictine tradition inadequate for new-fashioned spiritual needs. The Black Monks are seen, in the *Cronicon*, as powerful corporations with autonomous internal government and considerable influence outside the cloister, and yet sensitively vulnerable to attack.

Perhaps the fact that the *Cronicon* was so clearly intended for monastic readers explains why Richard created no picture of cloister life other than a few crises of office-seeking, and with the sympathy of his audience taken for granted, he offered no argument or *apologia* for the monks in their various embroilments with bishops and place-seekers. The resulting, unintended, impression is one of a jealous, power-obsessed institution whose only vital life was to maintain and extend its privileges. There is a degree of truth in that inadvertent view of late twelfth-century convents of Black Monks, but had he felt the need to defend his order, Richard would probably have argued for their superiority in useful service over seculars and other orders. In his anecdote in the Winchester Annals about the prior of Bath who became a Carthusian, the return to sanity and Benedictinism occurred when the prior realized how useful he had been to other souls at Bath.[54]

Even more selfish and useless than the semieremetical Carthu-

sians are prebendary cathedral clerks. In a lengthy account of
the expulsion of the monks from Coventry by Hugh of Nonant,
Richard creates a scathing caricature of the secular canons who
replaced the monks:

> Even the absent canons eagerly built large and splendid
> lodgings around the church, perhaps for their own use,
> in case any occasion should arise, even once in their
> lives, for visiting the place. None of the prebendaries
> lived a religious life there, as they do not do anywhere
> else, but some poor vicars were hired for a wretched
> stipend, as an insult to God.... This indeed is the true
> religious life: this every church should imitate and
> emulate. The secular canon will be permitted to be absent
> from his church for as long as he pleases and to squander
> Christ's patrimony where and when and in whatever
> pleasures he pleases. Let them see to it merely that a
> frequent uproar is heard in the Lord's house. If a stranger
> were to knock at such a man's gates, if a poor man cried
> out, the one who lived in front of the gates—and he would
> be the vicar, poor enough himself—would reply: "Go
> away and beg for food somewhere else, for the lord of
> the house is not at home." This is that glorious order of
> secular clerks, for whose sake the bishop of Coventry
> expelled his monks from Coventry.[55]

The outrage of Hugh's success prompted Richard to his single
explicit defense of the regular life, although his audience
probably included no one who was not already persuaded. In
contrast to the canons, the monks are men who serve: first the
Lord, next the traveler and the poor.

> [The bishop of Coventry] eliminated the monks at his
> pleasure: the monks who, not through a vicar but with
> their own mouths, praised the Lord, who lived and walked
> in the Lord's house in harmony all the days of their
> lives, who cared for nothing of this world beyond their
> bare food and clothing, whose bread was ready for the
> poor, whose door stood open at any time to the traveller.[56]

Richard's exquisitely phrased passage, the sentimental side of a
rather hardened sensibility, acquires an even more touching
pathos when compared with the jarring discord of his scenes of
actual monastic life.

Some monks of cathedral convents were forced by their bishops from whatever degree of simple, harmonious life they had achieved. These monks certainly could not be blamed for refusing to see anything but un-Christian malice in the efforts of hostile prelates to replace them with secular clerks. A monastic chapter inevitably increased the difficulties of episcopal administration, but the refusal of episcopal abbeys to give way without a fight was more than understandable. Still, the emotions aroused by these conflicts were bitter and ugly. Richard, whose chapter was never directly threatened, was fierce in his hatred of Hugh of Nonant and of William of Ely when, as legate, he helped Hugh install prebendary clerks at Coventry.[57] He depicts Hugh destroying the very buildings at Coventry and using up whatever monastic income was not allotted to his greedy, negligent, nonresident clerks.[58] Not satisfied by his evil victory, Hugh continued to revile and slander all monks, making use, for this purpose, of a monk as a kind of court jester *cum* chaplain— a man too weak or too corrupt to protest. This embarrassing traitor met a satisfying end when "a stone suddenly fell from the gable of the church and knocked the brains out of the monk."[59]

Less justifiable departures from Richard's sketch of cloistered harmony are his accounts of the efforts of houses to evade episcopal control, such as the successful fight of the abbot of Malmesbury against the bishop of Salisbury and the intermittent struggles at various houses for control of the office of abbot or prior.[60] The royal inclination to use abbeys as an economic reward for civil servants was another source of anger. The brother whom the chancellor, Longchamp, forced on Westminster Abbey found himself among a resentful flock who expelled him as soon as a safe opportunity offered.[61] Richard is sarcastic about the monks' belated courage.

All Richard's scenes of monastic life are variations on a theme of ambition and discord. By far the ugliest and most vivid are the internal struggles for office among the monks. With minor exceptions, the only times Richard singles out some individual monk for comment (as opposed to an entire house, which is his usual monastic unit), the individual is in the character of a renegade. When the reader sees a man step out of his corporate identity (or anonymity, depending on one's point of view), the monk is always violating the traditions and customs of his order, betraying them for the sake of wrongheaded and undisciplined ambitions. Robert, the prior of Winchester, and Walter, prior of Bath, are viewed in this character because of the—as Richard sees it—selfish absurdity of their decisions to be Carthusians. Another story told with great indignation concerns a Cluniac monk who obtained "by such arts as he was master of"—probably mere bribes—a letter from the abbot of Cluny authorizing him to supplant the virtuous prior of Montacute.[62] The usurper gives a pretentious, mock-humble oration ending with an exhortation to Christ to judge his worthiness to rule. "Behold a miracle! On that same day he lost his speech, on the next day he lost his life, and on the third day, when he was committed to the earth, he learned by experience and taught by example that 'in the long run, sordid booty brings no good.'" Another ambitious monk who invested in Count John's expensive goodwill in hope of promotion was killed by a falling beam.[63] It should be remembered that Hugh of Nonant's tame monk was killed by a falling stone. The only places in the *Cronicon* where Richard seems ready to believe in miraculous or at least providential events of a notably vindictive sort are the sudden deaths of these three monks, who betrayed the corporate integrity of their order.

A similar case is one of Robert, prior of Hereford, "a monk who held himself in no small esteem and gladly meddled in matters in which he had no business so that he might promote his own affairs,"[64] who obtained the abbacy of Muchelney through political favor against the convent's wishes. While he did not find himself in the path of a providential flying object, he was very ignominiously expelled by his monks: "They threw the coverings of his bed out after him and exposed him, heaped with insults, to the four winds of the island."[65]

Richard evidently finds nothing inappropriate in such violence, being, as it is, the action of the house as a corporate body to defend itself from outside control. He could not have noticed how sadly his vignettes of monastic bickering contrasted with his own ideal description of an unassuming life of steadfast service. A writer like William of Newburgh preferred to overlook most of the sordid politics of regular life (as visible to him as to Richard) and emphasized spiritual adventure, individual holiness, and new patterns of life. Richard's unashamed focus on place-seeking and politics reflects the entrenched loyalty of an older, now rigid order, absorbed in its privileges and the mechanics of its life. It is not that William's Cistercians were necessarily any less ambitious than Richard's Benedictines; but the differing focus of attention of the two writers allows us to see how minds formed by the age (or youth) and ideals of different orders see and judge.

The urban shrewdness discussed previously is not an incongruous mix with the closed, conservative standards of Richard's monastic life. The fact that Richard was insensibly attuned to some of the restless, changing currents of the late twelfth century does not mean that he was ready to see the institution at the center of his life attacked by secular clergy or, indirectly, by new kinds of monks. If anything, he seems disturbed and nervous in his overly quick defense against the enemies of the—to use an anachronism—right and left. His anger with monks who would damage the fabric of conventual life for their own advancement could be a response to increasing external criticism—the instinct to close ranks. There is in all his attitudes, whether, to the modern student, they seem to be moving with or resisting social and religious change, a pervading worldly sharpness, a vision limited (according to medieval standards) by the material and earthly, and a cleverness not aspiring to wisdom.

Such matters as the tone and point of view taken toward small but revealing subjects like monks, towns, and numbers may, I hope, tell something about Richard of Devizes's mind and character. But that kind of discussion does not, plainly enough, tell what the *Cronicon* is simply "about." To say that it is a chronicle that covers events in England and the Holy Land from 1189 to 1193 does and does not answer the question, mainly because modern readers of history demand to know more about sequence and arrangement than, apparently, medieval readers did. Trying to describe the *Cronicon* in a straightforward manner inevitably involves the infuriating stupidity of connecting events and anecdotes by "and then . . ." or "meanwhile" simply because that is how Richard wrote them down; a gross injustice is thereby done to the subtle, sophisticated writer one is so badly, yet, in a way, accurately describing. Straightforward monastic annals involve no such delicate betrayals, since less is

166

expected of that simpler genre of historical writing. Writers like Richard, because of their very evident learning and intelligence, are most vulnerable to hostile modern criticism for their neglect of causal connections and "structure" generally. Even a sympathetic critic must artificially isolate themes or topics for the sake of intelligible discussion and thus must distort and seem, however unwillingly, to "correct" the construction of the work as a whole. This situation has been caused by the passage of time and by the irrevocably changed expectations of historical writing and of narrative composition.

Richard of Devizes's *Cronicon* as a consecutive narrative is the result of a contemporary copyist working from the author's draft; Appleby's edition reproduces that fair copy with the valuable addition of typographical indicators to distinguish text from marginalia. As it stands, the *Cronicon* perfectly illustrates V. H. Galbraith's wonderful and devastating description of medieval histories as "just one thing after another."[66] That is how we and, I assume, everyone always registers the raw experience of life, but the recorders of life have always been expected to transform it—medieval recorders no less than ancient or modern. The great and often confusing differences lie in the expectations held about that transformation by the readers to whose judgment it is offered. And, since the Middle Ages generally was a period of particular reticence and banality concerning the expressed standards for historical writing, we can only infer as best we can from the finished works. Among the few steps I am willing to venture on that quicksand subject is the suggestion that medieval readers did not expect highly conscious attention to be given to the discovery of logical, much less causal, patterns dominating the sequence of secular events (either in life or in historical literature)[67] although they appreciated explication of the Christian meaning of individual events and sharp observations on human motivations. A few historians, such as Bede, did come very close to suffusing their books with a significant, integral order, but on the whole, it was not expected or, perhaps, really appreciated by readers.[68] An educated twelfth-century reader hoped an historian would work the crude stuff of experience into, at the best, literary elegance, polished by classical refinements and elevated by Christian sentiment; but that same reader would settle happily for a good story and a lot of information. Fineness of style, sharpness of perception, and a respectable level of intelligence applied to the narration and interpretation of relatively separate events lifted from a seemingly static world made medieval historians popular.[69] The narrative structure of historical literature was, during the twelfth century, dominated by the aesthetic conventions of fictional narrative; the same tastes and habits that led readers and writers to appreciate epic and romance were brought to the reading and writing of history, a matter that is discussed at greater length in chapter 8.

Richard's book is concerned with two major subjects: war in the Holy Land and politics at home, added to which are occasional digressions, which might more aptly be called divertissements, into other matters. The major subjects and the digressions run one after the other in the narrative, separated only by modulations of style and tone rather than by subordinating connections. The digressions are often told in the satirist's style; the events of the Third Crusade are elevated by a rather artificial, inflated, or even epiclike narration. Dead seriousness and the authentic "feeling" of observed reality enters only with politics at home. All Richard's natural sympathies were engaged by the spectacle of the acquisition, the manipulation, the keeping, and the loss of power, by the varieties and fate of personal ambition, by the arts of government on every scale from abbey to royal court—in short, by everything that we now loosely arrange under the term, *politics*. The most vigorous and closely observed actors in the *Cronicon* appear as "politicians" in what the *Oxford English Dictionary* calls a "sinister sense"—men who are scheming, crafty, shrewd, and resourceful or, in an earlier and even finer definition, men "of artifice" and "deep contrivance."[70] Richard judges individuals only as he judges their aims; he is never really shocked by any scheme whose end he disapproves (monks usurping abbacies, for example), and no contrivance is too questionable to forward some plan he approves.[71] His partisan instincts are deep. Bishops figure largely in the book because they were great public men and, of course, because Richard moved in ecclesiastical circles, which traditionally were dominated by the demands and rewards of royal service.[72] The pastoral duties attached to episcopal office are as absent from his book as from the lives of many of the men whose political careers he followed—or perhaps more absent from his book than from their lives. While he was naturally more interested in matters of large public importance, the intensity of his attention and his consistently serious tone for even small mundane affairs reveal nothing short of a wholly pure, amoral fascination with the grasping and loss of power and privilege. The almost ubiquitous mockery is silenced in face of the fickle attentions of the *gloria mundi*.

One sort of politics has already been discussed: the machinations after monastic office and the attempts of certain bishops to reduce the number of cathedral abbeys, and it has also been remarked that these skirmishes were the only activity in the monastic world Richard found interesting enough to record.

Viewed sympathetically, the gravity and closeness of Richard's attention to the political situation in England during the absence of the king is genuinely admirable. He was loyally devoted to the interests of Richard I[73] and, more important, was astute enough to understand that the king's chosen minister William Longchamp, however repellent some of his actions and all his manners, was the true representative of the legitimate royal power. (William of Newburgh was loyal to Richard I as well, but often was so disgusted with the overbearing chancellor that he seemed to lose a sense of the larger issues at stake.) Richard was never long distracted by ethical or even purely ecclesiastical questions, as William was, from the struggle between the absent king and his restless brother. As a token of that steady hold on the great matters, Richard always refers to Longchamp as "the chancellor," to remind his readers of what Longchamp was; William of Newburgh always refers to him as "the bishop," to remind us of what he was not. While Longchamp is never heartily praised in the *Cronicon*, and most of his egregiously high-handed acts are not excused ("he spared no-one and was more savage than a wild beast to everyone."),[74] Richard, with what, for him, must be acknowledged as notable restraint, passes by several opportunities for cruel satire. More correctly, he pauses briefly at the irresistible points and then passes on: "William, bishop of Ely and the king's chancellor . . . a remarkable person who made up for the shortness of his body with his mind." "I shall not mention that he was caught and held both in a monk's habit and in woman's clothing."[75] Longchamp's unattractive person, which everyone seemed to have found fascinating, and his more ludicrous adventures, in Richard's book, only make his stubborn efforts for his king almost heroic.

It is not that Richard shields any detail of Longchamp's steps, alternately buying and bullying his way, to complete secular and ecclesiastical authority, but he repeatedly reminds the reader that something more important is in question than the outraged feelings and privileges of individuals or even of the Church. Richard did not approve of Longchamp's jealous attack on Hugh of Durham's authority as justiciar and earl of Northumbria, but he is less outraged than many contemporaries. He reflects with a kind of worldly philosophy that "all power always has been, still is, and always will be jealous of anyone sharing it"[76] and goes on to note that, after appeals against the "tyrant" were sent to Richard I, Longchamp emerged more powerful than ever.[77] It was well, if grudgingly, known that Longchamp was the only minister in whom the king had full confidence,[78] and while that fact alone ensured his general unpopularity, Richard was clever enough to have realized at the time that no complaints from Englishmen or Normans could dislodge Longchamp from his lord's confidence. Even if hindsight was a "crib" to his wisdom, Richard wants his readers to know that he, for one, was never fool enough to believe that anyone would keep for long the extraordinary things their king pretended to sell before the crusade. "The king most obligingly unburdened all those whose money was a burden to them, and he gave to whomever he pleased whatever powers and possessions they chose.... He made this jest: 'If I could have found a buyer I would have sold London itself.' By this remark, if it had not later been forgotten, many people might have been warned."[79]

In Richard's eyes, Longchamp's worst offenses were his interference in monastic affairs (most notably his temporary support of Hugh of Nonant's policies), his actions against the interests of the bishop of Winchester, and his excessive aggrandizement of himself and his relations.[80] He is absolved, in the *Cronicon*, of direct, personal responsibility for the clumsy mistreatment of Bishop Geoffrey Plantagenet, and Count John is blamed for indirectly creating and then exploiting the situation to his own benefit.[81] The major confrontations that led, eventually, to Longchamp's exile in 1192, when he leaves the *Cronicon*, though not England, forever, are struggles between a dogged, crafty, increasingly desperate defender of the legitimate sovereign and a party of men variously self-interested, weak, shortsighted, or faithless led by the impatient heir to the crown.[82] Since it appeared likely that Richard I would never return from the crusade, men with an eye on the main chance follow John. As friends desert him and enemies maneuver with growing freedom and success, Richard's Longchamp succeeds to the personal dignity they discarded with their loyalty. Richard's tribute to the chancellor's tenacity and courage was to create for him two concise, strong speeches (using some elegant classical tags) that allow Longchamp a rhetorical triumph at moments of political failure. "In so far as you can, you have already given the count whatever was the king's in the realm. Tell him that Priam is still alive,"[83] is part of Longchamp's reply to the messengers who announce the decisions of the council that, under John's direction, deprived him of effective power. Facing John and his allies outside London, after hearing his numerous accusers, Longchamp offers a simple and dignified reply, beginning with a line from Juvenal, "Am I always to be only a listener, and shall I never answer?" and ending with calm recognition of political realities: "You are stronger than I, and I, the king's chancellor and justiciar of the realm, judged contrary to all law, give way to stronger men because it is necessary."[84]

The William Longchamp that Richard presents easily accords with our idea of the friend and patron of that other monk satirist, Nigel Wireker.[85] On the occasion of Longchamp's death several years later, Richard gave his final thoughts about the chancellor in the Winchester Annals: "In this year [1197] William Longchamp, Bishop of Ely and King's chancellor, by dying, entered upon the path he had earned while living . . .; a man distinguished by the high esteem for his prudence in the world, and the charm of his speech, than whom no one ever existed more faithful in the integrity of love once conceived; and who could be called father of monks by his merit except that he once gave in to the counsels of the enemies of religion so that at his great council at London he confirmed the ejection of the monks from Coventry as much as it was in his power to do so."[86]

Richard's account of the clash between Count John and the chancellor is the best argument that he understood policies and loyalties larger than the petty tyrannies and excesses incidental to them, but he followed many other affairs of less consequence with great attention to the personal dramas in the vacillations of power and favor. The smallest incidents reveal how substantial and immediate that aspect of life was for him. The fall of Stephen of Marzai, seneschal of Anjou (a principal in one of Newburgh's demon tales), "that great and powerful man," is related briefly but in telling detail: "[He was] loaded down with chains. He was forced to pay 30,000 pounds of Angevin money for his freedom and to promise to pay 15,000 pounds more."[87] Richard probably witnessed the transaction at Winchester. Ranulf Glanville, too, had occasion to buy back part of his freedom for "15,000 pounds of silver. And although this name of Glanvill had been so great on the day before . . . so that anyone to whom the Lord had granted it might speak amongst princes and be worshipped by the people, yet on the day after there was not one man left on earth who was willing to be called by that name."[88] He even notes as the ultimate humiliation that Glanville lost his unequaled fluency of speech when he lost place and power.[89] Stephen of Marzai is seen debilitated from hunger and chains; Glanville is stricken dumb; Longchamp faints and foams at the mouth when he realizes everything is lost. These broken men are not presented as exempla; no lesson is drawn and none seems implied. The reader merely observes with the author that the fall from office and influence is precipitate and terrible.

A small incident in Normandy between papal legates trying to make a visitation and two of Richard I's officials, which involved mutual threats and, finally, excommunication, causes Richard to remark as Longchamp had done, "Power had to be given in to."[90] The remark could stand as the theme of much of his book.

The practical arrangements of the secular world occupy the center of Richard's vision and are seen clearly in natural perspective. Various other subjects are seen, as it were, obliquely: enlarged, shrunk, distorted. His narrative of the Third Crusade is more grandiose in style and celebrates the virtues of Richard I and his victories over all his enemies, French, Greek, and "pagan" Moslems—generally in that order of precedence. While the story covers the whole of Richard I's crusade from his preparations in England almost to his departure from the Holy

Land, it is radically condensed in a peculiarly idiosyncratic way, being consecutive and detailed only through the conquest of Cyprus and thenceforth sketchy and haphazardly compressed. The slightly odd result (though it evidently did not seem so to the author) is that Richard I is shown chiefly in quarrels and in combat with Catholic and Orthodox Christians. The difference between a holy crusade and an ordinary military expedition is obscured almost totally in this account. In point of information, Richard's account is considered to be original—that is, not based on any known *written* sources—but not very inclusive or reliable.[91] However, compared with the *Itinerarium* or William of Newburgh's exposition, the really notable absence is not so much of facts as of Christian reflections on the Holy Land and the purposes and results of the Third Crusade.

Richard I's fleet and equipment are precisely described and counted—ships, crews, horses, and knights—and his military adventures in Sicily, which were provoked by his private quarrel with King Tancred and by general ill feeling between the English army and the Sicilians, are told with enthusiasm.[92] The king's address to his troops before the battle conflates the crusade with a private vendetta: "Will our right arms make a way for us to the ends of the earth after the Cross of Christ, . . . if we show our backs to these vile and effeminate Griffons? . . . As for me, I will either die here or get revenge for my injuries."[93] The effect here, as throughout, is to reduce the crusade to the level of ordinary warfare and, incidentally, to exaggerate the fighting in Sicily far beyond its real scope or significance. The more important exploit, the taking of Cyprus, is told as a brief and confused series of armed encounters, inadequately explained. The emphasis in both the Sicilian and Cypriot engagements is on money, and here the author's and the king's preoccupations coincide: Joanna's dowry, Tancred's payments, the booty of gold, silk, jewels.

"The king . . . came to the siege of Acre and was received by the besiegers with as much joy as if he had been Christ Himself returning to earth,"[94] but King Richard's godlike entrance is into a very earthly Holy Land. The theme of the siege of Acre emerges as the liberality and bellicosity of the English king, compared with the poverty and timidity of Philip Augustus, who allegedly has the letters from home forged to create an excuse to leave the crusade.[95] The ultimate failure of the crusading armies to recover Jerusalem is analyzed in purely material terms of climate and provisions: "The King's army grew weaker day by day in the Promised Land . . . many thousands of them died each month from the very great extremes of cold by night and heat by day. . . . On the other hand, the pagans' strength increased greatly. . . . They were accustomed to the climate, the place was their native land, the work was healthful, and the scarcity of food was curative."[96] Richard explains that the French and English habitually ate, and thus required, large amounts of food, and the English in particular drank extraordinary amounts of wine. Furthermore, the king suffered so terribly from fever that his followers became demoralized. The will of God is not explicit or active, and the bitterest contests are clearly among the Christians themselves.

Saladin does not appear at all, but his brother, whom Richard calls Safadin, figures nobly as the only praiseworthy leader other than the English king and as almost an ally: "a man of long military experience, very polished and wise, whom the king's magnanimity and munificence had won over to his friendship and to favouring his side." Richard's grandly fictive pagan delivers a long speech in which hs prays to the Christian God, "if You are God," to spare the life of the noble king stricken with fever. Safadin declares himself very knowledgeable about Henry II, "the outstanding man of his time," and about Richard's career as duke of Aquitaine; he is made to express the singular idea that Duke Richard was the favorite son of Henry II and fought his rebellious brothers on behalf of his father.[97] He also finds one more excuse for Richard's failure to take Jerusalem: "He was burdened with the king of the French and held back by him."[98] Safadin breaks off his speech, weeping bitterly over the king's illness. The fever breaks and abates when the king hears the happy news that the duke of Burgundy is sick. He had prayed, "May God destroy him, because he would not destroy the enemies of our faith with me, although he has been waging war with my money for a long time!"[99]

There seems to have been no doubt in Richard's mind that the failure of the Third Crusade was adequately explained by an unfortunate concurrence of natural and human causes. We may agree with him in a general way and still wonder how a twelfth-century monk could conceive of a specifically holy war so completely dominated by ordinary earthly considerations. If God were present at all to the author's imagination, He would seem to have been a sadly feckless partisan of His own cause. When the remains of the crusading armies refuse to make a last effort for Jerusalem, King Richard chews up his pine staff in rage and shouts to God that He has deserted His servants, all the "foolish Christians" there for His sake. "Oh, how unwillingly would I desert thee in such a grave hour of need, if I were to thee what Thou art to me, my lord and advocate!"[100] Having a clear feudal notion of deity, the king knows what is expected of his omnipotent overlord, and he has no patience with mysterious ways and movements. He remains sullenly proud to the last, elegant, lines of the *Cronicon:* "When they returned from the holy places, the duke and the bishop tried to persuade the king that he, too, should go up, but the proud swelling (*digna . . . indignatio*) of his great heart would not allow him to enjoy as a privilege from the pagans what he could not have as a gift from God."[101]

The fact that this portrait of King Richard as belligerent, hot-tempered, and not very pious appears realistic and accurate to us in light of other information does not argue for its "objectivity." It is not a balanced or impartial appraisal, and it does not contain any criticism, hidden or otherwise. The king on crusade is a heroic portrait consciously drawn to inspire unreserved admiration and to justify military failures. Richard's version of the crusade is as startlingly devoid of Christian feeling and implications as, perhaps, it was in reality.

Subjects that made his contemporaries think about the supernatural, whether in hackneyed or fresh ways, appear very different when Richard touches them. His avoidance of everything immaterial makes him, in many ways, a very attractive writer; he does not cant. One of these subjects seen through a distorting mirror, not to Christian or heroic, but to comic effect is that of the Jews. The grisly business of the alleged ritual murders of children by Jews scarcely lends itself to comedy, but Richard's presentation of the Winchester case in 1193 (a genuine accusation corroborated by independent evidence)[102] is lightened by the facts that there was no corpse and the accusation was eventually dismissed. The idea that the Jews murdered Christian children for religious purposes originated in its English version in 1144 with the accusations and events following discovery of the murdered child William at Norwich (later Saint William of Norwich). The history of that case by the monk Thomas of Monmouth became immensely popular and set the pattern for a variety of similar accusations against Jewish communities, most but not all in England. Each succeeding case, with its predictable similarity to all preceding ones, confirmed a general belief in such crimes.[103] These supposed child-martyrs appealed strongly to a strain of maudlin sentimentality in contemporary religious feeling to be typified, somewhat later, by Chaucer's Prioress. The taste for exaggeratedly sweet pathos and for stories evoking it was sufficiently developed in the twelfth century to make florid and pathetic child-martyr accounts widely read and appreciated as soon as they appeared.

Richard brought a new style to the child-martyr story by turning the very conventions of virgin innocence attacked by ancient hatred back on themselves to satiric effect. (Needless to say, he was the only exponent of this new style.) He uses the Winchester case, not to express any sincere opinion about Jews or ritual murders, but to air his amusement with the conventions of ritual-murder literature. He begins the tale with an equivocal introduction:

> Because Winchester should not be deprived of its just praise for having kept peace with the Jews, as is told at the beginning of this book, the Jews of Winchester, zealous, after the Jewish fashion, for the honour of their city (although what was done greatly lessened it), brought upon themselves, according to the testimony of many people, the widely known reputation of having made a martyr of a boy in Winchester. The case was thus.[104]

The story, in brief, concerns a Christian boy apprenticed to a Jewish cobbler in France. The boy complains of his poverty to another Jew, not his master, who suggests that he try his fortune in England. He gives the boy a letter of recommendation to a Jew in Winchester. The French Jew's description of the English towns, in which the author's voice and the invented character merge, is the satiric tour de force of the *Cronicon*. It ends with a panegyric of Winchester, comically leavened by the admission of one local fault: "There is one vice there and one alone. I would say, with all due respect to the learned men and to the Jews, that the people of Winchester lie like sentries. Indeed, nowhere else under heaven are so many false rumours made up so easily as there; otherwise they are truthful in all things."[105] We should remember as we are intended to, while reading what follows, that Richard is one of those learned men of Winchester. After the tour of cities, the tale resumes with the boy and a companion arriving at Winchester and taking work there with a Jew. "Wherever these poor lads worked or ate away from each other by day, every night they slept together in the same bed in the same old hut of a poor old woman."[106] Richard is playing here with exaggerated alliteration and diminutives to call attention to the silliness of the pathetic image: "pauperculi ... in uno unius uetule ueteri tugurio in uno lectulo quiescebant." When the first boy disappears, around the time of Passover, his companion, offering no evidence, accuses the Jewish employer of a terrible crime. All the sentimental conventions of childish purity hover behind the first quoted words of this innocent *pauperculus:* "You son of a dirty whore, you thief, you traitor, you devil." The result is a wonderfully pathetic pratfall after the little hut with its bed of (perhaps equivocal) innocence. The boy's confidence grows with his audience, and so does his diction: "See if there is a grief like unto my grief.... This man has cut the throat of my only friend, and I presume he has eaten him, too."[107] (It would account for the lack of a corpse.) Richard tells us that eventually the matter was brought to court, the evidence was inadequate, money changed hands, and the charges were dropped. The story is given an abrupt, anticlimactic ending and would seem to be a fiction if the Pipe Rolls did not prove it otherwise.

It is very interesting to trace certain parallels between Richard's story and the much longer, pious account of the first child-martyr, Saint William of Norwich, by Thomas of Monmouth—a long, digressing book filled with visions and miracles and cloyingly emotional in tone. It had great literary success and more than literary influence. Little William was a poor boy, apprenticed to tanners; he left his country village to seek greater prosperity in the city of Norwich, where he often did work for the Jews—all of which is told at great length and while he worked at Norwich, "a considerable space of time passed away," according to Thomas.[108] Richard says, after explaining how the French boy came to Winchester, "Day followed day and month followed month; and for our lad, whom we have so carefully brought thus far, time hastened on, whether he was present or absent," obliquely twitting Thomas's prolix, circumstantial style.[109] The companion of the French boy is disturbed by nightmares; Thomas's characters are always having visions. In a chapter called "A Warning to those who deride the miracles of St. William and who deny or doubt that he was killed by the Jews," Thomas argues against the idea (ascribed to doubters) that a poor little boy (*pauperculum*) could not accomplish miracles.[110] That chapter seems the likely specific source for Richard's *pauperculi* in the old hut. Thomas of Monmouth's book was sufficiently well known for quick allusions to register immediately. The death of William of Norwich and the accusation against the Winchester Jews were actual events, but Thomas of Monmouth's history is long, emotional, and credulous while Richard's story is brief, acerbic, and suggests that the whole business was one of Winchester's many "false rumours."

It would be a grave mistake to think Richard was concerned to vindicate the Jews about whom he has nothing good to say; he simply took the occasion of the Winchester case to satirize, in passing, a popular hagiographical book whose style and substance made an irresisitible target for his wit. He is consistently more concerned with literature and verbal style than with religion or crime among vulgar people. If one wants to determine Richard's genuine attitude toward the Jews, it might be better to reflect on one laconic sentence from the Winchester Annals for 1198: "The Lombard Jew loaned twenty-one marks to the convent in the vigils of Saint Swithun"[111]—a pragmatic, businesslike comment that expresses neatly what we know of the author and the ordinary, peaceful dealings so common between Jews and religious houses in the twelfth century.[112]

The twelfth-century mind that can dismiss a ritual murder as the excited fiction of vulgar and self-serving persons is unusual, and even in that singularly intellectual age, it was still uncommon to feel contempt for people who were awed by natural events that reason could explain (to some), such as eclipses. "Those who do not understand the causes of things marvelled

178

greatly that, although the sun was not darkened by any clouds, in the middle of the day it shone with less than ordinary brightness. Those who study the·working of the world, however, say that certain defects of the sun and moon do not signify anything (*aliquid non significare*)."[113] Richard claims no particular knowledge of astronomy for himself, but he accepts the authority of men who do, and it is clear that the authority of those who seek significance in such things is very small in his estimation. He is quite ready to believe that events—an eclipse, the failure of a crusade—"do not signify anything." There is, so far as one can infer from his historical writing, no supernatural dimension to his world, and his personal religion is the Church, not Christ. If Richard is amused and scornful at the ways men go about obtaining office and wealth and at the ways they squander or misuse what they have, he never scorns the very objects of ambition. He is the brilliant observer just at the edge of events, both intensely of and apart from his age, appraising the show by a standard at once conventional and idiosyncratic. His writings are too few and too brief to satisfy the questions he provokes. The *Cronicon* gives us a teasing entrance into an earthbound society of only temporal dimensions, where everything can be counted or calculated by some finite measure, and that which surprises does not, in the end, signify anything.

IV

THE WRITING OF HISTORY
IN TWELFTH-CENTURY ENGLAND

Seven

THE QUESTION

OF HISTORICAL EVIDENCE

In a very serious and once immensely popular and controversial novel of 1888 called *Robert Elsmere*,[1] an intelligent and devout young English clergyman begins to study the sources for medieval history and ends by losing his faith. In spite of his scholarly disposition and a university education, Robert Elsmere found medieval narratives, especially chronicles and saints' lives, totally unnerving.

> One day he was deep in the life of a certain saint. The saint had been a bishop of a diocese in Southern France. His biographer was his successor in the see, a man of high political importance in the Burgundian state, renowned besides for sanctity and learning. Only some twenty years separated the biography, at the latest, from the death of its subject. It contained some curious material for social history, and Robert was reading it with avidity. But it was, of course, a tissue of marvels. . . . [Here the author quotes, from the saint's life, a fairly conventional miracle involving demons.]
>
> Robert made a hasty exclamation, and turning to Catherine, who was working beside him, read the passage to her, with a few words as to the book and its author.
>
> Catherine's work dropped a moment on her knee.
>
> "What extraordinary superstition!" she said, startled. "A bishop, Robert, and an educated man?"
>
> Robert nodded.
>
> "But it is the whole habit of mind," he said half to himself, staring into the fire, "that is so astounding. No one escapes it. The whole age really is non-sane."[2]

Robert Elsmere's Anglican faith was temporarily secure in the face of discredited Roman miracles, but an intellectual process had begun that would not stop, and "the comparative instinct— that tool, *par excellence*, of modern science" (as the author terms what we would call historical criticism) refused to halt at Protestant ground and inexorably death-marched Elsmere through the Old and New Testaments until he could no longer believe in any revealed religion and had to take refuge in deism and good works. It was a route that many Victorians knew well.

We still value medieval biographies for their "curious material for social history," though we have lost the impulse to exclaim out loud at marvels, perhaps regrettably, since we really have no explanation of them more thorough or satisfying than Elsmere's charge that the whole age was "non-sane." We have simply grown patronizing and tolerant. We are also very like Robert Elsmere and everyone his character was based on (those, at least, who had learned the new biblical criticism), for whom liveliness and general intelligence in a medieval historian were not enough to compel respect if the writer could not also display an ability to find and critically evaluate a variety of historical evidence. And that is a test no medieval historian can pass very creditably. With Robert Elsmere, an articulate century milestone, we have somehow come an immeasurable distance from Eleanor Tilney's genial willingness to enjoy the invented speeches and edifying anecdotes of dubious provenance found in history books, "very well contented to take the false with the true," as she says, with a mild and undemanding skepticism. Admittedly, she would have found medieval histories distasteful and crude, but she would never, on their account, have ceased to be a Christian.

Since the Middle Ages and most noticeably since the nineteenth century, the writing of history has been strikingly transformed—and likewise its sensitive corollary art, the reading of history. Modern readers have acquired fairly rigorous expectations as to form and content, and we have come to hold them so unself-consciously that they seem part of the very framework of our minds. Medieval histories do tend, as a consequence, to feel unsatisfactory and, sometimes, positively baffling. There is, after all, something impenetrable, tiresome even, about books that promise a familiar array of contents, arrangement, and intentions, and then deviate in odd and irritating ways from expectations we consider not only proper but irresistibly natural. Classical histories, for all their occasional marvels, offer no serious affront to present sensibilities, while medieval histories often read like books from the other side of the looking glass—plainly recognizable, but altered in disturbing ways. It is not merely our high-minded rejection of entertainment in favor

of analysis that causes our dissatisfaction with medieval history (though that is part of it) but our basic assumptions about historical evidence and its organization into narrative sequence do not entirely help us to read medieval works with much sensitivity.

The key elements of historiography—evidence and narrative structure—were approached by medieval readers and writers with expectations very different (though not entirely different) from our own. During the twelfth century, when historical writing of all kinds proliferated, we must suppose, at the least, that readers and writers were satisfied with the genre as they knew it, and yet, to modern tastes, medieval expectations about written history seem terribly slack. Putting aside for the moment the matter of narrative structure, which depends heavily on formal literary conventions and partly on historical interpretation, the most obvious questions about medieval histories concern evidence: that is, after all, what so upset Robert Elsmere. It would seem that in an age of high intellectual sophistication, with a widely diffused taste for classical literature and inquiry of all sorts, the best-educated people could not tell truth from falsehood in the most obvious instances, accepted quantities of complicated, distant, or unusual information on the assurances of one informant, and, worst of all, had a sense of probability that apparently excluded nothing.

The lamentable spareness of the last two books of Henry of Huntingdon's history, the very books in which he promises to tell what he himself has seen or has heard from eyewitnesses, testifies to the practical difficulty of writing history in an age of difficult and slow communications. It required determination and patience, well assisted by luck and a large acquaintance, to acquire full information about an event, even if it happened only a few miles away. Henry was well situated and well connected, but perhaps his very immersion in the world—his time taken up by the claims of cathedral and archdeaconal business and the welfare of his family—made him resort to sketchy accounts and a lot of poetry when he came to write contemporary history. He was, in any case, a man of bookish tastes, inclined to elegantly derivative work. Probably, his Latin prose rendering of the Anglo-Saxon poem on the battle of Brunanburh shows him most comfortably employed. However, even an historian more inclined to look about him and report to his readers in detail

185

would not easily find many accounts of any single event, especially written accounts that could be considered at leisure. Reference bibliography was nonexistent, and contemporary or near-contemporary histories evidently moved into general circulation slowly and erratically. Henry's discovery of Geoffrey of Monmouth's book at Bec, although the men had shared the same patron in England, is at first surprising, but suggests a common circumstance; much older works with more copies stored in monastery and cathedral libraries were more readily at hand. If books were of limited access, reliable witnesses were more so. William of Newburgh frequently mentions that he learned something from several witnesses of good moral character, and he clearly regarded that as a circumstance deserving special notice. In general, if a medieval historian of contemporary events had refused to write until he had several accounts to compare, he would have had little enough to tell.

We should remember that practical problems, even trivial ones, can be overwhelming when there is no methodical discipline to point to solutions and to shame the expedients of laziness with a high and widely acknowledged standard of work. The amount of history read in the ordinary course of a boy's education was undoubtedly larger than it would seem from the circumstances of its not appearing formally in the trivium or quadrivium (it was subsumed under the category of Grammar), and we can be certain that all educated men had a clear idea of what ancient and modern history contained and sounded like. But casual reading of even the most scrupulously composed history books does not necessarily reveal their secrets, and without any formal or systematic study directed to some procedures and methods for composing history, prospective historians were left very much alone to cope with theory and practice according to their own lights. Henry of Huntingdon is exactly the instance of a highly educated man floundering in his task through the lack of any but the vaguest guidelines for accomplishing it. The absence of history writing from school lectures and exercises (as distinct from simple reading of history for general knowledge and exempla) ensured that its principles and methods as a special form of literature would not be debated, refined, and taught to every new writer to polish or supply the lack of his natural gifts. In compensation, history writing was left to develop freely, but too much freedom results more often in dreary, cautious sameness than in bold originality.

The reliance on uncorroborated, or very partially corroborated, testimony for natural events (to the almost complete exclusion of circumstantial evidence) and the acceptance of such testimony as evidence for supernatural events form a simple division of the subject of evidence that, however obvious to us, would not have been recognized in the twelfth century. Natural and supernatural events differed in immediate cause, intention, and frequency, but not in their inherent probability, and did not, at the time, require different kinds of evidence.

It is quite possible that the universal inclination to accept miraculous events on the basis of honest, or well-intentioned, testimony (inspired testimony, in the case of the Bible) had a pervasive effect, if one hard to define, on ideas about natural events and evidence for them. This acceptance generally tended to disarm suspicion about the worth of testimony and to eliminate any felt need for circumstantial or indirect evidence. I discussed this matter in particular relation to William of Newburgh and his struggles with the evidence for demonic agents and vampires, and those observations apply generally to twelfth-century historical practice. The complete and implicit belief in the frequent activity of supernatural beings in the natural order made necessary a trustful reliance on "moral truth" (which results "when you tell a thing sincerely and precisely as it appears to you") if anything at all were to be known about such important but elusive events. Miracles sometimes, but not often, left behind material clues. The attitudes and assumptions learned from religious study, reliance on the revealed truth of scripture and on those holy men of postbiblical authority, were naturally brought to the investigation of recent miracles; it was an easy, perhaps inevitable, step to the secular world. I am, for the sake of exposition, suggesting an artificial sense of logical or sequential progression from religious studies to secular, from supernatural events to natural; to suggest an untidier feeling for pervasive influences, for habits or states of mind, would be more accurate.

The acceptance of miracles on the basis of testimony was central to Christian faith and Christian history. It could hardly be expected that medieval Christians should have ready a radically different set of intellectual assumptions and habits to bring to the problems of their own, more recent, history. In a general way, standards for accurate knowledge were not derived from experience and probability in the natural order and then applied to the supernatural but, rather, the other way around. What was adequate for knowledge of the superior order may inevitably have seemed adequate for the lower. It was, as the astounded Robert Elsmere observed, "the whole habit of mind" and "no one escapes it." (Whether he was quite fair in thinking that the whole age really was "non-sane" is, of course, another kind of question.)

The development of procedures for studying historical events had to be somewhat discouraged by the universally held prejudice that the objects of such study were not very exalted. That persuasion was somewhat mitigated by another, equally universal, which held that the *saeculum* was theoretically dignified by an invisible cloak of the divine, and the most ordinary happenings might express, in some fragmentary way, an intention beyond immediate appearances—and historians certainly gave way often enough to the temptation to speculate about the eternal, "real" meanings of things before they had nearly exhausted the possibilities of the present and visible. It was, after all, a cliché of historical writing, but one sincerely held, that the major purpose of recording secular history was to expose the Divine Will working through lower agents. John of Salisbury, who wrote a first-rate history, the *Historia pontificalis*, a few years after Henry of Huntingdon died and a generation before William or Richard wrote, is particularly explicit about the relation of the natural to the supernatural world: "My aim, like that of other chroniclers before me, shall be to profit my contemporaries and future generations. For all these chroniclers have had a single purpose: to relate noteworthy matters, so that the invisible things of God (*invisibilia dei*) may be clearly seen by the things that are done."[3]

Theoretically, all of secular history, the visible "things that are done," was related to the "invisible things" by an ultimate cause and purpose, usually quite obscure, and the categories of natural and supernatural beings and events could be seen as though ranged along a continuum from grossness and instability to refinement and permanence. Henry of Huntingdon, not, so far as I can discern, a man given to theological speculation, was absorbed by the terrible impermanence of all human life (or at least human pleasures) and found consolation in thinking of the unchanging, unseen things that offered the true grounds for a Christian's hopes. Such a state of mind, however interesting and sensitive in itself, was not a promising beginning for history. Even William of Newburgh, a more critical man and a better historian, is most energetic and original in the pursuit of the supernatural or the explication of divine purpose in natural events. It is hardly wonderful that a preoccupation with the unseen, higher truths could be accompanied by a certain impatience with the minutiae of secular events, especially if it required tedious effort to discover and record them all. (High and low motives have always combined happily.) So long as an account seemed correct in its main elements, the main elements would have to suffice—unless the smaller aspects struck the writer as particularly apt or amusing. It would be a laughable illusion to think that all, or even most, medieval historians were of a devout or thoughtful temperament, given to deep reflections on the frangibility of human life; but the odd cursoriness and a kind of slackness of observation found, to some degree, in all the written history of the period may be the attenuated expression of a deeply felt view of the universe.

Historians also had to cope with the discouraging and again, pervasive, subtle assumption felt acutely throughout the twelfth century that nothing on earth would hold still, reveal itself in its true nature, and remain that way (Aelred of Rievaulx, who thought of life as a furious river, comes to mind). The highest objects of human knowledge were eternal and unchanging, complete and true, but everything beneath heaven was of a mixed nature, restlessly shifting and tossing up deceitful appearances. The human mind itself was gross and slow, so William of Newburgh complained, and incapable of penetrating even the secrets of the lower world.

Nonetheless, like the man who was astonished to discover that all his life he had been speaking prose without knowing it, all sorts of things only begin to exist once we have learned of them. Scarcely anyone in the twelfth century would have thought that "evidence" was a source of intractable problems. In common life a working method for determining the truth of things was always available. The law courts, which had no choice but to pronounce something to be the truth, had their own procedures for obtaining information and, increasingly during the twelfth century (and most rapidly in England) were discarding the old system of ordeals in favor of the sworn, evidence-giving jury. The ordeal was a temptation of God; William of Newburgh thought that the poor army of half-prepared crusaders who rushed into battle arrogantly counting on divine assistance were also tempting God and almost deserved their defeat. Sensible and sophisticated people in the second half of the twelfth century were generally coming to feel that complacent reliance on supernatural intervention was both impractical and morally suspect.[4]

The criterion that made evidence acceptable in a court of law was essentially similar to good historical evidence: "moral truth," unbiased and free from self-interest. In moving from ordeal to jury the courts had decided in favor of rationality and, incidentally, entered into all the difficulties faced by historians: "Witnesses are unreliable, corruptible, fearful, forgetful; the judges are not infallible, they are gullible."[5] Still, most court investigations were more systematic than those of most historians, and they had the advantage of dealing with clearly limited circumstances, specific questions, and matters that were, in fact, susceptible of being unambiguously known (at least, compared with vampires).

Both the courts and the historians were seeking "moral truth" from their informants, but a more active skepticism was built into the law whose activities were all adversary procedures. Historians often obtained their information from sources that disarmed suspicion: friends, ecclesiastical superiors, men of high rank, bystanders with, seemingly, nothing to gain by lying. (There were penalties for jurors who chanced to give wrong information, however innocently.) Both historians and courts characteristically directed their skeptical impulses toward exposing conscious deception. Even the "old books" mentioned by most historians were consulted in much the same spirit; the author's sources of information were not evaluated, especially if the book appeared rare and very old, nor was he scrutinized for unconscious bias. There was even a certain amount of inevitable confusion of fiction and nonfiction in an age when fiction was routinely prefaced by claims of historicity that, however conventional and artful, were often quite artlessly believed. When William of Newburgh attacked Geoffrey of Monmouth, it was for simple deception, consciously done for self-aggrandizing purposes. Geoffrey was, in William's humorless eyes, a false witness with pernicious intentions. Henry of Huntingdon, perhaps moved by his love of effective literature, simply thought that Geoffrey had written an extraordinarily interesting history book.

We cannot accuse any clever twelfth-century writer of being so naive as not to realize that one honest story might not be the whole truth of any matter, but there was no systematic or thorough effort to find ways to detect mistaken or biased "moral truth." The concepts of "trustworthiness" and "accuracy" were not sufficiently distinguished, just as the difference between "possibility" and "probability" in the twelfth century was less marked than it is now. There was, in historians and everyone else one encounters through twelfth-century sources, skepticism in a hearty measure but directed chiefly to credulity and deception. Perhaps, among historians, the universal interest in motivation has been described as part of the pervasive legacy of Sallust to the Middle Ages: ". . . his analysis of motive, informed by cynical pessimism: suspect the worst. . . . His lesson was well learnt. . . . Naive they often were in their views on causation; but many show an acute awareness of self-interest covered up by hypocrisy, which they revel in exposing."[6]

Self-interested frauds have to be complemented by credulous fools, and, then as now, clever men looked down on honest fools and were inclined to confound stupidity with wickedness or at least moral laxness. William of Newburgh was very severe with people who believed in every new marvel or every dubious saint. Cases such as the Christian looter of Jewish houses (at Stanford in 1190), who was killed in a squabble over the plunder and then revered as a local saint until Bishop Hugh of Lincoln forbade his veneration, may seem to us a bizarrerie of popular piety and crowd psychology; William characteristically looked first for deception on the part of someone with something to gain. In the case of the sainted thief, the cult began with the dreams of some poor, old person (not the sort of witness William trusts) and the "illusory appearance of false signs"; he uses the word *praestigiis*, which suggests tricks as well as illusions.[7] But if

191

the cult arose through suggestible ignorance, it was nurtured by venal fraud: "It was welcomed by certain clerks who saw that there was money to be gotten out of the superstition."[8] In that case, and in others, when there is a strong suspicion of fraud, William's kind of moral skepticism is very effective. However, even in very odd cases, if there seems to be no agent of conscious deception, no opportunity for profit (one thinks of the vampires), he generally does not question vigorously but proceeds to the next level of interpretation. Richard of Devizes was, if anything, more skeptical, but to different purpose; what could outrage and anger William merely amused Richard. His account of the supposed child-martyr of Winchester is a brilliant study in fools and scoundrels, with the author laughing at them all.

This fairly static picture of one aspect of twelfth-century thought must be broken apart to allow room for some new and different elements that are peculiarly characteristic of the age and suggestive of things to come. When William of Newburgh blames both Henry II and Becket for persevering in stubbornness to the detriment of Church and state alike, and when he suggests that the English bishop's lax enforcement of adequate laws governing clerks was ultimately to blame for the conflict, he has taken a step far beyond the simplicities of truthful or lying witnesses. He has described a situation that turns about a cause, not a motive, and has recognized the many shades of ambiguity between right and wrong. When he suggests a connection between well diggers hitting a vein of toxic gas and the deaths in the lime pit at Malton, he is allowing the regular course of nature some of the consequence it deserves instead of turning too quickly to the supernatural. William's painstaking efforts to understand marvels as thoroughly as he could and to find some explanation by himself (though not a natural one, of course) rather than to accept pious formulas, and his evident disgust with looters and murderers who attacked the richer Jews for the greater glory of Christendom and the destruction of the records of indebtedness—all attest to a new self-confidence of moral feeling, common sense, and inquiry.

Henry of Huntingdon comes to life only when hit closely by the attack on clerical marriage or when troubled by thoughts of loss and death. Richard of Devizes is all personality, confident and self-conscious. The effect of his cynical eye is enhanced by his resolute and urbane mundaneness; not many miracles dare to happen in his world. He is both fairly accurate and casually offhand about it; perhaps an increasingly secular point of view sharpened his judgment and powers of observation. Natural shrewdness and parochial concerns made him attend to what he knew best. In an age that liked its literature long and its authors reticent, he wrote a short book full of himself.

I have not intended to suggest a strict chronological progression through the century, but a kind of leavening—of resurgent personality, powers of observation, and an inclination to question (and to laugh)—that one notices more clearly in the second half of the century than in the first. It is an inchoate, growing taste for a more material, orderly, and original observation of the world, not transforming the selection of evidence, but blending new elements with the old.

Eight

THE QUESTION OF LITERARY FORM

ONE ESPECIALLY WITTY MODERN HISTORIAN HAS ROBUSTLY ACCUSED medieval histories of being just one damn thing after another (although in 1944 he said it a shade more politely)[1] and that uncompromising little phrase expresses exactly the experience of reading medieval histories. Of course, history has come a long way from the twelfth century. We are now perfectly accustomed to see a history book begin with the author's gratitude to his first mentors, present colleagues, and spouse, and end with an alphabetical index, and to find everything between in firm and logical order; we would be made slightly uncomfortable if it were otherwise. And with due allowance for the march of civilization, one might think that medieval readers, too, expected and recognized certain conventions of arrangement. Yet the best medieval histories, for all their success with vivid detail, sharp observation, and the like, seem to have no shape at all.

With certain internal lapses, backtrackings, and confusions, all medieval histories proceed chronologically, and that rudimentary principle appears to have been the only discipline to ensure anything like an orderly presentation. And orderliness, that modest substitute for logical structure, would seem the most we can hope to find in the twelfth century, because the modern reader assumes that the structure of historical narrative must be the result of some principle of causation informing and organically controlling the diverse materials of written history.[2] While even a limited understanding of causes, such as an exclusive interest in motivation, is enough to produce an intrinsic structure if it is pursued with strict consistency, we generally feel that some such concept is absolutely necessary if a work is to have any form at all. From this point of view, so natural and necessary to us, the apparent shapelessness of twelfth-century histories is the unhappy, inevitable corollary of the absence of natural causation from contemporary historical thought.

The fact that history was, in the past, a literary genre, a species of polite letters suitable for the practice of any person of decent education is known in an offhand way by everyone, but this commonplace premise suggests a way of looking at the question of narrative structure. The medieval expression of this idea was the inclusion of history in the category of Grammar, the third of the trivium that embraced all literary studies. Isidore of Seville, who always rewards consultation on many points of common knowledge and tradition, divides his book on Grammar into the two broad categories of poetry and prose and further divides prose into *fabula* and *historia*. *Fabula* is the story of fictional happenings; *historia* is the narration of things that have actually taken place.[3] The distinction is only one of content, not of form, much less of intellectual approach. "This discipline belongs to the category of Grammar because whatever is worthy of memory is committed to writing."[4] Isidore further distinguishes history from monthly or yearly notations (*kalendaria* or *annales*) by its larger chronological scope and by the fact that "annual memoranda are carefully expanded into books."[5] The position assigned to history in Isidore's time and throughout the Middle Ages was perhaps a little vague, but comfortable; it was distinguished from other narrative compositions only by the presumed truth of its contents. There was, as has been remarked before, no special set of rules for writing history, either with regard to content or to form. Just as medieval historians brought with them their common assumptions and habits to the task of selecting evidence, so they quite naturally brought the conventions of contemporary narrative literature, whether unconsciously or studiously accumulated, to the task of composition.

This admittedly simple relationship between history and fictional narrative has not been much explored, perhaps because literary critics do not find medieval histories aesthetically interesting and historians deplore what they consider an illicit and improper connection. The idea of history imitating, though at some remove, the conventions of narrative fiction is nonetheless easier to accept than the alternative idea that medieval historians merely picked up a quill and rambled on in some fluffy-minded way until they had run out of *res gestae*. The fact that the writings of the best historians all sound more or less discursive and disconnected to us and all sound substantially similar to one another suggests that the historians were writing in accord with tastes and standards recognizable to them and their readers, however obscure to us. Vernacular narratives, often treating similar subjects (heroes, wars, great exploits), were the natural contemporary models for history. The writer of history, like the writer of romance, was a trouvère—one who "found" stories and made them into literature.[6] There was nothing in literary tradition or contemporary thought to suggest that history required a new and special mode of discourse.

It is consoling to a historian to find the literary critics puzzling over "the rather loose and even disorderly appearance of much medieval literature"[7] and the absence of causality, and generally complaining about the same characteristics in epic and romance that disturb the historian of written history. Literary scholars have devoted a great deal of effort to the question of organization in medieval narrative, and it would seem reasonable to suppose that any general theories of narrative structure derived from imaginative literature should apply to history as well. Literary critics, however, have often approached the Middle Ages armed with stern Aristotelian or subtle Coleridgean ideas of artistic unity, and their analyses are often so abstruse or refined as to be inapplicable to the uses of simpler historians, past and present. Analyses of structure based on symbolism, numerical systems, or motif duplication, while perhaps suitable for certain works of the finest literary craftsmen, cannot be applied to history without doing gross violence to common sense. Still, general theories of medieval narrative that attempt to isolate and describe narrative conventions and techniques in the broadest and most inclusive terms must have their usefulness for historiography.

If twelfth-century history was a familiar form to its readers and not a mere jumble of content, it cannot be classed among the most sophisticated literature of the age with respect to formal technique. The best historians exerted much more than perfunctory control over their materials, but they pursued literature as knowledgeable imitators; they did not set the pace. The "other" writings of most twelfth-century historians tend to be biblical commentary, hagiography, and similar works of a religious nature, though it can be confidently assumed that monks and clerks were not above reading secular stories and poetry. Of the three under particular discussion here, Henry of

Huntingdon was most truly a man of letters, writing essays on many subjects, poetry, and formal epistles, but he has never been considered a writer of the first rank. William of Newburgh composed a commentary on the "Song of Songs"; Richard of Devizes lent his pen to the Winchester Annals for some years, and his *Cronicon* contains a poem of his own composition. Given the general nature of medieval narrative and the particular talents of the historians under discussion, I have not attempted to construct a complete analysis of any one historical work. The facts that Henry of Huntingdon continued his book on several occasions after it was, ostensibly, finished; that he removed and replaced the epilogue and finally left it off altogether; that William of Newburgh's history is apparently unfinished, and many similar others, suggest that these works are probably not susceptible to the kind of formal scrutiny appropriate to imaginative literature. The construction of a scheme that would integrate beginning and end and would provide logical or other connections for all the narrative material of a history might very well strain ingenuity and credulity too far. I think that it is more appropriate and useful to describe in broad strokes some of the commonest narrative techniques of the twelfth century and to indicate their application to contemporary history, and in this cautious way to try to understand how the conventions and aesthetic standards that governed the authors of epic and romance also guided the construction of historical narrative.

It seems to me that first steps toward the problem of structure can safely be made under the capable and comprehensive guidance of Eric Auerbach, whose term *parataxis*, discussed in several of the essays in *Mimesis*,[8] works as a focus for certain distinguishing characteristics of late classical and medieval literature. *Parataxis* in its basic sense is a grammatical term that indicates the juxtaposition of essentially equal elements without causal or temporal connectives and without the subordination of one element or another; *parataxis* is opposed to *hypotaxis*, which is the form of construction in which elements are connected in subordinative relations. Parataxis is the single characteristic that most strikingly distinguishes medieval from classical or modern narrative; encountered in historical narrative, it is profoundly disturbing, both aesthetically and intellectually.

Auerbach expands these terms far beyond clauses and con-

junctives. Hypotactic constructions, chosen with fine discrimination, are of the essence of classical thought exemplified by its
"literary language ... with all its ingenious and nicely shaded
conjunctions, its wealth of devices for syntactic arrangement, its
carefully elaborated system of tenses."[9] The rational arrangements of language and, by implication, of thought, gave way in
late antiquity to a simpler, less rational, but potentially more
dramatic method of juxtaposition: "Dixit Deus: fiat lux, et facta
est lux."[10] The paratactic style, which had been, in classical
terms, a "low" style suitable only for satire and comedy,
became, in the hands of the Christian Fathers, the vehicle of a
sublime subject matter once reserved for a formal, elevated (and
hypotactic) style. For Auerbach, the fact that Jerome preserved
the paratactic style of the Bible in his translation rather than
recasting it into a "high" classical style signaled the inevitable
dominance of a new literature that combined "low" style and
lofty subjects. The Bible, once a stylistic embarrassment to
educated pagan converts, became the model for a new, emotional, and powerful style whose connections were not causal or
temporal but somehow "vertical," linking earthly events to the
Divine Will.

Many examples are, I think, unnecessary, to illustrate the
change from classical gradations of relationship to the disconcerting abruptness and unexplained juxtapositions so familiar in
all medieval narrative, history not least of all. It is significant
that the jaggedness of Gregory of Tours's prose does not
disappear by the polished twelfth century, although so much else
had changed. "The chancellor went to Dover ... and the count
turned over all the fortified places of the land, which had been
surrendered to him, to whomever he pleased and most trusted.
The king of the French sailed ... home from Acre with a small
force."[11] This example of paratactic prose is from the subtle,
classically learned Richard of Devizes, and any page opened at
random in his book can furnish more. It is inconceivable that
Richard was unable to understand that there might be a better
connective than *et* to describe the relationship between the
chancellor's retreat to Dover and John's disposition of the
castles. He also knew enough Latin to write a plausible transition
for his next paragraph, which changes the scene abruptly from
England to the Holy Land. Richard is so artful a writer that one

is forced to conclude that he wrote by choice in this style and that it was acceptable and satisfying to him and to his cultivated circle of friends. They could not have experienced the unexplained shifts and missing connections as rough and clumsy, much less as simpleminded.

The patrons and readers of Henry of Huntingdon and of William of Newburgh, as well, were men of education and taste who thought highly enough of history to commission books. It can be a useful test of our own reactions to imagine them reading passages such as the following one from Henry of Huntingdon: "In this year the king led an army into Wales.... A huge comet appeared at the end of May. The king went across to Normandy and made all the nobles of the country swear fidelity to the lord William his son, and he returned to England."[12] Every conjunction is *et*. We would, at the least, prefer to be told that the king went to Normandy "in order to" make the nobles swear fidelity and "then" returned to England; we also feel the lack of some specified relationship between the comet and the king's activities, regardless of what we think of portents. We are not at all justified in thinking that twelfth-century readers felt the same. William of Newburgh shows a taste for more hypotactic constructions, frequently using the ablative absolute or subordinating conjunctions in sentences within the passages of exposition or anecdote; the overall construction of his book, chapter by chapter or episode by episode, is paratactic.

In this case of a change in taste so extreme that we cannot pretend to reconstruct intuitively the reactions of earlier minds, we are forced to accept a great deal "on credit," as it were. Paratactic prose came into increasing use in late antiquity and was the norm in the twelfth century, in spite of well-known classical models. The general absence of causality from medieval thought is simply not a sufficient explanation for the quality of hard juxtaposition that characterizes so much medieval literature, fiction and history alike, the work of scholars and trouvères writing in Latin and in the vernaculars. We have to accept, for example, that any characteristic of narrative style commonly found throughout the works of educated men had to be there because everyone at the time liked it, regardless of how repugnant we find it.[13] Perhaps the enhanced force of parataxis held a strong emotional appeal and classical hypotactic arrangements seemed long-winded and tedious, or seemed to weaken the overall effect, or were simply unnecessary—like saying "Paris, France." We can speculate that the homogeneous culture of a small literate class encouraged a shorthand style of writing, with the reasoned connections and much detail supplied by the reader or auditor.

Auerbach, with a well-earned largeness of vision, has speculated on the relationship between paratactic organization and Christian views of history. He sees in the Vulgate a signal literary concession to a lower style of syntax, "for the Latin translation of the Bible has preserved the paratactic character of the original,"[14] and a corresponding, more grave, concession of classical rationality to a providential, figural conception of history. Syntax, in this view, is a key to mind.

> For example, if an occurrence like the sacrifice of Isaac is interpreted as prefiguring the sacrifice of Christ, so that in the former the latter is as it were announced and promised, and the latter "fulfills" . . . the former, then a connection is established between the two events which are linked neither temporally nor causally—a connection which it is impossible to establish by reason in the hori-dimension (if I may be permitted to use this term for a temporal extension). It can be established only if both occurrences are vertically linked to Divine Providence, which alone is able to devise such a plan of history and supply the key to its understanding. . . . This conception of history is magnificent in its homogeneity, but it was completely alien to the mentality of classical antiquity, it annihilated that mentality down to the very structure of its language, at least of its literary language, which . . . became wholly superfluous as soon as earthly relations of place, time, and cause had ceased to matter.[15]

Thus Auerbach concludes that paratactic structure and "the figural interpretation of history" emerged victorious together. The first and obvious objection that this plausible grand scheme, which integrates language and theology, cannot easily be reduced to a level that applies sensibly to "the king went across to Normandy and made all the nobles of the country swear fidelity, . . . and he returned to England," has been anticipated by Auerbach. He explains that, since the figural interpretation of history "was no fully adequate substitute for the lost comprehension of rational, continuous, earthly connections between things"[16] and was too difficult to apply to most ordinary, everyday events, writers fell back on "passive observation, resigned acceptance, or active exploitation of whatever chanced to occur in the world of practical events—raw material which was absorbed in its rawest form."[17] That is, they exerted almost no control at all.

While Auerbach's ideas about language and historical thought are brilliant and suggestive and are clearly the best, most dignified approach to medieval history, even he seems to think that most postclassical history, aspiring to neither rationality nor *figura*, was written in a kind of stylistic and mental vacuum. In a way, he asks too much or sees too much in the growing dominance of paratactic prose; it must either aspire to vertical links with Divine Providence or lapse into nothing. Without denigrating Auerbach's powerful and convincing analogy between style and thought, a less highly charged level of discussion is possible.

Stylistic elements such as parataxis, and others as well, can be regarded simply as the formal conventions of literary composition. Psychological and philosophical interpretations in appropriate cases are not negated by a more formalist or descriptive approach, but neither are they necessary to it. One recent study, *Structure in Medieval Narrative* by William Ryding, has presented a descriptive analysis of the development and chief characteristics of medieval narratives, especially in the twelfth and thirteen centuries.[18] Ryding's study is based primarily (but not solely) on French vernacular literature, but its conclusions are intended to have more general application; the particular interest for students of historiography lies in the wonderful aptness of Ryding's observations for historical narrative.

Medieval Latin history shares with the great mass of medieval fictional narrative the appearance of "a string of juxtaposed, mutually independent episodes," which is called, in French, the *roman à tiroirs*, "a phrase that makes us think of a chest of drawers which are explored one after the other."[19] Such cohesion as these narratives have is often provided by a single hero whose adventures make up the different episodes of the, often long, story; the analogy for historiography is obvious, as the *roman à tiroirs* is a reasonably apt description of Henry of Huntingdon's or William of Newburgh's loose, episodic narratives of events in and concerning England. Ryding's comments on the *roman à tiroirs* organization apply equally well to fiction and nonfiction: "The structural pattern of such stories is basically repetitive and sequential, one event cluster after another; it is not developmental. Such stories have not a single beginning, middle, and end; each episode has its own beginning, middle, and end. Structurally unimaginative, stories of this sort may nonetheless prove very effective in the reading, depending on the quality and arrangement of the episodes."[20] The narrative that continued but did not develop is nicely exemplified by histories that only stopped but did not end and thus could absorb later additions by the author (Henry of Huntingdon's several editions) or even by another author. Single episodes from this sort of narrative could be discarded or rearranged without material damage to the logic of the whole. It was a comfortable form for the author who wanted to insert a favorite, if fairly unconnected, anecdote into his work, and for the historian who liked to place information of only private or provincial interest next to events of national importance.

The *roman à tiroirs* allowed for variations; there could be a frame of beginning and end with a string of episodes between, or more than one large episodic section, each with its own beginning and end. For history, one thinks of Henry's use of the idea of foreign invaders as divine retribution (successively Saxons, Danes, and Normans) as frames for books of looser, episodic, material. The range of artistry or simplicity found in the fictional episodic story is paralleled in history, from the simple chronological annal to the more focused and cohesive monograph, in which the basic *roman à tiroirs* form is controlled by a smaller period of time, a particular place, and/or a heroic figure. The basic narrative conventions were available to writers of varying skills, and more sophisticated and subtler artists than the historians could better manipulate the narrative and sometimes shape the multiplicity of events into a symmetrical balance. The essential point is simply the universality of episodic, nondevelopmental, serial organization—Auerbach's parataxis without the philosophic implications. It was clearly the preferred form for narrative of all kinds, the form readers and auditors expected and enjoyed. It was an aesthetic fact of medieval life, symptomatic of a profound difference in taste and not of a failure of mind. As Ryding remarks, the problem for modern readers is that "in every case we are faced with a multiplicity where we should like to see unity."[21] That dizzying, nonconnected multiplicity, so irritating to us, must have been a source of real enjoyment to twelfth- and thirteenth-century readers. Since we can no longer experience their enjoyment directly, perhaps we should learn to measure their pleasure by our annoyance.

The universal taste for compound narratives did not entirely rule out the possibility of some controlling design. The historians were not leaders in such artistic developments, but they were able to select some of the easier techniques, common throughout fictional narratives, that were appropriate and useful. The device of interlacing, which came into use during the twelfth century and grew especially popular in the thirteenth, was one in which the author began one episode, introduced a second episode before he had ended the first, and then returned to finish the first. More than two actions could be interlaced by a clever writer, who could thereby keep several different, simultaneous actions moving together at great length. Chrétien de Troyes was quite accomplished at this technique.[22] Interlacing had good possibilities for history, and it is commonly found in historical works; it solved, for example, the problem of introducing a crusade into an English history.

Henry of Huntingdon inserts a ten-page account of the First Crusade into Book VII, between William II's first expedition into Wales in 1096 and his second expedition in 1097. He prefaces the account of the crusade with a brief justification for so long a digression and ends that account, remarking: "They subdued the provinces and the adjacent cities for Christ, except Ascalon, which to this day perseveres in its sin."[23] The next paragraph simply picks up the train of English history where it had left off. The Second Crusade is woven more complexly into Book VIII: In 1147 the earl of Chester attempts to take Lincoln; the French king leads a new crusade; Bishop Alexander visits Rome, returns home, and dies in 1148 (his character sketch is placed here); in the same year the crusade fails badly and only a small English force has any success before returning home; a new bishop is elected to Lincoln.[24] Interlacing the crusade with English ecclesiastical affairs in a way that strikes us as disconnected and odd was not the only possible way of narrating that material; Henry undoubtedly chose it for the sake of elegance.

William of Newburgh uses the same stylistic device for three crusades, each one more elaborately interlaced than the last. Book IV is worked out very thoroughly. It begins with the coronation of Richard I, his preparations for a crusade, and important events in England; changes scene to crusading adventures in Sicily and the Holy Land; interlaces the capture of Richard with the collection of the ransom money in England; and ends with the king safe again in England, wearing his crown at Winchester. The basic material lent itself easily and appropriately to the interlacing technique combined with the additional element of design in the frame of the two coronations. By the early thirteenth century, when William was writing, narrative interlacing was coming into increasing favor, and readers of William's Book IV must have admired the felicitous meeting of elegance and truth.[25]

Richard of Devizes, whose book covers only the years 1189 to 1192, was a master of many styles. He understood classical satire and effective oration; he could parody the sentimentality of religious literature and yet compose a sincere, touching defense of the monastic life. The pervasive style of his book, as one should expect, conforms to contemporary taste, in that it is severely paratactic, with episode after episode in hard juxtaposition with paratactic construction (the dominance of *et* as conjunctive) of many sentences. His various and delightful *jeux d'esprit* (the child-martyr parody, the guide to English towns) are assembled episodically to create a compound narrative. Richard's work reports substantially the same historical events as William's Book IV, but he imposes a much more elaborate scheme of narrative interlacing on the basic materials.

In the first few pages of his book, after the prologue, Richard sets out his three major themes or subjects: the crusade of King Richard, the elevation of William Longchamp as royal chancellor, and the ambitions of the king's brother John.[26] When the book closes, the king has ended his crusade, Longchamp has been deposed from office and expelled from England, and Count John has been foiled in his attempts at usurpation. The book contains a variety of other subjects, but these three themes are laced together from beginning to end. Although Richard wrote an unusually short book compared with those of his contemporaries—only eighty-four pages in Appleby's edition—he manages to change scene at least twenty-eight times—a veritable skein of narrative interlacing, far more complex than William's use of the technique. The changes of scene from England to Sicily, Cyprus, Acre, and back are done quickly, paratactically, without transition, and they achieve some fine effects that even modern taste can enjoy. All the actions move forward simultaneously and are held in suspense. A typical sequence of events has King Richard waging war in Tancred's Siciliy while Queen Eleanor brings him the daughter of the king of Navarre to be his bride; meanwhile, back in England, John and William Longchamp are holding their first hostile conference; in Sicily, Richard negotiates his release from a promise to marry Philip Augustus's sister; in England, the priors of Winchester and of Bath decide to become Carthusians; Philip Augustus disembarks from Sicily for Acre—and so forth.[27] Because we find this technique somewhat disconcerting and difficult to follow, we can only guess at the effects intended; perhaps thinking of a cinematic montage, the pleasures of contrast and variety, and of suspense may help. At any rate, compared with the truly heroic feats of interlacing achieved by fiction writers (the early thirteenth-century prose *Lancelot* weaves numerous subplots for more than a thousand pages),[28] Richard was working in small and intelligible scale. In one truly splendid section, Richard interweaves the disastrous arrest of Geoffrey Plantagenet, archbishop of York, by Longchamp's men; the increasing tension between Phlip Augustus and Richard I at the siege of Acre; Count John's successful contrivances against Longchamp, who retreats to the tower of London; the taking of Acre; and Longchamp's trial *in absentia*.[29] The building tension of competing ambitions, hatreds, and violence is genuinely powerful.

Accepting the fact that many of the general aesthetic conventions of twelfth-century narrative are applicable to the written history of the period should help us to recognize, or at least be reconciled to, a profoundly different standard of taste. It remains true, of course, that aesthetic considerations cannot meet our serious intellectual objections to what we now must see as grave defects in medieval history, but historical writing (and fictional narrative) has had a radical development, and current standards can be applied to the Middle Ages only at the risk of grotesque anachronism. Our objection to the lack of causal or logical connections in history is met, in medieval aesthetic terms, by the taste for paratactic structure and compound or episodic literature. Our objection to the absence of a principle of design based on unity of action can be met by the recognition that unity as a literary quality was not highly prized and that techniques, such as narrative interlacing, which imposed some design on disparate materials, were considered interesting and sufficient. Even our confirmed grievances, that medieval histories seem to ramble along slackly and erratically, often at great and unnecessary length, that they are discursive and disorderly and filled with pointless material, can be explicated in terms of a basic medieval aesthetic impulse.

Amplification was the essential work of an elegant writer. Even when his materials were fictive, a fine writer did not stake his reputation on his inventive genius (fiction writers, trouvères, generally used received stories or claimed to have found new ones) but on his ability to recast received materials into a magnified, elaborated, more impressive form.[30] The identification of elegance with fullness and decorative elaboration may largely explain the contemporary disregard for tidy cohesiveness. The same literary qualities that distinguish the romances and epics of high literature from brief, popular tales also marked the difference between true history and the jottings of annal keepers. The common fate of many popular stories, which grew longer and more elaborate as each succeeding redactor "improved" them, is paralleled by the practice of historians copying or amalgamating the works of previous writers and then extending them to a new chronological limit. Both the trouvère and the historian found his basic materials and amplified them, to the best of his ability, in accord with current taste. Henry of Huntingdon's insertion of poetry into sections copied from Bede or the Anglo-Saxon Chronicle is a good example of purely ornamental amplification; seen in this aesthetic light, his inclusion of epistles, genealogies, and the like, in various editions of his history is not quite so egregious an act. Henry undoubtedly considered such—

to us—extraneous additions as reasonable and tasteful, as giving his book dignity, fullness, and interest. We do not have to relinquish entirely our own conviction that Henry's choice of literary ornaments was not especially sensible or felicitous. Given a firm cultural bias in favor of expansive narrative, different authors still had different degrees of taste, judgment, and skill.

William of Newburgh exhibited better taste and more common sense, working within the same canons of convention and fashion, than did Henry of Huntingdon. Ryding defines two primary categories of narrative amplification: rhetorical amplification, in which the writer reproduces received material but gives it fullness with greater detail of explanation, and material amplification, in which the writer introduces new narrative matter within or at either end of his work.[31] The distinction sometimes blurs a bit for historical narrative, but it is useful nonetheless. For example, William's frequent use of dialogue, especially invented dialogue, to liven an anecdote is rhetorical amplification, while his vampire episodes qualify as material amplification. Henry's poems, speeches, battle scenes, and his Latin translation of the Anglo-Saxon poem are instances of rhetorical amplification. A less frivolous sort of rhetorical expansion are William's thoughtful excursuses on moral or theological issues, such as the Becket controversy, the nature of demons, the spiritual fate of dead crusaders, or the value of Geoffrey of Monmouth's work. Such passages elevate the intellectual stature of the book and fill out many events to a more complex level. The same techniques of composition were available to Henry and William, but William displayed better judgment of aptness and of appropriateness.

Free association, dependent on the writer's particular resources and intuition, played a large and legitimate role in fiction and nonfiction narratives. "It stands to reason that in the absence of strict logical control over a narrative sequence, some form of association would from time to time dictate the development of an episodic sequence."[32] The historian was committed only to report "important" events of past or present time and was free to exercise his own intuitive judgment or his emotions in their selection. William tended to regard demons as important and interesting, and so he inserted all major demonic events

207

known to him into his history. If one event reminds him of another, he may write several in a row before taking up again the train of his original narrative. William ends his story of the London popular leader, William Fitz Osbert, with an account of how the misled populace tried to honor their demagogue as a martyr after he was executed by hanging. There immediately follows the first vampire story, although there seems to have been no direct chronological sequence. This sequence seems to have been the result of an associative process in William's mind that linked dishonorable death, sin, popular misfortunes with ominous consequences and an aura of spiritual unease.

Narrative could also be amplified quite logically in order to explain or elucidate some occurrence, as when William adds his special knowledge about the color of the teeth of the dead Archbishop William of York to disprove rumors of poison. Both commonsensical, explanatory amplification and looser digressions were regarded as legitimate and tasteful methods for creating important works of literature. The sacrifice, if it must be so regarded, of tight structure was an inevitable consequence of the preference for expanded narrative and was, apparently, of negligible importance to the twelfth-century reader.

A happy whim of fate has preserved the autographed manuscript of Richard of Devizes's *Cronicon* and, in preserving the author's draft, has given us a glimpse of the process of composition. In the editor's words:

A [MS 339, ff.25r–43v, Corpus Christi College, Cambridge] bears all the marks of an author's draft. It starts out as a conventional chronicle, with wide margins at the outside and bottom of the page and a line left blank after each entry. Then the author starts adding bits of information in the empty spaces. There is nothing in the context to distinguish text from marginalia; the story wanders from one to the other, apparently as the items occurred to the writer. Some bits in the margin are obviously intended to fit into the text and are so marked; others carry on an entirely different story. In the year 1190, for example, once the story is under way, the deeds of King Richard occupy the text and the misdeeds of Longchamp the margin. In 1191, on the other hand, Count John and Longchamp fill the text, and the king's deeds are relegated to the margin. By f.40v things have got so far out of hand that the margin is entirely filled, and the space left blank for the text is used for an addition to the margin.... The writing varies from entry to entry, now careful and stately, now hurried and dashing. The ink varies throughout the manuscript. Spaces are left blank for names or better turns of speech, which are sometimes added later in a different ink. Corrections and interlineations abound. All these points would indicate that A is in the handwriting of Richard of Devizes.[33]

The only other extant manuscript of Richard of Devizes's book, MS B, is a fair copy in a different hand. The visual impression of the manuscript, as described by Appleby, is entirely congruent with chief techniques and conventions of twelfth-century narrative art. The physical arrangement of parallel text and marginal material is a visual plan for interlaced narrative; the exploding, engulfing marginalia allow us almost to see the very process of associative and logical amplification.

Appleby has indicated marginal material and interlineations by typographical means, which permits the reader to notice, for example, that from the very beginning of the book, the marginalia combined rhetorical amplifications both explanatory and digressive, with vital narrative material.[34] The marginal material sometimes extends the subject of the text logically, as when the text is about Longchamp becoming papal legate and the margin adds that he held a council at Westminster;[35] or the margin can insert unconnected information of peculiar interest to Richard (often about monastic affairs) into a text concerned with major political or military events. One marginal story can, by clear association, lead to another. The marginal insertion about the usurping prior of Montacute who suffered a sudden and significant death, is followed directly, again in the margin, by the account of the improperly ambitious monk, who, well-deservedly, had a beam fall on his head.[36] Frequently, several marginal additions are grouped together, which is, I think, a natural occurrence, given the basic impulse to amplify. Margin and text are used, as noted before, for interlacing events in England with the crusade. The entire story of the child-martyr of Winchester is a marginal entry, and it is followed by another long marginal account of the bishop of Chester and his hatred for monks—a passage that presents Richard's defense of the monastic life.[37] The margin is also where King Richard's defiant speech to God, "Henceforth my banners will lie prostrate, not for me, indeed, but for Thee,"[38] is to be found.

I have stressed the importance of the marginal material in order to counteract the natural, modern expectation that marginalia must be extraneous or obliquely connected to the "real" matter or, at best, explanatory, such as the notes we jot in the margins of books. Richard's use of the margins reveals something of the approach to composition when canons of taste were focused, not on tidy and unifying structure, but on amplitude, variety, and multiplicity. In a spatial metaphor, his narrative does not move forward with much impetus, but expands sideways from text to margin and back in a leisurely zigzag motion. The burgeoning marginalia of the center of the *Cronicon* shows the associative, amplifying process gaining momentum, growing richer and fuller as it draws on the reserves of a clever and cultivated mind. Richard, in common with all historians of his period, came to his work ready-furnished with a minimal structure of limited time, place, and major events, and that structure (if we can so dignify it by the name) was as much as contemporary taste demanded. The very choice of a monograph on England over a universal history was a considerable step toward specificity and was probably one aspect of the larger impulse to realism and clarity in twelfth-century thought. Intellectual movements and aesthetic conventions are, however, hardly ever identical. The true writer's task was, not to contrive neat organization through a process of careful selection and stern elimination, but to enlarge and enrich his basic narrative. Richard's book is, for the age, uncharacteristically short, but it covers only a brief period and a limited scope of event and does so at a leisurely pace of digressions, additions, and all the resources of amplified or "high" literature. It is not a brief or terse book but a slice, as it were, of a very large one.

What we have come to experience as rambling discursiveness and irrelevance was once appreciated for its variety and elegance, for the general conventions of narrative literature in the twelfth century were easily applicable to history as it was then understood. The looseness of narrative structure, the universal taste for digression, the technique of interlacing, the basic impulse to juxtapose elements in accord with allusion or relations other than strictly logical or subordinating ones—all lent themselves to the materials and point of view historians commonly brought to their work. The expansiveness of narrative forms, their ability to include much diversity, along with an audience accustomed to understand connections or relations we find obscure, to read at length, and to appreciate ornament and digression—all conduced to fit history comfortably with existing narrative forms. History participated in the fashions and techniques of fictional narrative to the extent that historians were able to imitate the stylistic elements of "high" literature; nothing in an historian's education or cultural milieu would have prompted him to think that history needed a new and different set of techniques or forms.

Nine

THE QUESTION
OF CHRISTIAN HISTORY

EARLY IN THE *Historia pontificalis*, JOHN OF SALISBURY, conscientious as always and attentive to the single uniting purpose of all Christian historians as he understood it, gives one firm example of how "the invisible things of God may be clearly seen by the things that are done":

> It happened after the council [1148], while the pope [Eugenius] was celebrating mass in the cathedral and the chalice was being brought to him by his assistants according to Roman custom, that through some carelessness of the assistants the blood of the Lord was spilled on the carpet before the altar. The pope at once sent his chancellor, the cardinal deacon Guy of Pisa, to cut out the piece of carpet on which the blood had fallen, and place it among the other relics; and he imposed penance on the assistants for such negligence. But this event frightened many thoughtful men; for the prevailing belief was that such a thing could never happen in any church unless some serious evil threatened it; and since this time the Apostolic See was involved the whole Church seemed to be in danger. And indeed this belief did not err.[1]

John recognizes the fulfillment of this portent, explicitly and neatly, in the various disasters suffered by the French and German armies on the Second Crusade in that year.[2]

John of Salisbury was a thoroughly sensible man, and, for all the apparently genuine fright of the event, there is an air of calm and correctness about his relation of it; the terrible "accident" in the cathedral is dramatic in setting and action, and the explanatory unfolding in the Holy Land appropriate in scope and meaning. The dignity of this example of Christian explication (as rigorously "vertical" as Auerbach could demand) is only slightly unsettled by the persistent, vulgar, silly idea of that piece of wet carpet placed among jeweled bones. More seriously awkward is the fact, at the center of the event in many ways, that the pope punished his chalice-bearers for being clumsy. Presumably, the assistants were, as they tripped on the carpet, the instruments of a higher will, bearing a message to such thoughtful men as could "read" more than words; the bearers of such grave news were surely no more responsible for spilling the wine than for ruining the Second Crusade. Some explanation could be constructed with terms like *proximate* and *ultimate cause*, but would, I think, only explain away the central reality of the event—that Eugenius's impulse to punish his assistants was a natural one (in the full colloquial sense of the word); that that impulse of common sense radically contradicted his own and John's theological sense of the occasion; that a miniature tension that passed unnoticed in the flurry of its own moment stands eternally and interestingly unresolved in John's book.

This small matter may very well be the artificially sensitive observation that betrays irrecoverable distances from writer to reader, but it nonetheless sets forth plainly enough the terms of a question that, for medieval historians, was neither small nor artificial. If historians at all times in the Middle Ages agreed that God did manipulate the natural world for purposes of His own, that principle never was adequately extended to account for particular cases; the explanation for any event that hesitated between natural and divine agency depended very much on the temperament and persuasions of the individual reporter. John himself held some deeply complicated views about portents, believing that genuine omens did occur as warnings from God to mankind, but that portended misfortunes would not necessarily follow, because God might, in the interval, alter His judgment— but without thereby impeaching the validity of His portent.[3] There were undoubtedly many people whose minds could not conceive such complicated possibilities, who were restrained by innate reasonableness from overeager belief in signs and casual interferences by the Divinity. Many degrees of scrupulous caution and ordinary skepticism were available to the intelligent observer of John's age, but no one could simply deny the supernatural possibilities in human life, and no one could comfortably assume the guarded posture available to the modern Christian historian, as so forthrightly expressed by one of the most noted: "Hold to Christ, and for the rest be totally uncommitted."[4] For the twelfth-century observer, the question of supernatural forces, phrased in its simplest and most intractable form (who did, in effect, spill the consecrated wine?), was always waiting for the resolution that could never, finally, be given.

From a cavalier hindsight, the writing of history in accord with a Christian consciousness after the fifth century (and especially during the literate twelfth) would not seem to have been such a formidable undertaking. A great deal in the way of large design and clear example had been offered by Orosius, especially to prospective writers of history in the Christian era; Orosius's optimistic simplifications passed for Augustinian history—the bishop's thoughts about human history and Christianity being far too dense and subtle to be easily understood, much less imitated.[5] One might theoretically expect—and according to a few modern students, may actually be able—to read postclassical histories as so many variations on a firmly set theme.[6] In fact, the peculiarity of medieval histories is not that they are so thoroughly Christian but that they are so little so, and that those particularly Christian elements in them are so often perfunctory or odd. Following the loss of classical Latin syntax, which is itself a figure for the loss of rational, classical causality, Auerbach judges historical writing as bleak, with "vast regions of event . . . without any principle by which they might be classified and comprehended,"[7] revealing the inadequacy of figural, Christian modes as a replacement for what had been lost.

The most commonplace instances of twelfth-century historians describing and explaining small but presumably supernatural events tell, in their own oblique way, more about Christian history than the bland clichés found in prefaces; at least they reward close attention more interestingly. The most frequent and cursory moments of divine interference with the world consisted of bizarre or unexpected variations on natural phenomena and were interpreted as warnings of future misfortune or adverse judgments on the present. These fleeting signs from God were naturally quite similar to pagan omens, except that the pagans sometimes foresaw good luck. Natural portents or prodigies or signs, their most common names, are the set pieces of medieval Christian histories—highly conventional in form—and yet, for all their banalized rigidity, they do reveal something of an historian's mind. The following passages were chosen as being characteristic of their authors and similar in content.

In his entry for 1098, Henry of Huntingdon notices, with his usual assiduity for the subject, that royal taxation was particularly unbearable that year:

> The younger William in the eleventh year of his reign was in Normandy . . . all the same he was not merely abrading but excoriating the English people with the worst taxes and exactions ever. In the summer, blood was seen to bubble up from a certain pool in the Finchamstead in Berkshire. After this the sky looked as though it were burning almost all night.[8]

Several years later, King Henry I took his brother Robert prisoner and incarcerated him for the rest of his life; this, the historian explains, was God's punishment for Robert's refusal to govern the recaptured Jerusalem:

> In that year a comet appeared as a sign of this event. Two moons were seen at Pentecost, one in the east, the other in the west.[9]

Two passages by William of Newburgh, chosen for their similarity to Henry's subjects, are to be considered in direct comparison. The first concerns an unusual red sky that first occurred in January of 1193; William seems to have been an eyewitness.

> Through these storms occasioned by the capture of the king [Richard I], England groaned under multiple afflictions—so great they could not have been anticipated. The horror of this misfortune was made evident in recent times, it is believed, by prodigies of the sky. It happened in January of the very year in which the king fell into enemy hands that we saw a terrible sign in the sky, without any doubt a presage of our future affliction. For about the first vigil of the night, a middle zone of the sky, between the north and east, grew so red that it seemed to be burning.[10]

William proceeds to describe the appearance of the sky very exactly: the stars were not obscured but were reddened also and glowed with a blood-red light. This appearance lasted for "almost two hours" and then gradually faded. An exactly similar event occurred again in February, when the king's detention in Germany was not yet widely known; the fiery sky reflected in

215

glass windows so startled the monks at Lauds (William presumably among them) that they ran from church to see which of their buildings was on fire, and then, horrified, ran back to their prayers.[11] The same thing happened again in November, just before morning. The witnesses were less frightened this third time, "but the question and suspicion of a portent increased."[12]

In 1196 William again saw an interesting astronomical sight— a double sun. There was some question as to which was the true and which the false sun, but he thought that point was settled by the motion of the two bodies, in that one seemed to lead and the other to follow.[13] "I saw the sign with my own eyes in company with certain others who were with me," he says; while they stood there staring, the second sun vanished. It was recognized as a portent of misfortune, and, not long after, war broke out again between Richard and Philip Augustus.[14]

Modern science would hardly be put to any difficulty to explain these four little "prodigies" as infrequent but quite natural events; still, the real phenomena in question are men, and not the aberrations of fire, earth, and water. Henry could have been only about fourteen when the pond of blood and the red sky were reported, and he was not a witness to either; his information was taken almost verbatim from the Peterborough Chronicle, suggestively rearranged.

The Peterborough Chronicle reports some seven events for the year 1098: King William II's stay in Normandy, the deaths of a bishop and two abbots (including the abbot of Peterborough), the appearance of a bloody pond in Berkshire during the summer, the murder of an earl by northmen, the red sky at the end of September, and generally heavy taxes and too much rain—in that order.[15] Henry tightens and colors the scant material, having the absent king "excoriate" the English with his shameful exactions, and then he conflates the two prodigies to underline the royal rapacity. In fact, the Peterborough chronicler probably intended to indicate some relation between the bloody pond and either the death of his abbot just previously or the death of the earl reported immediately after (a little farther on in the chronicle, blood from the Berkshire earth clearly portends the death of William II);[16] he also indicates slightly more concern over rainfall and crop failure than over taxes.

Henry's rendition of these assorted facts makes slightly better reading; he freely altered the relations between supernatural signs and their earthly counterparts to suit his own taste. In this case and in many others scattered throughout Henry's work, no particular attention is paid to the sign itself; its validity is assumed, its significance stated or implied with matter-of-fact simplicity. He uses these flickering signals from heaven as a kind of moral punctuation.

To turn from Henry's burning sky, blazing with divine indignation at a king's fiscal policy and reported in nine words, to William's anxious, wordy, circumstantial report of the same sight in 1192–1193, thoughtfully compiled from the evidence of three events separated by many months, is to move from innocent complacency to something almost approaching intellectual morbidity. William is both more thoughtful and more emotional. His careful detailing of circumstance and his concern, very like John of Salisbury's, to fit an appropriately monumental misfortune to his omen are characteristic of the man and suggest doubts, the felt need to argue, to overwhelm objections. William invariably found things problematic that would not, one feels, have presented any problem to others. The emotion of the witnesses is what he most wants to convey: "We saw a fearful sign in the sky"; "this horrible sight ... had held the eyes and minds of the witnesses fixed with stupefaction"; "seeing the horrifying sign, the amazed monks ran back to their psalms."[17] This reaction is the basis of his own conviction, the unprovable proof, the shocked inner assent to a supernatural event. William did not take such things lightly.

It remains to remember what William's contemporary Richard, similar in all things but mind, had to say about seeing significance in the sky: "Those who do not understand the causes of things marvel greatly that, although the sun was not darkened by any clouds, in the middle of the day it shone with less than ordinary brightness. Those who study the working of the world, however, say that certain defects of the sun and moon do not signify anything."[18] If one is to group the three men by their reactions to natural signs, Henry is the one who must stand apart. He was always inclined to see meaning in any infrequent occurrence, to accept it in good faith, and, probably, to think very little of it; he wasted very few words on the terrible sign he himself saw at Ramsey in 1144. His attitude toward such things was the uninquiring and old-fashioned one that Richard, fifty years later, dismisses. Yet Richard's and William's minds are not so far apart as they first appear. Their treatment of portents— William's anxious wordiness, Richard's inattention—are both consonant with sophistication, generalized skepticism, and increased information. The mature alternatives to Henry's easy, somehow cheerful acceptance of fearful omens are greater seriousness about them or impatient disregard.

The other pair of portents quoted above, Henry's double moon and William's double sun, follow the same pattern. Henry takes his basic information from the Peterborough Chronicle, adding comments and rearranging the order of events to shift the comet and moons into a more satisfying alignment with earthly sin.[19] William was again an eyewitness, with companions; he gives the date, the time of day, the movement of the celestial bodies, and his state of mind. He wonders which is the true sun, stands in amazement for a long time, says they recognized the sight as a portent of evil. He offers the resurgence of Richard I's and Philip's chronic war as an explanation.

One step up, as it were, from signs were sudden deaths by accident, especially when effected by inanimate objects. These events were very like natural portents but much stronger in the effect they had on moral, thoughtful, or suggestible minds. The fatal accident, with its startling, saddening effect on observers, was the most persuasive example of God's judgment—inexorable and, given the usual state of human nature, unambiguously proper. Most victims met their sudden deaths in a satisfyingly sinful state, or if not, there was always the ancient theme of vanity, vanity to edify the conventional moralists. (Only the prosperous, well-born, or eminent attracted attention by untimely deaths; the illiterate and poor presumably all died without divine interference.) The well-deserved death, violent and swift, was an irresistible occasion for Christian (and some not very Christian) reflections. Even Richard of Devizes, scorner of portents, includes three extremely satisfying cases: a Cluniac monk who usurps the office of prior from its rightful holder is struck dumb and dies after his hypocritical speech of introduction to the monks; an ambitious monk who tries to bribe his way to unearned promotion is hit on the head by a falling beam; a traitorous monk who plays the dupe and fool for Bishop Hugh of Coventry's antimonastic vituperation is brained by a falling stone.[20] These three providential acts were the expression of Richard's secure conviction that God loves the regular life in all of its tradition, privilege, and autonomous self-government—this conviction being the closest thing to religious passion Richard apparently felt.

The terrible descent from prosperity to the grave was the very heart of Henry's elegiac history. His *De contemptu mundi* is a virtual roll call of sudden, mortal falls from power, position, and happiness, and even natural death in old age is seen as the ultimate judgment on little human ambitions and fragile joys: vanity and emptiness, violence and disease. Throughout the *Historia*, its presence naturally more diffused, the judgmental death strikes often, teaching what Henry clearly believed, that God was not ever asleep or away (the desperate grumbling repeated by the Peterborough chronicler) but was the true *deus irritatus*, ever ready to strike in anger.[21] The wicked Sigebert of Wessex, unrecognized and killed by a swineherd—"Behold the manifest judgment of God . . ."; the noblemen at Calne, fallen through a collapsed floor, leaving Dunstan, holy and unharmed, clinging to a beam; Henry I's homosexual son, dead in the drunkenly navigated White Ship; the fall of majesty in the young Philip of France's fatal riding accident—"Behold this great eminence, how quickly, how lightly it is annihilated";[22] these are Henry's favorite moral vignettes and only a few chosen from many. His particular theme, his characteristic signature, was the cultivated gloom, the edgy distrust of his own and everyone else's happiness; it was a habit of mind that was more widespread and perhaps more fashionable at the period of his birth than at his death.

William, as his readers come to expect, was willing to attempt the hard cases. The spectacle of interesting persons dying in striking circumstances did not allow much scope for the Christian imagination, but a few instances did present difficulties. The death of Emperor Frederick I, who rode his horse into a river in Asia Minor at the very outset of the Third Crusade and drowned before he ever saw a pagan, was a puzzle and an embarrassment to the Christian world. The judgment of God visited on the emperor at that most meaningless of moments is conceded to be very obscure: "By the hidden judgment of God, a miserable accident (and one which no one could have anticipated) removed that man of great eminence from the world"; and "O great abyss of the judgments of God! That such a man, prompted by a divine fervor, having left behind his imperial pleasures and wealth and exposed himself to a thousand dangers for Christ, is killed in so quick and wretched an accident."[23] Those expressions of real, felt pain before the mystery of God's punishments (for William, like John, knew that a crusade involved the whole Christian world) are followed by some attempt at explanation. He finally, and awkwardly, reconciles fact with belief by suggesting that Frederick's great act of devotion to Christ, which took him to his wretched death in Asia Minor, effected the only sufficient atonement for his past sins and thus won his salvation.[24] It is a strangely complicated explanation, but it does not gloss over anything and has none of the complacency of Henry of Huntingdon's exclamations over fatal accidents.

In unusual coincidence with Richard of Devizes, William too has his own example of a monk hit on the head by a falling stone, in judgment on his violation of the dignity and propriety of his order. Richard's monk was the hapless wretch who let himself be used as the "straight man" to a routine of anti-monastic jokes. William's monk was a Premonstratension hermit and priest who joined in the siege of the Jews in the tower of York in 1190 with loud and bloody enthusiasm: "He had so persuaded himself in his blinded mind that he even labored to persuade others, that the work under way was quite religious." He was crushed by a stone from the catapult because his guilt was greater than that of others "by reason of his profession and order."[25] The differences between William's and Richard's notions of the true dignity and propriety of regular life should by now be apparent and predictable.

So much concentration on these small issues, the briefest manifestations of divine intelligence in the twelfth-century world, may seem to be begging the larger question of Christian history, of God's relation to human society. But if Christian history did not consist of exactly those moments of startling and mysterious information, it is difficult to see in what exactly it could have consisted. During the lifetime of all the historians mentioned, and before and after them as well, no educated man was satisfied with the conception of God working only in movements so ineffable, so large, and so deliberate that no individual could ever hope to see anything of it in his own time. The idea of a God who is "there" but never precisely here or there is suitable only for modern minds, embarrassed by too provincial a deity. Those who watched their world in the twelfth century for signs of the living presence took them as they found them. The very sporadicness and even triviality of most of the events that prompted medieval historians to open affirmation of their belief in divine superintendence of the world—a seepage of rusty water, the aurora borealis, the accidents so common around building sites and war machinery—are a kind of inverse measure of how much else was allowed to go assumed and unexpressed, and perhaps only half understood.

The specialness of human history in the Christian era, however any particular writer had learned of it and understood it, was, with a few exceptions, the most sketchily treated of historical themes. After a few prefatory remarks about history and God, graceful reference to previous writers, assurance of the propriety of the author's didactic intentions, most medieval histories get quickly under way, shedding almost cavalierly as they approach the author's lifetime every trace of dogmatic coherence in favor of increasing dependence on portents, demons, and all the debris of popular belief for a Christian tone.[26] Only the most strenuously philosophic of minds would attempt to work out the implications of their historical religion for their own, invariably disordered, time.[27] European Christendom was old by the twelfth century, its institutions stable or rigid, according to point of view; the urgent occasions for Augustine's *City of God* and Orosius's *Against the Pagans* belonged entirely to the past. The insistent and present sense of a large and inclusive plan for mankind, the need for that sense, had subsided into a quiet acceptance of the *idea* of such a plan without the need for very specific understanding of its provisions. Narrower problems dominated the mental and moral leisure enjoyed by the world. Only a very few historians seemed to have had the intellectual confidence or the interest to make systematically known their own understanding of any higher purpose informing recent history.

The incalculable effects of aesthetic conventions on the exposition of an historical theology must also be weighed, however imprecisely, into the cultural milieu that produced these works of apparently uncertain philosophical nature. The dominant literary conventions of the age, the taste for abrupt, paratactic composition, for episodic, compound narratives, had to make the conception of an orderly, linking theme of providential history as foreign to nonfiction as the well-made plot was to contemporary fiction. An unbroken web of reasonable and plausible motivation was not considered necessary to the most elegantly composed romances; history being an analogous, subsidiary kind of high literature, the genre carried no intrinsic necessity of a thoroughly exposed plot, even though its plot would be both divine and real. Any regular pattern of historical development, secular or spiritual, had to be brought into history from outside the dominant literary conventions that shaped the genre. An historian could expand or modify the prevailing conventions of narrative to accommodate larger historical or theological conceptions if he so chose, but the merely episodic and compound was perfectly acceptable to an educated audience. Christian history presented as a series of disconnected, startling events fit so well into the aesthetic habits of the twelfth century that it is not very surprising that so many historians ventured so little beyond what they felt, if not exactly thought, to be necessary.

The basic authority of the idea that all secular history is included in, and eventually explained by, a purpose only partially visible to men, and the basic impulse toward a Christian exegesis of history had not diminished since late antiquity; but the laborious and open insistence on those themes had been replaced by a more comfortable reliance on assumptions generally understood among all Christian readers. The best and the most serious-minded of twelfth-century historians allowed their own sense (it is usually too much to say "philosophy") of Christian history to surface occasionally, under the influence of special experiences or information. Between an author's vaguest prefatory remarks and the didactic purposes of written history, and his particular catalogue of demons, ponds of blood, and comets, there is usually a rather empty middle distance containing little that connects the movements of the empyrean with life in Berkshire. The prodigies and signs and amazing occurrences that irregularly mark the surface of twelfth-century histories are the self-explanatory expressions of each author's special conscious-ness of the relation between his God and his world—the scattered and often unlikely pieces of a whole that can be only partially reconstructed.

The patterns through which a Christian consciousness of the meaning of human history was expressed at this period had been long since fixed: the alternations of sin and punishment, the pilgrimage of life, the warning signs from an outraged heaven. But even medieval religiosity had its fashions, and changing assumptions and encroaching questions seem to fill the distance between Henry of Huntingdon and William of Newburgh. When Henry acquires, from some unknown source, knowledge of an interesting portent whose application is unclear (a rare event), he offers only a brief, tepid gesture at interpretation. In the year 786 the sign of the cross appeared on certain peoples' clothing—a miracle to be sure, but whether it was some premature sign of a crusade to take place three hundred and nine years later or a sign to mark off some people from the suffering soon to be inflicted by the Danes, Henry is not sure. "We, however, do not venture to make our own definition, but leave God's secrets to God."[28] This is a hasty, prim retreat from the field of divine mysteries, almost suggesting that it would be impolite to inquire more aggressively. The recurring themes of God's stern relationship to His creation, of man's sin and vainglory, of the hopelessness and pain of the world, of waves of cruel conquerors succeeding one another at England's shores, and of disappointment and death overtaking individual happiness, anchor Henry's history in a secure and predictable, if pitiable, universe. Hie elegiac sensi-bility ("See how the honors and pleasure and glory of the world come to nothing"),[29] which favors the word *nihil*, with its flat, depressing sound, is expressed so consistently and so often that the whole effect is finally one of complacency—the comfortable gloom of a rich man whose family is on the ascendant. Every sign from heaven, every intelligible pattern in human history repeats the same lesson, without puzzles or mysteries.

More than the differences between an uninquiring or satisfied mind and an inquisitive one separated Henry and William, or at least their differences were more than merely personal and individual traits. Henry's world and his God were thoroughly

223

traditional (from an early twelfth-century point of view); they immediately invoke the pictorial representations of the enthroned God of Judgment typical of a somewhat earlier age. It was not unreasonable for him to excise all the saints and their miracles from Bede's history and combine them with similar contemporary stories to make a separate book; saints did not quite fit in a dark world of sin and punishment. William's world, full of disturbing and half-explained things—demons, vampires, toads with golden collars—is also filled with calmness and goodness—Thurstan, Saint Godric, Gilbert of Sempringham, the Cistercian houses. Satan and his legions, so active a part of the later history, play virtually no role in Henry of Huntingdon's world; God alone is responsible for everything severe and painful.

Conventional patterns of Christian explication had not changed between Henry's death at mid-century and the time William was trying to fit his strangely more diverse world into them. The sheer effort required by this well-intentioned and thoughtful man to make form and content fit is what compels the reader's attention and sympathy. Our difficulties in trying to define and place those mental and moral efforts, at once so rational and so perversely misdirected, are caught up in the assumptions directing our choice of language. The growing impulse in the twelfth century, exposed through the various literary and plastic arts, to notice and record the natural world has been well documented.[30] It is true that observing reality and observing nature are identical activities now, but if "reality" and "nature," with their corresponding styles, methods, or intellectual systems of "realism" and "naturalism," are allowed to coincide in our descriptions of the twelfth century, the very words will enforce distortions and a kind of blunted sensitivity. The William of Newburgh who described Scarborough Castle will be included as one of the best of the new sort of observer in his own time, but the William who applied the same perspicacity to the investigation of vampires must be excluded, and misunderstood. If naturalism is regarded, with good dictionary authority, as a style or method characterized by close adherence to and faithful representation of nature, and if realism, by that same authority, is taken to mean an attachment to what is real and an inclination to render the precise details of some fact or experience that actually existed or occurred,[31] then the two words need not be rigidly synonymous when used to describe a society characterized by universal belief in the supernatural. No one in the twelfth century believed that the natural world encompassed all of the real world. Reality, in the firm and knowledgeable belief of intelligent people, contained a great many actually existing facts and experiences that nature knew nothing of; such facts and experiences could be made the objects of the same kind of attention usually employed in the understanding and manipulation of the natural world, with, admittedly, a great deal more difficulty and some odd results.

What may be observed throughout William's work is an attempt, though not consciously conceived as such, to extend the standards of bold mental activity appropriate to energetic life in the natural world to supernatural "reality." One may even, with the addition of many more authors, generalize this observation to a view of the twelfth century's peculiar feeling of energy and tension as the encroachment of the demands of "naturalism" into the supernatural realities of the traditional Christian world. In the end, the facts and experiences William tried to explain were not susceptible to the standards of probability, consistency, and concreteness taught by mundane existence, however informally. The result was that many of his best intellectual efforts look foolish, though not much more foolish than many subsequent attempts at the problem of "Christian evidence." He struggled on many occasions to rationalize what could not, ultimately, be rationalized, and his failure is less important than the fact of his attempt.

The effort that William gave to recording subjects like the green children who appeared in a ditch was not solely the impulse of a story collector; every painstakingly described grotesque was an expression of his felt conviction that God's governance of His creation is reasonable and intelligible. Clearly, the old, formal patterns of a universe ruled by a justly cruel lord whose presence was felt through punishments, never anticipated but always deserved, were no longer satisfying, and neither were the dark mysteries of arbitrary event and human helplessness that must accompany such a strict but distant dominion. The kind of Christian universe that Henry appeared to accept as strong, at once sorrowful and comforting, must have seemed to another generation as banal, inadequate, and superstitious. William talks often about superstition; Henry, never.

Devout and thoughtful, William insisted on a detailed, living, bold *saeculum* informed with meaning—a world more emotional and rational than anything Henry had described. He was one of the most complete and unflinching reporters of the anti-Jewish horrors of 1189–1190, telling with unhidden disgust the base motives and vile conduct of the Christian townsmen. While William cannot be expected to have regarded the Jews with sympathy or understanding, his distaste for the violence and looting was still not the same as Richard of Devizes's fastidious recoil. He despised the Premonstratensian hermit who emerged to encourage the besiegers around the tower at York; he exposed the venality and foolishness that created a martyr out of a murdered looter at Stanford; but an attack on Jewish infidels had to mean something more than Christian dishonor. From the sad welter of a conscientious religious purpose and the ugly facts (which he did not try to conceal or soften) of Christian greed, violence, duplicity, and bloodiness, William found his way by resorting to a "rule" for historical interpretation—employed only once in his book.

> The first day of the reign of the most illustrious King Richard was marked by this hitherto unheard-of event in the royal city, both by the uncompleted destruction of a notoriously perfidious people, and by a new confidence of the Christians against the enemies of the Cross. Clearly this was a presage of the advancement of Christianity in Richard's own time, not only according to the rule (*regulam*) which prescribes that ambiguous meanings (*ambigua*) be derived in the better rather than the worse sense, but even according to the most appropriate meaning.[32]

This rule, whose original application was perhaps grammatical, is placed firmly at the beginning of several chapters given to a full and explicit chronicle of murder, looting, riot, impotent royal officers, false saints, in city after city, all told in pitiful (and perhaps pitying) detail. He warns the reader not to be distracted by the incendiary violence of the mobs from the certainty that the pious interpretation is the correct one: "The

Omnipotent One may fulfill His supremely good will through the will of the most depraved men and thoroughly wicked acts."[33] There must, after all, have been some question about it. The full effect of William's unyielding insistence on such events as a happy presage for Christendom, combined with his scenes of Jews killing their wives and children and then themselves rather than face baptism or murder by a Christian mob, is more than distasteful. But the strength of that revulsion by the modern reader is itself the result of William's relentless, one may say even courageous, clarity of vision—the scenes in London, York, Stanford, Lincoln are repulsive because he was repulsed and because he did not conceal anything. Once William had committed himself to thinking about such *ambigua*, he arrived, unsurprisingly, at the only Christian interpretation available to him, regardless of any rule he thought applied. No rule of history or theology impelled him to report the shabby and revolting story as honestly as he did. His emotional and intellectual attachment to a standard of realism as unflinching as any we now know was fully equal to his commitment to the other realities of a Christian universe.

William's confidence in the ultimate intelligibility and goodness of the world and of every perceived manifestation of divine intelligence is the implication gradually drawn from his essentially benign attentiveness to whatever the world offered, so different from Henry's conventional pessimism, is very like the tone that informs John of Salisbury's historical writing. The spilled wine at the pope's Mass is exactly the kind of problem to attract William.

Richard of Devizes, William's contemporary, always enters as a counterpoise and an astringent. In his book is found an almost completely natural world, an even defiantly secular approach to life against a permanent backdrop of a secure Christian society. He, like Henry, was a traditionalist, his loyalties and religious feelings engrossed by the institutions rather than by the dogmas of Christianity. His God is occasionally moved to the defense of His favorites, the monks of the established orders, but for the most part He remains at a polite and reserved distance. Richard's reaction to the new orders and the new enthusiastic devotion is the recoil of offended propriety. Sensitive men of Richard's generation found their world unfeeling and constricting; he and

227

probably many like him regarded with fastidious suspicion any sort of emotive religiosity or mysteries. Religion had already been thoroughly and suitably accounted for in the rule and traditions of his own order. If William's resort to a rule for reconciling the imperative realities of Christian history to the murk of observed life was one way of meeting the demands made on his faith by a world more compelling and various than his ancestors had encountered, Richard's mundaneness and cold wit was another way. His God, one feels, would not be so vulgar as to work His will through the instruments of city mobs and the burning and looting of houses. The same events that for William were *ambigua* and horrible because of Christian depravity and that yet solemnly, painfully affirmed the triumph of Christendom, were for Richard merely crude riots, the uncivilized in pursuit of the unholy.

God had retired to His ancient homes and did not push the celestial bodies out of their accustomed courses, or put blood in country ponds, or insist that men live in squalid huts in order to worship Him. He left the world to its own ways and purposes; the part of mature wisdom, implied by Richard's words and tone, was to accept the world on its own terms and to preserve the ancient, dignified forms of Christian life as they had been inherited. It must be remembered that Richard cannot be considered an irreligious man: he attacked the Carthusians because they were presumptuous and excessive; the Benedictines were quite sufficiently Christian for the occasions of modern life. An account by Richard of Devizes of Pope Eugenius's accident-crossed Mass would, one feels, be instructive in many ways.

The existence, during the twelfth century, of a literary genre that may, not too inaccurately, be called Christian history is indubitable, but the exact nature of the quality that made written history "Christian" is very elusive. It is true that the bare recognition of supernatural influences on earthly life is a tacit affirmation of belief in some kind of providential history, but that affirmation is left, by most authors, very bare, promising a doctrinal fullness that is never given. The Augustinian or Orosian suggestions for historical pattern and the simplified variants like Henry of Huntingdon's *deus irritatus* and the vainglorious world were never challenged during the twelfth century; neither were they applied very thoroughly by working historians. (It is useful to think about how vividly Otto of Freising stands out when he merely attempted the obvious—or so it seems now.) History was, after all, conventionally considered an easy kind of literature to write, and perhaps it was; it has merely grown harder to read. The writers who originally set the basic doctrinal patterns for Christian history had strong, polemical motives for creating a clearly patterned Christian course of history; they had urgent moral impulses, which overrode the trivial business of reporting the peculiar details of men and events and which justified any distortion or simplification necessary to the full defense of their still-threatened religion. In a world irrecoverably secured for the Church, with the pagan infidels off to a poetic biblical distance, a few men who had addressed themselves to the ancient task of writing history might very well begin again to notice that their world was immensely various and solid, and oddly resistent to easy interpretation.

The impulses toward Christian exegesis and toward history are not mutually repulsive, but in practice they seem to be combined only with great effort and great tact. Few historians have been able to do justice to both, even in the presumably Christian centuries. Augustine wrote one true work of Christian history, and that was his autobiography, for which he had the supreme advantage of interior knowledge of the events of his own life; autobiography may be the only entirely satisfactory form of Christian history. Autobiography, however, was not a popularly acceptable form of literature in the twelfth century (although it interestingly begins to appear then), and history was.

Christian history was being written during the twelfth century, but only with increasing difficulty. One way of expressing that observation, the cumulative experience of reading, is to say that the habits of mind, the expectations and involuntary judgments we associate with the word *naturalism* were beginning to encroach, however insensibly, upon a reality that passed the boundaries of the natural world. The cold division between religious and secular experience, almost to the exclusion of the supernatural from the world, found in Richard of Devizes's history is one contemporary expression of, and solution for, a pervasive cultural tension. That same tension impelled William of Newburgh to strenuous efforts of investigation and inner debate to force the supernatural to take on some of the straight-forward plausibility of natural objects and events. Richard's radical solution, being our own, has the air of intrinsic rightness, while William's conscientious efforts to find a workable com-promise fix him for eternity in solemn foolishness. The *invisibilia dei* that John of Salisbury wanted historians to expose bravely to the light were receding again into indecipherability, not as in a combative, half-pagan antiquity, but to a new and more unreachable distance.

Notes

INTRODUCTION

1. Jane Austen, *Northanger Abbey* (1971), 34; the opening quotation is on pp. 97–98.

2. Oliver Goldsmith, *The History of England*, 1:iv.

3. Isidore of Seville, *Isidori Hispalensis episcopi etymologiarum sive originum*, ed. W. M. Lindsay, 1:xl–xliv.

4. See William Nelson, *Fact or Fiction*, for the ambiguous borderline between fact and fiction from antiquity through the Renaissance.

5. Goldsmith, *History*, 1:1.

6. A. E. Roy and E. L. G. Stones, "The Record of Eclipses in the Bury Chronicle," *Bulletin of the Institute of Historical Research* 43, no. 108 (1970): 125–33.

7. Antonia Gransden's survey, *Historical Writing in England c. 550 to c. 1307*, will be the starting point for all studies of medieval English historiography; an interesting briefer survey is by C. N. L. Brooke, "Historical Writing in England between 850 and 1150," in *La storiografia altomedievale*. The best interpretive essays on medieval historiogaphy are Sir Richard Southern's four presidential addresses to the Royal Historical Society, "Aspects of the European Tradition of Historical Writing," *Transactions of the Royal Historical Society*, 5th ser.: 1. "The Classical Tradition from Einhard to Geoffrey of Monmouth," 20 (1970):173–96; 2. "Hugh of St. Victor and the Idea of Historical Development," 21 (1971): 159–79; 3. "History as Prophesy," 22 (1972): 159–80; 4. "The Sense of the Past," 23 (1973): 243–63. These essays are rich, pointed, and sensitive about history writing, past and present.

8. R. W. Southern, "The Place of England in the Twelfth-Century Renaissance," *History* 45 (1960): 201–16 is thoroughly excellent; see p. 203 for his discussion of the dominance of Bede in English intellectual life, and pp. 207–13 on the historical impulse in post-Conquest England.

9. Colin Morris, *The Discovery of the Individual 1050–1200*, contains many well-chosen illustrations of emerging twelfth-century individuality; see also Walter Ullmann's discussion of changes in historical writing during the twelfth century in *The Individual and Society in the Middle Ages*, 110–11, 142–43.

10. Herbert Butterfield, *Man on His Past*, 16.

11. Gransden, *Historical Writing in England*, discusses Henry of

Huntingdon, 193–201, Richard of Devizes, 247–53, and William of Newburgh, 263–68; also useful are J. C. Russell, "The Renaissance of the Twelfth Century," in *The Development of Historiography*, chap. 4; Herbert Butterfield, "Historiography," in *Dictionary of the History of Ideas* 2 (1973): 464–98; Jean Leclercq, "L' Humanisme des moines au moyen age," *Studi medievali*, 3d ser. 10 (1969): 69–113, and "Monastic Historiography from Leo IX to Callistus II," *Studia monastica* 12 (1970): 57–86; useful studies not specifically historiographical are James S. Beddie, "Libraries in the Twelfth Century: Their Catalogues and Contents," in *Anniversary Essays in Medieval History by Students of Charles Homer Haskins*, 1–24; R. W. Hunt, "English Learning in the Late Twelfth Century," *Transactions of the Royal Historical Society*, 4th ser. 19 (1936): 19–42; Urban T. Holmes, "Transitions in European Education," in *Twelfth-Century Europe and the Foundations of Modern Society*, 15–38; Eva Sanford, "The Study of Ancient History in the Middle Ages," *Journal of the History of Ideas* 5 (1944): 21–43.

12. Robert W. Hanning, *The Vision of History in Early Britain from Gildas to Geoffrey of Monmouth;* rather less successful full-length treatments of historiography are William M. Brandt, *The Shape of Medieval History*, and C. A. Patrides, *The Grand Design of God: The Literary Form of the Christian View of History.*

13. Beryl Smalley, "Sallust in the Middle Ages," in *Classical Influences on European Culture*, 165–75; see also Robert Brentano's excellent discussion of thirteenth-century historical writing in *Two Churches*, 326–45; any student of historiography of any century may profitably read Peter Gay's *Style in History* (New York, 1974).

14. Erich Auerbach, *Mimesis;* and Arnaldo Momigliano, *Studies in Historiography;* "Pagan and Christian Historiography in the Fourth Century A. D.," in *The Conflict between Paganism and Christianity in the Fourth Century*, 79–99; "Popular Religious Beliefs and the Late Roman Historians," *Studies in Church History* 8 (1972):1–18; "Tradition and the Classical Historian," *History and Theory* 11 (1972): 279–93.

15. Samuel Johnson, Preface to the *Dictionary of the English Language.*

CHAPTER ONE

1. Henry of Huntingdon, *De contemptu mundi*, ed. Thomas Arnold, Rolls Series 74 (1879): 314; cited henceforth as *De contemptu.*

2. Henry of Huntingdon, *Historia Anglorum*, ed. Thomas Arnold, Rolls Series 74 (1879): cited henceforth as Huntingdon.

3. Huntingdon, 237–38, "Eodem anno Nicholaus, pater illius qui hanc scripsit historiam, mortis legibus concessit, et sepultus est apud Lincoliam. De quo dictum est:

'Stella cadit cleri, splendor marcet Nicholai;
Stella cadens cleri, splendeat arce Dei.'
Hoc ideo scriptor suo inseruit operi, ut apud omnes legentes mutuum
laboria obtineat, quatenus pietatis affectu dicere dignentur, 'Anima ejus
in pace requiescat. Amen."

4. *De contemptu*, 302.

5. *Liber Eliensis*, ed. E. O. Blake, 229. R. M. Wooley, *Catalogue of
the Manuscripts of Lincoln Cathedral Chapter Library*, v.

6. A good general account of the history of clerical celibacy is by E.
Vacandard, "Les Origines du célibat ecclésiastique," in *Études de
critique et d'histoire religieuse*, 69–120; see also Émile Herman, "Célibat
des clercs," *Dictionnaire de droit canonique* 3:132–56; a somewhat
unreliable but lively and full treatment is H. C. Lea, *An Historical
Sketch of Sacerdotal Celibacy in the Christian Church*; an important
related subject is E. Jombart, "Concubinage," *Dictionnaire de droit
canonique* 3:1513–24. For the history of clerical celibacy in England, I
am much indebted to the discussion and bibliography of C. N. L.
Brooke, "Gregorian Reform in Action: Clerical Marriage in England,
1050–1200," *Cambridge Historical Journal* 12 (1956): 1–21; see also
R. R. Darlington, "Ecclesiastical Reform in the Late Old English Period,"
English Historical Review 51(1936): 385–428; B. R. Kemp, "Hereditary
Benefices in the Medieval English Church: A Herefordshire Example,"
Bulletin of the Institute of Historical Research 42 (1970): 1–15; W. A. C.
Sandford, "Medieval Clerical Celibacy in England," *The Genealogists'
Magazine* 12 (1957): 371–73, 401–3; Charles A. Frazee, "The Origins of
Clerical Celibacy in the Western Church," *Church History* 41 (1972):
149–67; Filippo Liotta, *La continenza dei clierici nel pensiero cano-
nistico classico, da Graziano a Gregorio IX* (Milan, 1971).

7. *De contemptu*, 299.

8. *De contemptu*, 299.

9. *Registrum antiquissimum of the Cathedral Church of Lincoln*, ed.
C. W. Foster and K. Major, in *Lincoln Record Society* 3:263.

10. Arnold, Introduction to *Historia*, xxi–xxii.

11. A. Grea, "Essai historique sur les archidiacres," *Bibliothèque de
l'école des Chartes* 12:220. For the development and duties of the
archdeaconal office, see also A. Amanieu, "Archidiacre," *Dictionnaire
de droit canonique* 1:948–1004; discussions of the archdeaconry in
England are A. Hamilton Thompson, "Diocesan Organization in the
Middle Ages, Archdeacons and Rural Deans," *Proceedings of the
British Academy* 29 (1943): 153–94; Jean Scammell, "The Rural Chapter
in England from the Eleventh to the Fourteenth Century," *English
Historical Review* 86, no. 338 (1971): 1–21; Margaret Deanesly,
Sidelights on the Anglo-Saxon Church, 140, 145–70; C. R. Cheney,
From Becket to Langton, 145–46, 150–53; Cheney, *English Bishops'*

Chanceries, 1100–1250, 7–8, 110–18, 145–46; G. V. Scammell, *Hugh de Puiset, Bishop of Durham*, 126–27, 162; R. Brentano, *Two Churches*, 66–68, 66 n.8.

12. Colin Morris, "A Consistory Court in the Middle Ages," *Journal of Ecclesiastical History* 14 (1963): 151 n.4, for evidence of archdeacons of Lincoln having synods of their own. Dorothy M. Owen, *Church and Society in Medieval Lincolnshire*, 35–36, discusses the typical concerns of archdeacons as being the parochial clergy and church property.

13. Amanieu, 976.

14. Jean Scammell's "Rural Chapter" gives an exciting, vivid idea of the functioning of a rural chapter and its power; G. V. Scammell offers the fine illustration of the repute in which archdeacons were held, which I have quoted. *Hugh de Puiset*, 92 and n.1.

15. *De contemptu*, 305.

16. Brooke, "Gregorian Reform," 7–11; Darlington, "Ecclesiastical Reform," 404–7, cites only a few examples of reformers attempting to impose celibacy on clerks and no evidence of any success; Deanesly, *Sidelights*, 134–36, gives interesting evidence for the respectability of married clergy in Anglo-Saxon England.

17. *Cartularium monasterii de Rameseia*, ed. W. H. Hart, 3 vols., Rolls Series 79 (hereafter cited as *Cart. Ram.*); information from the Ramsey Cartulary of Henry's family history seems to have been found and published first by D. L. Powell, writing on the parish of "Little Stukeley," in *History of the County of Huntingdon* 2 (London, 1932): 235, and later was used by Charles Clay in his detailed biographical sketch of Henry's grandson Aristotle, "Master Aristotle," *English Historical Review* 76 (1961): 303–8. The information does not seem to have been known by T. Arnold, editor of the *Historia* for the Rolls Series, by T. D. Hardy, *Descriptive Catalogue of Materials Relating to the History of Great Britain and Ireland*, Rolls Series 26 (1865), or by Henry R. Luard, "Henry of Huntingdon," in *Dictionary of National Biography* 9 (1917).

18. *Cart. Ram.* 1:392: "Et pertinent ad eandem [ecclesia] decem acrae terrae, que Henricus Archidiaconus, feodi firmarius de Stivecleya, ipsam ecclesiam fabricari fecit et dedicare"; and 2:260: "Carta Reinaldi ejusdem Abbatis, . . . in Giddinge, praeter eam partem quam habet Henricus Archidiaconus."

19. *Cart. Ram.* 1:396: "De Sticecleya . . . Henricus filius Thomae tenet unam dimidiam virgatem, quae aliquando fuit de dominico, per Henricum Arch[idiaconum], qui quondam fuit firmarius, illam contulit Henrico le Stiward, avo ipsius Henrici, ad reddendum pro ea per annum quatuor solidos. Quo Henrico Stiwarde mortuo, successit ei Thomas filius suus, Archer in firma de Stivecle. [The editor adds that Archer is "a mistake for Archidiacono. Most probably Henry of Huntingdon the

historian."] Idem autem Adam remisit eidem Thomae tres solidos";
3:274–75: "Adam filius Henrici Archidianoconi tenet modo ipsam
villam (Stivecle) pro octo libris." The scribe was at obvious pains to
specify the various Henrys and their heirs as clearly as possible.

20. *Cart Ram.* 1:328: "Adam de Stivecle tenet unam virgatam. . . ."

21. *Cart. Ram.* 1:106: "Conventio inter Robertum abbatem [A.D.
1180–1200], et Adam de Stivelce, et Aristotilem filium ejus, de firma de
Stivecle"; and 230 (A.D. 1206): ". . . Styvecle Aristotle. . . ." Henry's
grandson and great-grandson, Nicholas, appear to have been in priest's
orders and to have suffered no penalty for their uncanonical descent.
Clay, 304–6.

22. *Cart. Ram.* 2:217–18.

23. *Cart. Ram.* 2:336–37 (A.D. 1228–1231): "Sciant praesantes et
futuri, quod ego Nicholaus de Stivecle, filius Aristotilis. . . ."; and p.
351. Feet of Fines, 12 Hen. 3, with this endorsement, "Et Adam de
Stivecle apponit clameum suum"; and 1:396: ". . . cum nepte magistri
Adae. . . ."

24. Huntingdon, 3.

25. *De contemptu*, 298.

26. Arnold, Introduction to *Historia*, xviii–xxiv.

27. Arnold, Introduction to *Historia*, xxiv–xxx.

28. Leland, cited by Arnold in Introduction to *Historia*, xvii.

29. Huntingdon, 3.

30. See Arnold, Introduction to *Historia*, xi–xvi, for his analysis of
the successive editions.

31. Arnold, Introduction to *Historia*, xiv–xv.

32. Huntingdon, 1.

33. Huntingdon, 2.

34. Huntingdon, 2.

35. Huntingdon, 4: "Aspice, magne pater, quo devenere potentes: /
Aspice quam nihili sit honor, lux, gloria mundi."

36. Arnold, Introduction to *Historia*, lii–lix.

37. Huntingdon, 115.

38. Huntingdon, 156.

39. Huntingdon, 277.

40. Huntingdon, 159–60.

41. Arnold, Introduction to *Historia*, lxiii.

42. Arnold, Introduction to *Historia*, lxiii.

43. Samuel Johnson, Preface to *A Dictionary of the English Language*.

44. Huntingdon, 8.

45. Huntingdon, 63.

46. Huntingdon, 66.

47. Huntingdon, 103.

48. Huntingdon, 103.
49. Huntingdon, 137.
50. Huntingdon, 173.
51. Huntingdon, 214.
52. Huntingdon, 290.
53. Huntingdon, 211.
54. Huntingdon, 208.
55. Huntingdon, 193–96.
56. Huntingdon, 197.
57. Huntingdon, 188–89.
58. Huntingdon, 208–9.
59. Huntingdon, 232–33.
60. Huntingdon, 255–56.
61. Huntingdon, 256, 258, 267, 288.
62. Huntingdon, 265–66.
63. Huntingdon, 216–17.
64. Huntingdon, 280.
65. Part 4, chap. 8, "The Question of Literary Form."
66. Huntingdon, 4.
67. Huntingdon, 252.
68. From the epilogue to the *Historia*, quoted by Arnold in Introduction, xix: "Hanc cum adeptus fueris, habes; mundanam cum adeptus fueris, ut aqua vase terebrato defluit, et nihil habes."
69. Huntingdon, 37.
70. Huntingdon, 62.
71. Huntingdon, 66.
72. Huntingdon, 113.
73. Huntingdon, 117–18.
74. Huntingdon, 118–19.
75. Huntingdon, 256–57.
76. Huntingdon, 257.
77. Quoted by Arnold in Introduction, xix: "Dic, Henrice, dic, hujus auctor historiae, qui fuerint illius temporis archidiaconi. Quilibet eorum, sive fuerit nobilis vel ignobilis, clarus vel fama obscurus, laudabilis vel infamis, elatus vel oppressus, sapiens vel indiscretus, quid refert? Si aliquis eorum causa laudis et gloriae aliquid laboris praesumpserit, cum jam nulla possit super eo esse memoria, major quam super equo vel asello suo, cur in vanum miser animum suum afflixit?"
78. Henry of Huntingdon, in Arundel 48. lib. VIII, Brit. Museum ms.
79. Perhaps the major modern work on *contemptus mundi* literature is that of Robert Bultot, *Christianisme et valeurs humaines; la doctrine du mépris du monde;* see also Donald R. Howard, *The Three Temptations: Medieval Man in Search of the World,* 68–75, 158–60 et passim, for interesting remarks relating the genre of *contemptus mundi* to

late-eleventh- and twelfth-century life; and for a large, miscellaneous selection of mostly anonymous poems on *contemptus mundi,* useful for supplementing the well-known treatises, see Edelstand du Méril, *Poésies populaires latines du moyen age.*

80. For a brief but excellent account of the subgenre of *contemptus mundi* called *ubi sunt,* see E. Gilson, "De la Bible à François Villon," and "Tables pour l'histoire du thème *ubi sunt,*" in *Les Idées et les lettres,* 9–38. Gilson's article has been supplemented by M. Liborio, "Contribuit alla storia dell' 'ubi sunt,'" *Cultura neolatina* 20 (1960): 141–209; both Gilson and Liborio stress the continuity of thought and poetic expression in the genre over a long period of time.

81. Gilson, "*Ubi sunt,*" 19.

82. Peter Damian, *De fluxa mundi gloria et saeculi despectione, Patrologia Latina,* henceforth *PL* 145:807–20; see also his *Liber Gomorrhianus,* 159–90; and *Apologeticum de contemptu saeculi,* 251–92.

83. Francesco Lazzari, *Il contemptus mundi nella scuola di S. Vittore,* especially his Introduction, 11–30, which describes his special approach to the genre (the notes furnish an excellent chronological bibliography of *contemptus* writers through the late Middle Ages); and his *Monachesimo e valori umani tra XI e XII secolo,* which is a collection of essays on *contemptus mundi* literature and scholarship; Lazzari cites Donald Howard very favorably throughout and is very forthright in his distaste for the approach taken by Bultot, Gilson, and Liborio; see especially *Monachesimo e valori,* 45–48, 99–104.

84. Lazzari, *Contemptus mundi,* 22.

85. Lazzari, *Contemptus mundi,* 22, 26–28.

86. Donald R. Howard, "Renaissance World-Alienation," in *The Darker Vision of the Renaissance: Beyond the Fields of Reason,* ed. R. Kinsman, 53, 53 n.11.

87. *De contemptu,* 297.

88. Lazzari, *Contemptus mundi,* 51 n.48.

89. *De contemptu,* 297.

90. *De contemptu,* 298.

91. *De Contemptu,* 319.

92. *De contemptu,* 297: "Exemplar autem tertiae epistolae de contemptu mundi per ea que ipsi vidimus hoc est:...."

93. *De contemptu,* 300–305.

94. *De contemptu,* 318.

95. *De contemptu,* 319.

96. D. Howard, *Three Temptations,* 68–69.

97. Some of Henry of Huntingdon's poems are printed in *Anglo-Latin Satirical Poets,* ed. T. Wright, Rolls Series 59 no. 2 (1872): 163–74;

De contemptu visibilium

Mors properat, torpes; mors pulsat ad ostia, torpes;

Ingreditur, torpes; vir, memor esto tui.
Cur tua dum servas, te perdis? num tua mecum,
Perdes? quod si te non habeas, quid habes?
Te minus, illa magis curas, ut vel moderata
Praecipiam, cura te magis, illa minus. (p. 171)

98. Howard, "Renaissance World-Alienation," 48.

99. Huntingdon, 234. Text of the council in J. D. Mansi, *Sacrorum conciliorum nova et amplissima collectio*, 20:1150.

100. Brooke, "Gregorian Reform," 7–11; Darlington, "Ecclesiastical Reform," 404–7, cites only a few examples of reformers attempting to impose celibacy on clerks and no evidence of any success; M. Deanesly, *Sidelights*, 134–36, gives interesting evidence for the respectability of married clery in Anglo-Saxon England; Lea, *Sacerdotal Celibacy*, 161–69, 175; Cheney, *From Becket to Langton*, 14–15, 137–38, for comments on the later period that imply lax enforcement in the earlier; J. C. Dickinson, *The Origins of the Austin Canons*, 91 and n.1, quotes the Merton Annals for 1074: "Gregorius papa ... celebrata synodo symoniacos anathematizauit, uxoratos sacerdotes a diunino officio remouit et laicis missam eorum audire interdixit, noco exemplo sanctorum patrum sentenciam" (CCC Camb. MS. 59 f. 152 r.) as an example of "that distrust of the Hildebrandine reform which pervaded the English Church of his [Gregory VIII's] day."

101. Darlington, "Ecclesiastical Reform," 406; N. Cantor disagrees with Darlington's views on reform in the pre-Conquest church in *Church, Kingship, and Lay Investiture in England, 1089–1135*, 34–35 n.109.

102. David Wilkins, *Concilia Magnae Brittaniae* 1:367.

103. Z. N. Brooke, *The English Church and the Papacy*, 59–79.

104. In *The English Church and the Papacy*, Z. N. Brooke discusses the knowledge and acceptance of canon law in eleventh- and twelfth-century England; for the twelfth century, see S. Kuttner and E. Rathbone, "Anglo-Norman Canonists of the Twelfth Century," *Traditio* 7 (1949–1951): 270–358; Charles Duggan, *Twelfth-Century Decretal Collections*; Geoffrey Barraclough, review of S. Kuttner, *Repertorium der Kanonistik*, in *English Historical Review* 53 (1938): 492–95; M. Cheney, "The Compromise of Avranches of 1172 and the Spread of Canon Law in England," *English Historical Review* 56 (1941): 177–97, in which, on p. 178, Henry of Huntingdon's complaint about unaccustomed appeals to the papal curia is cited as evidence for the increase of papal jurisdiction; see *Historia*, 282.

105. Anon. of York, "An liceat sacerdotibus inire matrimonium," *Monumenta Germaniae historica, libelli de lite* 3:646; for the history of scholarly opinion of the provenance and authorship of the tractates, see Cantor, *Church in England*, 174–95, who argues for the authorship of

Gerard, archbishop of York. Since Gerard was one of the few prelates who tried to enforce celibacy in his diocese after the council of 1102, it is unlikely that he wrote in favor of clerical marriage about 1100—the date given to the tractates. A Morey and C. N. L. Brooke, *Gilbert Foliot and His Letters*, 175, comment that in the twelfth century "it became increasingly rare for anti-papel views to be stated in writing," as the strength of conservative opinion declined. Some later attempts to combat clerical celibacy are discussed by John W. Baldwin, "A Campaign to Reduce Clerical Celibacy at the Turn of the Twelfth and Thirteenth Centuries," *Études d'histoire du droit canonique dediées à Gabriel le Bras* 2:1041–53.

106. Cantor, *Church in England*, 42.

107. Anselm, *Opera omnia*, ed. F. S. Schmitt, IV, epp. 254, 255, 256, 257.

108. Wilkins, *Conciliae*, 1:387.

109. Eadmer, *Historia novorum in Anglia*, ed. M. Rule, Rolls Series 81 (1884); 193: "Quod incontinentiae crimen rex subvertere cupiens...."

110. Mansi, *Conciliorum*, 20:1150.

111. Mansi, *Conciliorum*, 23:XXIII, 1225, dates the fifty questions of the "Inquisitiones per archidiaconatus episcopatus Lincolniensis, a singulis archidiaconis faciendae" as ca. 1233 with no further information; questions 3, 4, 5, 6, 8, 20, 32, and 46 concern incontinent clerks.

112. Mansi, *Conciliorum*, 20: 1229–30, 1, 7, 8; both Nicholas and Henry were prohibited from marriage in any case by virtue of their status as canons of Lincoln. The fact that even clerks in minor orders could not marry if they were also canons has been discussed by T. P. McLaughton, "The Prohibition of Marriage Against Canons in the Early Twelfth Century," *Mediaeval Studies* 3 (1941): 94–100.

113. Jean Scammell, "Rural Chapter," 6.

114. Huntingdon, 237: "Obierat autem Anselmus archiepiscopus, Christi philosophus, in Quadragesima."

115. Huntingdon, 237–38.

116. Huntingdon, 245–46.

117. By 1125, about the time the *Historia* was being written, the marriages of men in higher orders were no longer valid. Calixtus II, at the Lateran Council of 1123, had declared that marriages contracted by clerks in higher orders were nullified, and subsequent popes repeated that law; Vacandard, "Célibat ecclésiastique," 119; Herman, "Célibat des clercs," 135. Regardless of whether Henry knew of Calixtus's decree, he must have known that the reformers' rhetoric tended to degrade and insult clerical wives, with the purpose of creating an aura of immorality and sin about clerical marriage. Henry's consistent use of *uxor* is, I think, quite conscious, and leads me to consider that his

personal arrangement was that of marriage rather than simple concubinage.

118. *The Peterborough Chronicle*, trans. H. A. Rositzke, 151; other
hostile chroniclers did relate even more unlikely versions of the legate's
lust; for example, the *Annals of Winchester*, in Rolls Series 36:2, 47–48.

119. Brooke, "Gregorian Reform," 19 n.62; Morey and Brooke,
Gilbert Foliot, 240–41.

120. Huntingdon, 250–51.

121. *Anglo-Latin Satirical Poets*, 174:

In Seipsum

Sunt, vates Henrice, tibi versus bene culti;
Et bene culta domus, et bene cultus ager.
Et bene sunt thalami, bene sunt pomeria culta,
Hortus centimodis cultibus ecce nitet.
O jam culta tibi bene sunt, sed tu male cultus;
Si quicunque caret, dic mihi, dic quid habet?

CHAPTER TWO

1. William of Newburgh, *Historia rerum Anglicarum*, ed. Richard
Howlett, Rolls Series 82 (1884–1885); to be referred to henceforth as
Newburgh.

2. Kate Norgate, "William of Newburgh," *Dictionary of National
Biography* 21: 316–62; Edward Freeman, "Mr. Froude's Life and Times
of Thomas Becket," *The Contemporary Review* 33 (August–November
1878): 216: "William of Newburgh, the father of historical criticism, as
Giraldus is the father of comparative philology, held his court on King
and Primate, and, while ruling that the zeal of both was praiseworthy,
gave sentence that the zeal of both had sadly outrun discretion."

3. Norgate, "William of Newburgh," 362. For another similar judgment, see J. Taylor, *Medieval Historical Writing in Yorkshire*, 10.

4. T. M. Fallow, "Priory of Newburgh," in *The Victoria History of
the County of York* 3 (1913): 226–30.

5. Newburgh, 51.

6. J. C. Dickinson, *The Origins of the Austin Canons and Their
Introduction into England*, 179.

7. Giraldus Cambrensis, *Itinerarium Kambriae*, ed. J. F. Dimock,
Rolls Series 21 (1868): 46–47: ". . . plus aliis mediocritate contentus
atque modestia, . . . et in mundo positus, mundi pro posse contagia
vitans, nec crapula notabilis nec temulentia, pro luxu rerum sive
libidine publicum in populo scandalum incurrere tam verecundatur
quam veretur."

8. Dickinson, *Austin Canons*, 179.

9. Dickinson, *Austin Canons*, 186: "There would, however, seem
little doubt that there was at any rate in the first few generations a

strong studious tendency within the order. We have already had occasion to remark that the regular canons had of necessity been driven to study to justify the very novel programme of life with which they confronted a highly critical age," and 187.

10. R. W. Hunt, "English Learning in the Late Twelfth Century," *Transactions of the Royal Historical Society,* 4th ser. 19 (1939): 34.

11. R. W. Southern, "The Place of Henry I in English History," *Proceedings of the British Academy* (1962), 138.

12. Dickinson, *Austin Canons,* 90.

13. Taylor, *Medieval Yorkshire,* 7–10.

14. Newburgh, 3–4; *William of Newburgh's Explanatio sacri epithalamii in matrem sponsi, A Commentary on the Canticle of Canticles,* ed. John C. Gorman, 71–72, to be referred to henceforth as *Explanatio.*

15. Gorman, Introduction to *Explanatio,* 3.

16. Howlett, Introduction to *Historia,* xviii, xix.

17. Newburgh, 19: ". . . ut a successore ejusdem Henrici Stephano, cujus anno primo ego Willelmus servorum Christi minimus et in Adam primo ad mortem sum natus, . . ."

18. Howlett, Introduction to *Historia,* xviii, xxvi.

19. Howlett, Introduction to *Historia,* xxiii–xxiv.

20. Kate Norgate, "The Date of Composition of William of Newburgh's History," *English Historical Review* 19 (1904): 288–97.

21. Newburgh, 52.

22. Philip, abbot of Byland, *Fundatio domus Bellalandae,* in *Monasticon Anglicanum,* ed. W. Dugdale, V: 350–54, cited by Gorman in Introduction to *Explanatio,* 8–9, 9 n.1.

23. Gorman, Introduction to *Explanatio,* 9 nn.2, 3, 4, 5, cites the relevant passages from Philip's chronicle; Norgate, "Date of Composition," 289–90.

24. Gorman, Introduction to *Explanatio,* 10; Norgate, "Date of Composition," 289.

25. Gorman, Introduction to *Explanatio,* 10.

26. Norgate, "Date of Composition," 290–97; Gorman, Introduction to *Explanatio,* 11.

27. Howlett dismisses a few vaguely traditional but wholly unfounded assertions about William's identity and life: Introduction to *Historia,* xviii–xxi.

28. Newburgh, 85: "In provincia quoque Deirorum, haud procul a loco nativitatis meae, res mirabilis contigit, quam a puero cognovi. Est vicus aliquot a mari orientali milliariis distans, juxta quem famosae illae aquae, quas vulgo *Gipse* vocant, . . ."

29. John Leland, *De rebus Brittanicis collectanea,* ed. T. Hearne, 4 (1770): 19, cited by Gorman, Introduction to *Explanatio,* 4, 6; Norgate, "William of Newburgh," 360.

30. Newburgh, 51.

31. D. Knowles and R. N. Hadock, *Medieval Religious Houses, England and Wales* (London, 2d ed. 1971), 167.

32. H. E. Salter, "William of Newburgh," *English Historical Review* 23 (1907): 510–14. Gransden does not accept the Salter thesis: *Historical Writing in England*, 264; and C. N. L. Brooke, in a brief review of Gorman's book, states, "His conclusion, that the identification cannot be proved is reasonable; indeed, one could surely go further, and say that it is highly improbable that a twelfth-century English layman could have acquired the skill in Latin revealed in all William's works, the theological learning of the commentary, or the title *magister* given him in an early thirteenth-century manuscript. Neither chronicle nor commentary read like the work of a layman." *English Historical Review* 77 (1962): 554; and note D. Knowles, C. N. L. Brooke, and V. London, *The Heads of Religious Houses in England and Wales*, 177: "The identification of his brother William with William of Newburgh the chronicler cannot be accepted."

33. In addition to the *Historia* and the *Explanatio* there are three sermons ascribed to William which are found in two of the manuscripts of the *Historia*. They were printed by T. Hearne with his edition of the *Historia* in 1719.

34. Newburgh, 3–4.

35. *Explanatio*, 71.

36. Newburgh, 18.

37. Newburgh, 72.

38. Newburgh, 294.

39. Book I contains 32 chapters; Book II, 38 chapters; Book III, 28 chapters; Book IV, 42 chapters; Book V, 34 chapters in an unfinished state.

40. Newburgh, 19.

41. Newburgh, 69.

42. Newburgh, 78.

43. Newburgh, 286.

44. Howlett, Introduction to *Historia*, xxiv; Norgate, "Date of Composition," 294–95.

45. Howlett, Introduction to *Historia*, xi–xii.

46. Howlett, Introduction to *Historia*, xxiv.

47. Howlett, Introduction to *Historia*, xxv–xxxvi.

48. Newburgh, 326.

49. Newburgh, 86, 440, 136–39, 206–23, 245–47, 267–70, 320, 273–74, 457–58, 93.

50. Newburgh, 187.

51. Newburgh, 498.

52. Newburgh, 64; and see 28, 67, 434, 451, 457, 469.

53. Newburgh, 187, 80, 226-27, 67.

54. Newburgh, 72, 104, 482, 150.

55. Newburgh, 4.

56. With the partial exception of Bede, whose history he consulted for a description of Ireland and the history of the Canterbury-York dispute.

57. Giraldus Cambrensis, *Itinerarium Kambriae*, 208-9, claimed that Gildas had written a book about Arthur which he threw in a river when Arthur killed his brother, but that Geoffrey was a fraud. *Itin. Kam.* 57-58.

58. Newburgh, 11.

59. Newburgh, 11.

60. Newburgh, 11.

61. Newburgh, 18.

62. Newburgh, 11.

63. Newburgh, 11-12.

64. Newburgh, 18.

65. R. W. Barber, *Arthur of Albion*, 38: "We begin to get an idea of Geoffrey's object in writing the *Historia*. He seems to be attempting to provide the Britons with an emperor-hero to whose golden age they could look back with pride"; and 21-23 for evidence of the wide existence of the Arthur stories before Geoffrey's book; Roger S. Loomis, *Wales and the Arthurian Legend*, chap. 10, "The Arthurian Legend Before 1139," discusses the extent and sources of the Arthur saga before Geoffrey; see also E. K. Chambers, *Arthur of Britain*, especially chap. 4, "The Acceptance of Arthur"; and generally, Robert H. Fletcher, "The Arthurian Material in the Chronicles," in *Studies and Notes in Philology and Literature* 10 (1906); Robert W. Hanning, *The Vision of History in Early Britain*, chap. 5.

66. Bede, *Ecclesiastical History of the English People*, ed. B. Colgrave, R. A. B. Mynors (Oxford, 1969), 47-49; F. Barlow, in *Edward the Confessor* (Berkeley, Calif., 1970), 204, suggests that the typical twelfth-century attitude toward the Welsh as unreliable, irrational, etc., takes definitive form during northern border warfare in the second half of Edward's reign.

67. Loomis, *Wales and the Arthurian Legend*, 184: "Britones ... its reference in the twelfth century was uniformly to their Continental descendants in Brittany, and even Lot admitted this as a general rule, though he vainly tried to point out that in this instance the evidence is overwhelming."

68. Newburgh, 132.

69. Newburgh, on the Scots, 76, 182-83; on the Welsh, 107; on the Irish, 166; on Irish superstition, 239.

70. Newburgh, on the Bretons, 146-47 and 235.

71. Newburgh, 16, "Inde fabulator ille. . . ."
72. Newburgh, 13–15.
73. Newburgh, 16–17.
74. Newburgh, 17.
75. Newburgh, 12.
76. Richard Bernheimer, *Wild Men in the Middle Ages*, 13, discusses Merlin as part of the medieval topos of the "wild man" endowed with the power of prophecy; Fletcher, *Arthurian Material in the Chronicles*, 91: "While no conclusion seems likely to be reached as to his real existence, or as to the origin of his name, there is no doubt that he was known in Celtic tradition before Geoffrey's time," and 92.
77. Ralph of Coggeshall, *Chronicon Anglicanum*, ed. Joseph Stevenson, Rolls Series 66 (1875): 146: "Itaque hoc anno, juxta prophetiam Merlini, 'Gladius a sceptro separatus est,' id est, ducatus Normanniae a regno Angliae."
78. Giraldus Cambrensis, *Itin. Kam.*, 197, and, generally, 196–200.
79. Newburgh, 12.
80. Henry C. Lea, *Materials Toward a History of Witchcraft*, 1 (1957), 53–56.
81. Newburgh, 86.
82. Augustine, *De civitate Dei*, in *Corpus scriptorum ecclesiasticorum latinorum* 40 (1889): Book 9, 22: "Daemones autem non aeternas temporum causas et quodam modo cardinales in Dei sapientia contemplantur, sed quorundam signorum nobis occultorum maiore experientia multo plura quam homines futura prospiciunt; . . ."
83. Augustine, *De divinatione daemonum*, in *Corpus scriptorum ecclesiasticorum latinorum* 41 (1900): Book 5, 9: ". . . sed quae naturalibus signis futura praenoscunt, quae signa in hominum sensus venire non possunt, ant praedicunt."
84. Augustine, *De divinatione*, Book 6, 10: "In ceteris autem suis praedicationibus daemones plerumque falluntur et fallunt"; compare Newburgh, 12: ". . . in suis . . . conjecturis saepe falluntur et fallunt. [esse oportebat, feminarum multitudo versabatum."]
85. Isidore of Seville, *Isidori Hispalensis episcopi etymologiarum sive originum*, ed. W. M. Lindsay, Book 9, 3: "Castra sunt ubi miles steterit. Dicta autem castra quasi casta, vel quod illic castraretur libido. Nam numquam his intererat mulier."
86. Isidore, *Etymologiarum*, Book 8, 11: "Praesciunt enim futura multa, / . . . Inest enim illis cognito rerum plus quam infirmitati humanae, partim subtilioris sensus lumine, partim experientia logissimae vitae, partim per Dei iussum angelica revelatione."

CHAPTER THREE

1. Newburgh, 76–78.

2. Newburgh, 147: "et tanquam terrenum quendam angelum."

3. R. L. Graeme Ritchie, *The Normans in Scotland*, 417.

4. Newburgh, 77.

5. Ritchie, *Scotland*, 416–17, and see 354–57.

6. Gorman, Introduction to *Explanatio*, 22; for Roger of Byland's connection with Aelred, see C. T. Clay, "The Early Abbots of the Yorkshire Cistercian Houses," *Yorkshire Archeological Journal* 38 (1951): 11.

7. The most recent edition of Aelred of Rievaulx's *Speculum caritatis* is in the series *Corpus Christianorum continuatio mediaevalis, Aelredi Rievallensis operia omnia*, ed. A. Hoste and C. H. Talbot (1971).

8. Aelred, *Speculum* Book 1, chap. 31: "sed in caritate perfecta castitas, ideoque nulla libido . . ."

9. Aelred, *De vita et miraculis Edwardi Confessoris*, in *Historiae Anglicanae scriptores* 10 (1652): 369–414.

10. Ritchie, *Scotland*, 357.

11. Ritchie, *Scotland*, 357: "Some maintained that he [Malcolm] should take the monastic vows of chastity, obedience and poverty, like the Templar. Such views were in accordance with Cistercian thought. It was with the powerful help of St. Bernard that the Templars obtained recognition as an order."

12. Newburgh, 71. Cf. the similar story of the King of Aragon who, having been a monk, is persuaded to accept his throne and marriage for the sake of his country but returns to celibacy after the birth of one child, 124; in contrast, William considers lust a serious defect of character of both Henry I and Henry II, 30, 280.

13. Aelred, *De sancto rege Scottorum David*, printed as a preface to his *Genealogia Regum Anglorum* in *Historiae Anglicanae scriptores*, Book 10, 348: "rex justus, rex castus, rex humilis"; for David I's virtuous court, see Ritchie, *Scotland*, 252; "Splendor reigned at Roxburgh. Decorum likewise. The royal couple set an example of domestic unity. Queen Maud of Scotland was much respected, and her death, in 1131, was widely mourned. Afterwards, as before, David was universally regarded as a model of the virtuous life." A source for both William of Newburgh and Ritchie is the continuator of Symeon of Durham, John of Hexham, who said of David, "Gloriosius dixerim, quod frugalitate quotidiana victus et vestitus, sanctitate honestae conversationis, disciplina morum etiam viris coenobialibus se imitabilem praebuit." *Historia regum*, ed. T. Arnold, Rolls Series 75:330.

14. Compare Newburgh, 72: "Sicut enim ille post multa virtutum insignia in adulterium simul et homicidium, . . . incidit: . . . Scottorum gentem ex effrenata barbarie sanguinis avidam, . . . licet eo nolente et frustra prohibente," with Aelred's claim, "Unde tota illa gentis illius barbaries mansuefacta tanta se mox Regi benevolentia & humilitate

245

substravit, ut naturalis oblita saevitiae," *De David*, 10, 348.

15. Newburgh, 28–29. Cf. Symeon of Durham, *Historia regum*, who does not tell the anecdote but does mention perfect virginity as one of Thomas's virtues: "... etiam in virginitatis puritate perrexit ad Dominum," 248; for Cistercian rules against the use of medicines and consultation with physicians, see Alice M. Cooke, "The Settlement of the Cistercians in England," *English Historical Review* 8 (1893): 673 n.312.

16. Note also William's regard for Gilbert of Sempringham: "propriae castitatis conscientia," 54, and his disdain for Bishop Hugh of Durham who left several bastard children, 440.

17. Newburgh, 66: "... tam contra Christianam quam contra castrensem etiam disciplinam, mala increverant, ut mirum non sit, quod eis tanquam pollutis et immundis favor nequaquam divinus arriserit. Castra enim a castratione luxuriae discuntur"; for William's use of Isidore of Seville's etymology of *castrum*, see chap. 2 n.85.

18. Newburgh, 92–93.

19. Note William's apology for Richard I's marrying while on crusade. Newburgh, 346–47.

20. Newburgh, 149.

21. Newburgh, 151.

22. Newburgh, 311.

23. Newburgh, 471: "Quomodo vulgis voluerit hominem illum tanquam martyrem honorare, et quomodo error iste exstinctus sit."

24. Newburgh, 472.

25. Newburgh, 234: "Denique post mortem ejus, quidam mentiendi libidine atque impudentissima vanitate, famam late sparserunt,..."

26. Newburgh, 149.

27. Newburgh, 150: "hominem simplicissimum ..."

28. Newburgh, 150.

29. Newburgh, 151.

30. F. W. Maitland, "William of Drogheda and the Universal Ordinary," in *Roman Canon Law in the Church of England* (London, 1898), 100–131.

31. For discussion of the close ties between the papacy and England in the twelfth century, see Z. N. Brooke, *The English Church and the Papacy*; M. Cheney, "The Compromise of Avranches"; and for an excellent and sharply focused survey, Charles Duggan, "From the Conquest to the Death of John," in *The English Church and the Papacy in the Middle Ages*, ed. C. H. Lawrence, 63–116.

32. Newburgh, 56.

33. Newburgh, 56 and cf. 60.

34. Newburgh, 60.

35. Newburgh, 111.

36. Newburgh, 79. Eugenius died 8 July 1153, Bernard on 20 August, and Henry Murdac on 14 October.

37. Duggan, "Conquest to Death of John," 86: "The rapid expansion of the monastic and canonical orders throughout Europe, and within England in full proportion, contributed beyond measure to the increase of papal influence. In this context, the growth of the Cistercian Order, . . . was of outstanding importance: the advance of papal power in the mid-twelfth century in the extent of its permeation of the Church was at least in part linked with the higher pitch of religious fervor achieved by the Cistercians. The great moral force of St. Bernard, especially in French society, had its counterpart in England too; and English society was confronted for the first time on a very large scale by an order decisively conceived on a supra-natural basis, and markedly detached from the structure of the feudal kingdom."

38. See Bernard's *De consideratione;* Saint Bernard, epistle, "De consideratione," in *Sancti Bernardi opera omnia,* ed. J. Mabillon, 1:1005–96.

39. John K. Cartwright, "St. Bernard and the Papacy," *The Catholic Historical Review* 9 (1923): 393–400 is polemical in tone but does argue around Bernard's own words.

40. Newburgh, 109–12.

41. The *Historia* is used extensively for information of Hadrian's early life by Horace K. Mann, *The Lives of the Popes in the Middle Ages* 9 (1925): 237–40; by Raymonde Foreville and Jean Rousset de Pina, *Histoire de l'église,* 9, pt. 2 (Paris, 1953), 5 n.1, 9, and, in a more complex way, by R. L. Poole, "The Early Lives of Robert Pullen and Nicholas Breakspear," in *Essays in Medieval History Presented to Thomas Frederick Tout,* 64–68.

42. Poole, "Early Lives," speculates on the possible influence of Robert Pullen in advancing Nicholas Breakspear's career, 68.

43. Poole, "Early Lives," 64–65.

44. Poole, "Early Lives," 66–68.

45. Newburgh, 112; and see Mann, *Popes,* 9:249–52.

46. Newburgh, 118: ". . . cardinales in summi pontificis electione discordes ecclesium sciderunt, . . . in orbe quoque terrarum vinculum ecclesiasticae pacis ruperunt"; Duggan, "Conquest to Death of John," 74–75: "But the problem of canonical elections provoked the use of a sword of two edges, since the legality of papal elections was often itself in dispute in the period. Gradually, through many crises, there evolved the basic canonical rules which were designed to place beyond question the validity of papal elections in the future. . . . After a long and dangerous instance of such confusion, the canon *Licet de vitanda* of Alexander III, in the Lateran Council of 1179, established the principle of a two-thirds majority of the total body of cardinals"; a recent general

essay is Marshall W. Baldwin, *Alexander III and the Twelfth Century*, with selected bibliography.

47. Newburgh, 119.

48. Newburgh, 121.

49. Mary Cheney, "The Recognition of Pope Alexander III: Some Neglected Evidence," *English Historical Review* 84 (1969): 474–97, includes a survey of scholarly opinion on the question.

50. Cheney, "Alexander III," 497; see also Kate Norgate, *England Under the Angevin Kings* 1 (1887): 499–501.

51. Cheney, "Alexander III," 493–96; see also Mann, *Popes*, 10:42–43.

52. Newburgh, 158 ff.

53. Duggan, "Conquest to Death of John," 76.

54. Newburgh, 119, 205.

55. Newburgh, 245–47, 267–70, 369–70, 345.

56. Newburgh, 271.

57. Newburgh, 43–44.

58. Newburgh, 79: "animi vere Romani"; 206; "Romanae avaritiae"; see also 239 for the behavior of a legate in Ireland.

59. Newburgh, 79, 459, 488, 32.

60. Newburgh, 136, 207.

61. Newburgh, 440, 423.

62. Newburgh, 37, 187; see also 47–48 on Robert Marmion and William of Albemarle as desecrators of monasteries.

63. Newburgh, 421.

64. Newburgh, 451: "quam a viro veraci audivi."

65. Newburgh, 451–53.

66. Newburgh, 453: ". . . ita quidem cum nostris illis visus est ludere."

67. For the monastic recolonization of the north, see L. G. D. Baker, "The Desert in the North," *Northern History*, 5 (1970): 1–11.

68. Bennett D. Hill, *English Cistercian Monasteries and Their Patrons in the Twelfth Century*, 38–39: "They brought to England austere ideals and a fervently emotional asceticism especially suited to the physical climate of those areas . . . all these ideals fitted well with the atmosphere of the barren moors and bleak ridings of the west country and Yorkshire. This helps to explain why the Cistercian abbeys, although they were evenly distributed throughout the entire island, had their greatest influence in the north and west." Hill's passage seems to have been inspired by a similar one in Cooke's important, seminal article, "Cistercians in England," 648: "The true interest of the Cistercian settlement lies in the north, and, at a somewhat later period, in the west . . . the southern and midland parts even of twelfth-century England, where, moreover, the older orders were in possession of the

soil, offered no free scope for the newborn restless energy of the monks of Citeaux. It is not here, therefore, but among the Yorkshire dales and moorlands, and the deep valleys of Wales, that we must seek for the spirit which animated the founders of Citeaux. With it reappear some of the characteristic features of the early movement in Burgundy."

69. See the map in Cooke, "Cistercians in England," opposite p. 632; for general information on the influence of the Cistercians in Yorkshire, see Francis A. Mullin, *A History of the Work of the Cistercians in Yorkshire.*

70. David Knowles, *The Monastic Order in England,* 356: "Thus by the end of the twelfth century an atmosphere of commerce and litigation was beginning to surround the white monks in England. As will be seen elsewhere, there is some reason to think that in this respect the Cistercians of this country were among the first to lose the original purity of their order. How far discipline and observance were affected for the worse is not so clear. . . . The Yorkshire families, in particular, with all their ramifications, were still a powerful spiritual force in 1200. Rievaulx, Fountains, and Byland were the luminaries of the north"; the last image is taken from Newburgh, 53.

71. Newburgh, 49–51.

72. This inconspicuous, tidy narrative device is characteristic of William's skill in building a text with connections that are very logical and yet flexible; it is a very different mind from the kind that repeats "eodem anno" over and over.

73. L. G. D. Baker, "The Genesis of English Cistercian Chronicles: The Foundation History of Fountains Abbey I," *Analecta Cisterciensia* 25 (1969): 25. Baker also says that William's account is of "some value," but he does not say what he thinks it is; see also by the same author, "The Foundation of Fountains Abbey," *Northern History* 4 (1969): 29–43; brief accounts of the foundation of the northern Cistercian houses are also in Hill, *English Cistercian Monasteries,* and Cooke, "Cistercians in England."

74. Newburgh, 50.

75. Newburgh, 50.

76. Newburgh, 51.

77. Baker, "English Cistercian Chronicles," 21.

78. The *Exordium magnum,* though not the earlier *Exordium parvum,* describes Citeaux as "locum horroris et vastae solitudinis," *PL* 185, cap. xiii; William of Saint Thierry, in the *Vita prima,* describes Clairvaux upon Bernard's arrival as "loco horroris et vastae solitudinis," *PL* 185: col. 241; a similar description is given for Fountain's site in Hugh of Kirkstall, *Narratio de fundatione Fontanis monasterii in comitatu Eboracensi,* J. R. Walbran, in *Memorials of the Abbey of Saint Mary of Fountains,* Surtees Society Publications 42 (Durham,

London, 1863): 2; see also Cooke, "Cistercians in England," 650; and Baker, "English Cistercian Chronicles," 21.

79. *Vita secunda*, comp. Alanus Autissiodorensis, *PL* 185:469–524; *Vita tertia*, Geoffrey of Clairvaux, *PL* 185:523–30.

80. *Vita prima*, 261: "Et petentur undique fratres et mittuntur, . . . civitates et regiones, . . . Ultra homines, usque ad barbaras nationes, . . ."

81. Newburgh, 51.

82. Another fainter suggestion of a source is found in the *Vita secunda*, *PL* 185: 494: ". . . rete verbi Dei in manu piscatoris Dei tam copiosas piscium rationalium multitudines coepit concludere"; cf. Newburgh, 51: "tanquam quaedam rationalium apum examina"; the parallel is an admittedly oblique one consisting of animal imagery used to express the multiplication of Cistercians, with the simile introduced by the word *rationalium* in both cases. William uses the image of bees, which had acquired the allegorical significance of contemplatives; see Alexander Neckham, *De naturis rerum*, ed. T. Wright (London, 1863), 268: "Per apes, viri contemplativi designantur, qui utilibus exercitiis quandoque invigilant." William may have consulted the *Vita secunda* in addition to or instead of the *Vita prima* (both contain the "loco horroris" phrase) and, characteristically, recast it into his own imagery.

83. Baker, "English Cistercian Chronicles," 22–23.

84. *Exordium Cisterciensis cenobii* (*exordium parvum*), ed. Philip Guignard, *Les Monuments primitifs de la régle Cistercienne*, 61–75.

85. Aelred of Rievaulx, *De bello standardi* in *Historiae Anglicanae scriptores* 10:337–46.

86. Newburgh, 51.

87. Newburgh, 51.

88. Newburgh, 52: "Cumque ex his tribus quasi radicibus servorum atque ancillarum Dei per diversas provincias religiosa germina pullularent."

89. Newburgh, 51–52.

90. Newburgh, 52.

91. Newburgh, 53: "unitatem disciplinae regularis, arctiori quoque animorum nexu"; for an entirely different version, see Hill, *English Cistercian Monasteries*, 104–9.

92. Newburgh, 53.

93. Newburgh, 53.

94. Newburgh, 53.

95. Hill, *English Cistercian Monasteries*, 27–29, and see n.43 for a survey of scholarly opinion.

96. Newburgh, 54–55.

97. Newburgh, 392.

98. Newburgh, 235: "mediocriter literatus sed laudibiliter innoxius."

99. Newburgh, 236.

100. Newburgh, 303.

101. See Everett U. Crosby, "The Organization of the English Episcopate under Henry I," *Studies in Medieval and Renaissance History* 4 (1967): 1–88, for a close, detailed study of "civil-service" bishops in the first half of the twelfth century.

102. Newburgh, 280–81.

103. Knowles, *Monastic Order*, 314.

104. Donald Nicholl, *Thurstan: Archbishop of York (1114–1140)*, 181 ff., 91.

105. Crosby, "Episcopate under Henry I," 46.

106. Nicholl, *Thurstan*, 211.

107. Newburgh, 226.

108. Newburgh, 393.

109. Newburgh, 393–94.

110. See Knowles, *Monastic Order*, 322–24.

111. Newburgh, 395; Knowles, *Monastic Order*, 324, 324 n.5.

112. Newburgh, 396.

113. Bernard of Clairvaux, *De moribus et officio episcoporum, epistola XLII ad Henricum archiepiscopum senonensem*, in *Sancti Bernardi opera omnia*, ed. Mabillon, vol. I 1:1101–30.

114. Saint Bernard, epistle 64, in *Opera omnia* 1:208–10.

115. Bernard of Clairvaux, *Officio epis.*, 1104: "Honorificabitis autem non cultu vestium, non equorum fastu, non amplis aedividiis, sed ornatis moribus, studiis spiritualibus, operibus bonis. Quam multi aliter."

116. Bernard of Clairvaux, *Officio epis.*, 1108: "Praesulum potissima et dignissima ornamenta, castitas, charitas, humilitas."

117. Newburgh, 36.

118. Newburgh, 36.

119. Newburgh, 38.

120. Newburgh, 303; for the ecclesiastical and political career of the bishop of Durham, see G. V. Scammell, *Hugh de Puiset, Bishop of Durham*.

121. But see Scammell, *Hugh de Puiset*, 49–50.

122. Newburgh, 304–5; William's account of the tumultous career of Wimund, bishop of the Isles, is another sort of exemplum of the vanity of secular ambitions in bishops, 73–76.

123. Newburgh, 437.

124. Newburgh, 440–41; Scammell, *Hugh de Puiset*, 311–13, demurs at least on the number of women.

125. Newburgh, 440–41.

126. See Bertie Wilkinson, "The Government of England During the Absence of Richard I on the Third Crusade," *Bulletin of the John*

Rylands Library 28 (1944): 485–509. He argues that Longchamp was only part of Richard's delegated government, which was an early experiment in conciliar forms to replace the old justiciarship.

127. Newburgh, 490.

128. Newburgh, 55–56, 79–81.

129. D. Knowles, "The Case of Saint William of York," *Cambridge Historical Journal* 5 (1936), 162–77, 212–14, for an account of the whole "case" and, on Newburgh as detective, 176–77: "If a formal process had ever been concluded we should scarcely find William of Newburgh thirty years later endeavoring—not, we may think, very efficiently—to elicit for himself and for posterity the truth of the matter from isolated survivors of the circle of archbishop William . . . taken as a whole, his evidence does little to clarify the question. He convinced himself, though it can scarcely be said that he proved, that the charge [of murder] was without foundation." A further comment along the same lines was made by Adrian Morey, "Canonist Evidence in the Case of Saint William of York," *Cambridge Historical Journal* 10 (1952): 353: "Finally, this new evidence strengthens the criticism of William of Newburgh's historical skill made by Prof. Knowles. Thirty years after the event William attempted to ascertain the truth from such survivors as might have known the inner history. It is indeed a reflection on his ability that he should have failed to obtain evidence of the canonical process, . . ." For a few more factual pieces of the William of York puzzle, see C. H. Talbot, "New Documents in the Case of Saint William of York," *Cambridge Historical Journal* 10 (1950): 1–15; and R. L. Poole, "The Appointment and Deprivation of Saint William, Archbishop of York," *English Historical Review* 45 (1930): 273–81.

130. For an interesting speculation on the cases of animosity against William Fitz Herbert, see Derek Baker, "*Viri Religiosi* and the York Election Dispute," *Studies in Church History* 7 (1971): 87–100.

131. Newburgh, 56.

132. For the early twelfth-century history of the dispute, see Nicholl, *Thurstan*, 35–40, and Denis Bethell, "William of Corbeil and the Canterbury–York Dispute," *Journal of Ecclesiastical History* 19 (1968): 145–59.

133. Newburgh, 204.

134. Newburgh, 203–4.

135. This one between Geoffrey Plantagenet, archbishop of York, and Hugh of Durham is explained succinctly by Decima L. Douie in *Archbishop Geoffrey Plantagenet and the Chapter of York*, St. Anthony's Hall Publications no. 18 (1960): 6–7; Newburgh, 371.

CHAPTER FOUR

1. Newburgh, 280–83, for his reflections on the death and character of Henry II.

2. Newburgh, 399, 416–17.

3. Newburgh, 500.

4. Newburgh, 174.

5. Newburgh, 422–23.

6. Newburgh, 192–94.

7. Newburgh, 223: "paulo autem simplicior quam deceret principem."

8. Newburgh, 369.

9. Newburgh, 144, 329–30.

10. Newburgh, 387.

11. Newburgh, 51.

12. See Alexander Bugge, "The Norse Settlements in the British Islands," *Transactions of the Royal Historical Society*, 4th ser. 4 (1921), and Henry Goddard Leach, *Angevin Britain and Scandinavia*.

13. Newburgh, 111.

14. For Sverre's full career, see G. M. Gathorne-Hardy, *A Royal Impostor: King Sverre of Norway*. William, along with many of the other English ecclesiastics, undoubtedly learned the story of Sverre's rebellion when Archbishop Eyestein of Norway (1155–1188) spent three years of exile in England after his defeat by Sverre in 1180; see Leach, *Britain and Scandinavia*, 89–92. William calls the archbishop "vir magnus," 231–32.

15. Newburgh, 229; "Christiana quadam simplicitate."

16. Newburgh, 326, and see 65, 350.

17. Newburgh, 172: "Igitur mense Junio, quando solent reges ad bella procedere, . . ."

18. Newburgh, 248–49.

19. Newburgh, 460.

20. Newburgh, 484.

21. Newburgh, 131.

22. Newburgh, 496.

23. Newburgh, 69.

24. Newburgh, 446.

25. Newburgh, 487: "reges nostri."

26. Newburgh, 57–60.

27. Giles Constable, "The Second Crusade as Seen by Contemporaries," *Traditio* 9 (1953): 213–79, describes the variety of opinions held by contemporaries as to the reasons for the failure of the crusade. Some accepted a natural (Greek perfidy and physical difficulties) explanation; a few (Otto of Freising and Bernard of Clairvaux) accepted an inexplicable though good judgment of God; and some "lesser spirits" including Henry of Huntingdon found a reason in the sins of the crusaders, 266–71.

28. Huntingdon, 280: "Ascendit enim in conspectu Dei incontinentia eorum, quam exercebant in fornicationibus non occultis; in adulteriis

etiam, quod Deo valde disciplicuit, postremo in rapinis et omni genere scelerum."

29. Newburgh, 66: "Porro in nostro illo exercitu tanta, tam contra Christianam quam contra castrensem etiam disciplinam, mala increverant, ut mirum non sit, quod eis tanquam pollutis et immundis favor nequaquam divinus arriserit. Castra enim a castratione luxuriae dicuntur. At castra illa nostra casta non erant: in quibus utique infelici quadam licentia multorum spumabant libidines"; for the derivation of the word *castrum* according to Isidore of Seville who is William's authority in these matters, see chap. 2, n.85.

30. Newburgh, 92–93.

31. See Howlett in the Introduction to *Historia*.

32. William took a different liberty when he considerably abridged and hardened Richard the Canon's lamentations for the death of Emperor Frederick I; compare Newburgh, 329–30, with *Itinerarium Regis Ricardi*, Rolls Series 38 (1864), 54–56.

33. Newburgh, 249–55.

34. Newburgh, 250.

35. Newburgh, 251.

36. Newburgh, 254: "tolerat gentem immundissimam Agarenos usque ad tempus, procul dubio et hos devoratura cum Deus voluerit."

37. Newburgh, 275.

38. Newburgh, 374.

39. See James A. Brundage, *Medieval Canon Law and the Crusader*, 145–53, for the development and popular notion of the crusade indulgence.

40. Cited by Brundage, *Crusader*, 150.

41. Newburgh, 374.

42. Newburgh, 375.

43. Newburgh, 380.

44. Newburgh, 183–84.

45. Newburgh, 185.

46. Newburgh, 126.

47. Newburgh, 126–27.

48. Newburgh, 130.

49. Newburgh, 383.

50. Newburgh, 194, 114.

51. Newburgh, 144.

52. Newburgh, 466–73 for the entire account.

53. Gwyn A. Williams, *Medieval London* (London, 1963), 2–4.

54. William Stubbs, *Historical Introduction to the Rolls Series*, ed. A. Hassall (London, 1902), lxxxix–xc; see also the *Dictionary of National Biography*, "William Fitz Osbert."

55. Richard Vaughan, *Matthew Paris*, 149, cites Paris, *Chronica majora*, 2:419.

56. Newburgh, 466.
57. Newburgh, 466.
58. Newburgh, 468.
59. Newburgh, 471, 472.

CHAPTER FIVE

1. Arnaldo Momigliano, "Tradition and the Classical Historian," *History and Theory* 11 (1972): 281.

2. Newburgh, 82.

3. See, generally, Edward Langton, *Satan, A Portrait*, for biblical and patristic sources for the existence and actions of demons.

4. Newburgh, 86: "Haec et hujusmodi incredibilia viderentur, nisi a dignis fide testibus contigisse probarentur."

5. Ralph of Coggeshall, quoted by H. L. Ward, *Catalogue of Romances in the Department of Manuscripts in the British Museum* 2 (London, 1893): 493.

6. James Boswell, *Boswell's Life of Johnson*, ed. G. Hill, rev. L. F. Powell, 4:6.

7. Boswell, *Life* 4:290.

8. Boswell, *Life* 3:230; and compare Joseph Addison in *The Spectator*, ed. D. F. Bond, no. 110, arguing in favor of the existence of ghosts and specters by means of "the Reports of all Historians sacred and prophane, ancient and modern, and to the Traditions of all Nations . . . this general testimony of Mankind."

9. Newburgh, 474, 479, 500, 434.

10. Newburgh, 104; the translation used is by Antonia Gransden.

11. Antonia Gransden, "Realistic Observation in Twelfth-Century England," *Speculum* 47 (1972): 42.

12. Newburgh, 81–82; his reliance on medieval medical expertise has been roundly ridiculed by David Knowles, "The Case of Saint William of York," *Cambridge Historical Journal* 5 (1936): 176–77, and A. Morey, "Canonist Evidence in the Case of Saint William of York," *Cambridge Historical Journal* 10 (1952): 352–53.

13. Newburgh, 380, and see 118 and 154–55 for two more examples of William's contempt for superstition.

14. Newburgh, 32.

15. Compare Newburgh, 130, for the motives, divine and human, behind the massacre of the citizens of Béziers.

16. See, for example, G. G. Coulton, *Five Centuries of Religion* 1 (Cambridge, 1923), for the most vivid expression of rational disgust with the demons of medieval guilt in objectified form.

17. Newburgh, 84: "Dicat quisque quod voluerit, et ratiocinetur de his ut poterit; me autem prodigiosum mirabilemque eventum exposuisse non piget."

18. Newburgh, 308: "Interpretatur quisque ut voluerit signum mira-

bile, cujus utique didici simplex esse narrator, non etiam praesagus interpres; quid enim Divinitas eo significare voluerit nescio."

19. Newburgh, 22–23.

20. Newburgh, 45–46; compare Henry of Huntingdon, 277.

21. R. W. Southern, "The Place of England in the Twelfth-Century Renaissance," *History* 45 (1960): 212–13, notices that many English historians were fascinated by marvels of all sorts and that this interest is closely related to the revived interest in science proper, "for science and marvels, it must be remembered, are almost interchangeable terms."

22. Jeffrey B. Russell, *Witchcraft in the Middle Ages*, 110–12, suggests an explanation for the indubitable increase in the attention paid to Satan and his demons throughout the eleventh and twelfth centuries can be found in dualist, heretical ideas.

23. Newburgh, 82–84.

24. Newburgh, 83.

25. Newburgh, 83.

26. Newburgh, 84–85: "Alia quoque aeque mira et prodigiosa nostris temporibus contigerunt, ex quibus pauca retexam. Mira vero hujusmodi dicimus, non tantum propter raritatem, sed etiam quia occultam habent rationem."

27. Newburgh, 85.

28. Newburgh, 85.

29. Newburgh, 85; and compare Robert de Monte (or de Torigni), *The Chronicles of Robert de Monte*, trans. J. Stevenson, 724, who tells of the discovery of a toad in a hollow stone at Le Mans in 1145.

30. Newburgh, 85.

31. Newburgh, 86.

32. Newburgh, 87.

33. Augustine, *De genesi ad litteram*, PL 34: Book 9, 15: "quia nec agricolas creatores segetum . . ."

34. Augustine, *De Trinitate*, PL 42: Book 3, 8: "nec agricolas creatores frugum."

35. Augustine, *Quaestionum in Heptateuchum libri VII*, *Corpus scriptorum ecclesiasticorum latinum*, 28 (Prague, 1895): Book II, 21: "sicut nec agricolae segetum . . . ; deus vero solus unus creator est."

36. See Langton, *Satan*, for specific citations.

37. Langton, *Satan*, 61.

38. The *PL* index to Augustine contains three full columns of references to demons.

39. Rabanus Maurus, *De magicis artibus*, PL 110: 1095–1110; Burchard of Worms, *Decretorum liber*, PL 140: 537–1053; Ivo of Chartres, *Decretum*, PL 161:59–1022; Gratian, *Decretum*, PL, 187.

40. J. S. Beddie, "Libraries in the Twelfth Century: Their Catalogues and Contents," in *Anniversary Essays in Medieval History by Students of Charles Homer Haskins*, 17.

41. Isidore of Seville, *Etymologiarum*, Book 8, 11: "Ante transgressionem quidem caelestia corpora gerebant. Lapsi vero in aeriam qualitatem conversi sunt, nec aeris illiiis puriora spatia, sed ista caliginosa tenere permissi sunt, qui eis quasi carcer est usque ad tempus iudicii. Hi sunt praevericatores angeli, quorum Diabolus princeps est."

42. Newburgh, 12.

43. Newburgh, 86–87: "convertere," "producere," "admovere . . . sic exeat quod creatur," "valeant exhibere."

44. Newburgh, 87.

45. Newburgh, 87.

46. Burchard, *Decretorum*, X, 44, "Nec ideo quisquam credere debet, quolibet magicis artibus aliquid facere posse, sine permissu Dei, qui omnia quae fiunt, aut justo judicio facit, aut permissu suo ita fieri sinit"; and compare Rabanus in the opening passages of the *De magicis;* and Ivo, *Decretum*, XI, 69.

47. Russell, *Witchcraft*, 110.

48. Newburgh, 151.

49. On the Devil as a black man, see Russell, *Witchcraft*, 87, who also refers to Orderic Vitalis's inclusion of Ethiopians in the night procession of purgatory, 97; see also Langton, *Satan*, for the Ethiopian as Devil in patristic writings, 114.

50. Newburgh, 151.

51. Langton, *Satan*, 68.

52. Newburgh, 153.

53. For Éon's career and the value placed on William's account of it, see Norman Cohn, *The Pursuit of the Millennium* (New York, rev. ed. 1970); F. Vernet, "Éon de l'Étoile," in *Dictionnaire de théologie catholique* 5 (1913); and T. de Morembert, "Éon de l'Étoile," in *Dictionnaire d'histoire et de géographie ecclésiastiques* 5 (1963).

54. Newburgh, 62 and 64.

55. Russell, *Witchcraft*, 95, cites Éon as one example of the growing association of heresy and witchcraft in the eleventh and twelfth centuries.

56. Arnaldo Momigliano, "Popular Religious Beliefs and the Late Roman Historians," *Studies in Church History* 8 (1972): 17.

57. Newburgh, 60: "sermone Gallico."

58. Newburgh, 60–61.

59. Cohn, *Millennium*, 45.

60. De Morembert, *Dictionnaire d'histoire:* "Sans doute, Éon feignit-il à folie, se sentant perdu"; and Newburgh, 64.

61. Newburgh, 60.

62. Newburgh, 61.

63. Newburgh, 61 and 62.

64. Compare Augustine on demonic transformation in *De Trinitate*, Book 4, 11: "Facile est enim spiritibus nequissimis per aerea corpora

facere multa, quae mirentur animae terrenis corporibus aggravatae, etiam melioris affectus, . . . quid magnum est diabolo et angelis ejus, de corporeis elementis per aerea corpora facere quae care miretur. . . ."

65. Newburgh, 62.

66. See, for example, *De diversibus quaestionibus ad simplicianum, libri II, PL* 40: quaest. 3, 6; *De civitate Dei,* Book 9, 22.

67. Augustine, *De diversibus quaestionibus,* Book 6, "De spiritu vero mendacii, per quem deceptus est Achab (III Reg. xxii, 20–23) hoc intelligamus, . . . Deum scilicet omnipotentem et justum distributorem poenarum praemiorumque pro meritis, non solu, bonis et sanctis ministris uti ad opera congrua, sed etiam malis ad opera digna; cum illi pro sua perversa cupiditate nocere appetant, sinantur, autem tantum quantum ille judicat, qui omnia in mensura et porȵdere it numero disponsit."

68. Newburgh, 424–25.

69. Newburgh, 425-26.

70. Newburgh, 426–27.

71. Newburgh, 477.

72. *The Travels of Three English Gentlemen, from Venice to Hamburg, being the Grand Tour of Germany in the Year 1734,* in *The Harleian Miscellany* 4 (London, 1809): 375–77.

73. For further information about the history and characteristics of vampires, see R. H. Robbins, *The Encyclopedia of Witchcraft and Demonology;* E. S. Hartland, editor of Walter Map's *De nugis curialium,* includes a great deal of historical and bibliographical information in a note to Map's text, p. 110 n.2; John C. Lawson, *Modern Greek Folklore and Ancient Greek Religion,* discusses the Greek and related Slavic traditions at length, 361–484; Ernst Havekost, *Die Vampirsage in England* (Halle, 1914), begins with William and is chiefly concerned with more modern literature. For an approach that has the merit of not being condescending and allows a rather disturbing insight into the state of mind that nurtures vampires, try Montague Summers, *The Vampire, His Kith and Kin* (London, 1928).

74. Lawson, Greek Folklore, 397–412; and see Bruce Dickins, "A Yorkshire Chronicler," Trans. of the *Yorkshire Dialect Society* 5 pt. 35 (1934).

75. Russell, *Witchcraft,* 97.

76. Robbins, *Encyclopedia,* "Vampire"; Havekost, *Vampirsage,* 15.

77. Map, *De nugis curialium,* cap. 27–28.

78. Newburgh, 477–79.

79. Newburgh, 479.

80. Newburgh, 479.

81. Langton, *Satan,* 32.

82. Langton, *Greek Folklore,* 410–12.

83. Newburgh, 474–75.

84. Newburgh, 475.
85. Newburgh, 474–75.
86. Robbins, *Encyclopedia*, "Vampire."
87. Newburgh, 476.
88. Newburgh, 476.
89. Newburgh, 480–82.
90. Newburgh, 497–99.
91. Newburgh, 498–99.

CHAPTER SIX

1. Richard of Devizes, *Cronicon Richardi Divisensis de tempore Regis Richardi Primi*, ed. John T. Appleby (1963); this edition will henceforth be referred to as Devizes; for previous editions and translations, see Appleby's Introduction, xxiv.

2. Appleby, Introduction to Devizes, xviii.

3. *Annals of Winchester*, ed. H. R. Luard, Rolls Series 36:2 (1865); J. T. Appleby, "Richard of Devizes and the Annals of Winchester," *Bulletin of the Institute of Historical Research* 36 (1963), 70–77.

4. Appleby, Introduction to Devizes, xviii.

5. Appleby, Introduction to Devizes, xiv.

6. Appleby, Introduction to Devizes, xx–xxiii.

7. Appleby, Introduction to Devizes, xxiii–xxiv.

8. Appleby, Introduction to Devizes, xvii–xviii.

9. Appleby, Introduction to Devizes, xiv.

10. Beryl Smalley, "Sallust in the Middle Ages," in *Classical Influences on European Culture*, ed. R. Bolgar, 171–72.

11. Charles Witke, *Latin Satire*, 249, 251.

12. See chapter 8.

13. Ernst Curtius, *European Literature and the Latin Middle Ages* (New York, 1953), 83–85, for the topic of "affected modesty."

14. Devizes, 1; I am using Appleby's translation for all quotations and therefore will not, in this chapter include any Latin text in the notes.

15. Devizes, 1.

16. Devizes, 1–2.

17. Devizes, 2.

18. Devizes, 2.

19. *Annals Win.*, 68: "Walterus prior Bathoniae, vir multae scientiae et religionis, apud Werewellam vitam in Christo finivit. Hic de subpriore Hidensi pro bona sanctitatis suae fama prior Bathoniae factus, postquam monachos monastico ordini ad unguem informaverat, cogitans intra se
'quam frivola gloria mundi,
Quam rerum fugitivus honor, quam nomen inane,'
praelatus mallens sibi tantum prodesse quam aliis praesse, contulit se ad

Cartusienses; ubi cum quidam monachus Hidensis venisset causa visendi eum, et vidisset eum circa ollas et olera valde intentum, qui multum paulo ante intenderat, circa salvanda animas. Ille autem ad se reversus post non multos hos dies, tam prece quam praecepto magnatorum intelligens quod sanctius est multas animas quam solam salvare, ad prioratum suum reversus est, et ibi se strenue usque ad obitum suum habuit, . . ."

20. Devizes, 2.

21. Witke, *Latin Satire*, 257, for the persona of the satirist.

22. Jean Leclercq, *The Love of Learning and the Desire for God*, trans. C. Misrahi, 77–80.

23. Leclercq, *Love of Learning*, 80–83.

24. Devizes, 49, 51, 65.

25. This applies chiefly to the *Historia novella*; but also see D. H. Farmer, "Two Biographies by William of Malmesbury," in *Latin Biography*, ed. T. A. Dorey, 157–76.

26. Devizes, 3, 4, 18, 35.

27. Devizes, 8.

28. Devizes, 15.

29. Devizes, 17.

30. Devizes, 28.

31. Devizes, 42, 51, and see also 5, 6, 7, 17, 26, 28, 33, 35.

32. Devizes, 9.

33. Richard Vaughan, *Matthew Paris*, 145.

34. Vaughan, *Paris*, 145–46.

35. Vaughan, *Paris*, 137.

36. Vaughan, *Paris*, 137.

37. Vaughan, *Paris*, 138.

38. Vaughan, *Paris*, 137.

39. Walter of Henley, *Walter of Henley and Other Treatises on Estate Management and Accounting*, ed. Dorothea Oschinsky, 309, and 149–50, 190 for the audience of the treatise.

40. Walter of Henley, 144–45.

41. Walter of Henley, 3–4.

42. Walter of Henley, 224.

43. Walter of Henley, 224.

44. Devizes, 49.

45. Devizes, 49.

46. Devizes, 51.

47. Devizes, 4.

48. Devizes, 9.

49. Jane Austen, *The History of England from the Reign of Henry the 4th to the Death of Charles the 1st, by a partial, prejudiced, and ignorant Historian*, in *The Works of Jane Austen*, ed. R. W. Chapman 6 (1954): 139–50.

50. Devizes, 65.

51. Devizes, 65, 66–67.

52. Devizes, 67.

53. Devizes, 66.

54. Devizes, 27.

55. Devizes, 70–71.

56. Devizes, 71.

57. Devizes, 13.

58. Devizes, 69–70.

59. Devizes, 72–73.

60. Devizes, 14, 27, 28.

61. Devizes, 29, 39, 54–55.

62. Devizes, 18.

63. Devizes, 18–19.

64. Devizes, 40.

65. Devizes, 55.

66. V. H. Galbraith, "Good Kings and Bad Kings in Medieval English History," *History* n.s. 30 (1945), 119–32.

67. Georges Poulet's abstruse presentation of the conception of time in the Middle Ages in *Studies in Human Time*, trans. E. Coleman, 3–8, does, although it is based entirely on thirteenth-century scholastic sources, seem congruent with (or at least does not contradict) my smaller-scaled remarks about the lack of causal structure in medieval historical writing.

68. Bede's history suffered the same fate as Saint Anselm's theology; they evoked interest and admiration but were not sufficiently understood to produce "schools" of successors.

69. Erich Auerbach, "Roland Against Ganelon," in *Mimesis*, trans. W. Trask, 96–122, discusses the use of "paratactic" structure in the "Chanson de Roland" and in medieval literature generally, that is, the simple juxtaposition of events without the subordinating or causal connections found in "hypotactic" structure: ". . . the representational technique (and this means more than mere technical procedure, it includes the idea of structure which poet and audience apply to the narrated event). . . strings independent pictures together like beads," 115; see also 109–10, 119–22.

70. Samuel Johnson, *A Dictionary of the English Language*.

71. See, for example, the quarrel between the abbot of Malmesbury and the bishop of Salisbury, Devizes, 14.

72. The two bishops Richard had to know well, Richard of Ilchester (1173–1188) and Godfrey de Lucy (d. 1204), were important royal servants, each of whom was closely attached to the court for many years before being rewarded with the bishopric of Winchester; see Charles Duggan, "Richard of Ilchester, Royal Servant and Bishop,"

Transactions of the Royal Historical Society, 5th ser. 16 (1966): 1–21, and Edmund Venables, "Godfrey de Lucy, Bishop of Winchester," *Dictionary of National Biography*.

73. Appleby, Introduction to Devizes, xvi.

74. Devizes, 10.

75. Devizes, 9. I differ with Appleby's translation of *animo* as "arrogance" and render it as "mind"; 53.

76. Devizes, 10.

77. Devizes, 10.

78. Stubbs, *Historical Introduction to the Rolls Series*, ed. A. Hassall (London, 1902), 216–18; Kate Norgate, "William of Longchamp," *Dictionary of National Biography:* "His loyalty to his royal friend seems in truth to have been at once his most conspicuous virtue and the source of his gravest political errors."

79. Devizes, 9.

80. Devizes, 13, 29, 39–40, 9–10, 12–13, 4, 9–10.

81. Devizes, 39–45.

82. Devizes, 29.

83. Devizes, 50.

84. Devizes, 51–52.

85. G. W. Regenos, translator of *The Book of Daun Burnel.the Ass* (Austin, Texas, 1959), remarks that Nigel Wireker "was on terms of intimate friendship with William Longchamp. . . . Nigellus seems to have had a genuine affection for this prominent man and to have held him in the highest esteem," 5; the *Tractatus contra curiales et officiales clericos*, ed. A. Boutemy (Paris, 1959), was dedicated to Longchamp.

86. *Annals Win.*, 64: "Hoc anno Willelmus de Longo Campo, Eliensis episcopus et regis cancellarius, viam ingressus est moriens quam vivens promeruerat, . . . homo quidem prudentia saeculi et gratia labiorum mira aestimatione insignis, et quo nemo unquam in integritate semel conceptae dilectionis fidelior extitit; qui et merito pater monarchorum poterat appellari, nisi cum olim utrumque tenerat gladium apostolica auctoritate et regia, consiliis consensisset religioni adversantium, ut in magno concilio suo apud Londonias ejectionem monachorum de Coventre quantum in ipso fuerat confirmasset."

87. Devizes, 5.

88. Devizes, 5.

89. Devizes, 7.

90. Devizes, 58.

91. Appleby, Introduction to Devizes, xvii–xviii.

92. Devizes, 16–17, 19–25.

93. Devizes, 20–21.

94. Devizes, 39.

95. Devizes, 48.

96. Devizes, 73.

97. Devizes, 75–76.

98. Devizes, 78.

99. Devizes, 79.

100. Devizes, 82.

101. Devizes, 84.

102. Cecil Roth, *A History of the Jews in England*, 22 n.1.

103. See chapters 5–7 of the Introduction to Augustus Jessop and Montague James, eds. and trans., *The Life and Miracles of Saint William of Norwich*; Gavin I. Langmuir, "The Knight's Tale of Young Hugh of Lincoln," *Speculum* 47 (1972): 461–64.

104. Devizes, 64.

105. Devizes, 67.

106. Devizes, 68; one should not ignore the possibility of a sexual allusion in the relationship of the two boys.

107. Devizes, 68–69.

108. Jessop and James, *Saint William*, 14–15.

109. Devizes, 68.

110. Jessop and James, *Saint William*, 85: "Commonitorium illis qui miraculis sancti Willelmi derogant et qui eum a iudeis occisum vel negant vel dubitant"; 86: "Primus igitur qui miraculis insultant, qui ficticia autumant, et sanctificatum non credunt, quoniam pauperculum fuisse audiunt, respondemus."

111. *Annals Win.*, 68: "Lumbardus Judaeus commodavit conventui viginti et unam marcam in vigilia Sancti Swithuni."

112. Henry Richardson, *The English Jewry under Angevin Kings*, 47–48.

113. Devizes, 35.

Chapter Seven

1. Mary Augusta Ward's (Mrs. Humphrey Ward) novel, *Robert Elsmere*, contains some interesting sections that dramatize the struggle between faith or traditional Anglican observance and reason represented by historical criticism; it is virtually unread now, with reason, but it attracted immense attention in the author's lifetime, very interestingly described by Basil Willey in "How 'Robert Elsmere' Struck Some Contemporaries," *Essays and Studies 1957* (1957), 53–68.

2. *Robert Elsmere*, 277; Mary Ward, daughter of the Rolls Series editor of Henry of Huntingdon and niece of Matthew Arnold, did some research into early medieval saints' lives; the "live" quality of this passage is perhaps the wonderful result of that experience of scholarship.

3. John of Salisbury, *Historia pontificalis*, trans. Marjorie Chibnall, 3.

4. John W. Baldwin, "The Intellectual Preparation for the Canon of 1215 Against Ordeals," *Speculum* 36 (1961): 613–36, specifically p. 623.

5. See, generally, R. Van Caenegem, "The Law of Evidence in the Twelfth Century: European Perspective and Intellectual Background," *Proceedings of the Second International Congress of Medieval Canon Law*, ed. S. Kuttner and J. Ryan (1965), 297–310.

6. Beryl Smalley, "Sallust in the Middle Ages," in *Classical Influences on European Culture*, ed. R. Bolgar, 172.

7. Newburgh, 311.

8. Newburgh, 311: "... sed tamen gratum erat clericis ex eadem superstitione provenientium gratia commodorum."

Chapter Eight

1. V. H. Galbraith, "Good Kings and Bad Kings in Medieval English History," *History* n.s. 30 (1945), 119–32.

2. See, as only one example, though one that enunciates a common assumption very firmly, Paul Conkin, "Causation Revisited," *History and Theory* 13 (1974): 7; if we are unwilling to try to relate past events by some form of causal connections, we have no histories. For if we are unwilling to try to make some sense out of an otherwise overwhelming flux of events in the past, if we are unwilling to seek some enduring coherence or pattern, we have no histories: "Even from a literary standpoint, the narrative form requires causal relationships. They alone make possible a convincing history, one that an audience will believe or take seriously."

3. Isidore of Seville, *Etymologiarum*, ed. W. Lindsay, Book 1, xl–xliv.

4. Isidore, 1, xli: "Haec disciplina ad Grammaticam pertinet, quia quidquid dignum memoria est litteris mandatur."

5. Isidore, 1, xliv: "... annui commentarii in libris delati sunt."

6. M. L. Levy, "As Myn Auctour Seyth," *Medium Aevum* 12 (1943): 25–39, explores the modes in which medieval fiction and history overlapped one another.

7. Arthur K. Moore, "Medieval English Literature and the Question of Unity," *Modern Philology* 65 (1968): 285–86.

8. Erich Auerbach, *Mimesis*, trans. W. R. Trask, 70–75, 99–101, 166 ff.

9. Auerbach, *Mimesis*, 74.

10. Auerbach's discussion, p. 70.

11. Devizes, 52–53.

12. Huntingdon, 239.

13. As Moore remarks on the more inclusive matter of unity, "Whatever the unity of the vernacular literature of the Middle Ages may consist in, it is obviously neither the elegant balance and symmetry of classical verse nor the relentless causality of, say, modern detective

fiction; but there is no reason for doubting that on this score medieval writers somehow satisfied the expectations of their audiences," 286.

14. Auerbach, *Mimesis*, 75.

15. Auerbach, *Mimesis*, 73–74.

16. Auerbach, *Mimesis*, 75.

17. Auerbach, *Mimesis*, 76.

18. William W. Ryding, *Structure in Medieval Narrative*; reviewed very favorably by Morton Bloomfield in *Speculum* 48 (1973): 584–87; discussed also in a review article by Tony Hunt, "The Structure of Medieval Narrative," *Journal of European Studies* 3 (1973): 295–328, which comments on three books on medieval narrative and is especially favorable to Ryding as being "full of common-sense and refreshingly eschews excesses of any sort . . . ," 319; I have also benefited in a more general way from the sensitive and illuminating discussions of medieval narrative by Eugene Vinaver in *The Rise of Romance* and in "Form and Meaning in Medieval Romance," his presidential address to the Modern Humanities Research Association, 1966. Bloomfield reviews *The Rise of Romance* in unfavorable comparison with Ryding's book in the same review, but I think that Vinaver's work should be regarded as an essay in sensibility and thus different in its aims from Ryding's work.

19. Ryding, *Structure*, 43.

20. Ryding, *Structure*, 44.

21. Ryding, *Structure*, 61.

22. Ryding, *Structure*, 139–54.

23. Huntingdon, 230.

24. Huntingdon, 279–81.

25. Ryding, *Structure*, 139.

26. Devizes, 3–6.

27. Devizes, 23–27.

28. Ryding, *Structure*, 145.

29. Devizes, 40–49.

30. Ryding, *Structure*, 62–63.

31. Ryding, *Structure*, 65–66.

32. Ryding, *Structure*, 82.

33. Appleby, Introduction to Devizes, xx–xxi.

34. Devizes, for example the marginalia on pp. 4–5, includes an "omen" (told satirically) and information about Longchamp.

35. Devizes, 13.

36. Devizes, 18–19.

37. Devizes, 64–73.

38. Devizes, 82.

Chapter Nine

1. John of Salisbury, *Historia pontificalis*, 11; I have changed Chibnall's translation slightly in the direction of explicitness.

2. John of Salisbury, *Historia*, 11–12.

3. John of Salisbury, *Frivolities of Courtiers and Footprints of Philosophers*, trans. W. R. Trask 74, 120–23.

4. Sir Herbert Butterfield, *Christianity and History*, 146.

5. For Augustine's ideas about history and human society, shown in their full complexity and gradual development, see R. A. Markus, *Saeculum: History and Society in the Theology of Saint Augustine*, especially 162 ff. on the relation of Orosius to Augustine.

6. See, for example, C. A. Patrides, *The Grand Design of God: The Literary Form of the Christian View of History*, and Floyd S. Lear, "The Medieval Attitude Toward History," Rice Institute Pamphlet 20 (1933): 156–77. Lear frankly mourns the change in historical writing from classical models: "History had meant an interesting account of human society, its customs, and its institutions. . . . But now something has happened to history. It is no longer *historia*, research, inquiry, critical investigation; it has become God's purpose revealed in man," 166, and thinks, interestingly, that he sees history "dissolve into a dream," 164.

7. Auerbach, *Mimesis*, 76.

8. Huntingdon, 231.

9. Huntingdon, 236.

10. Newburgh, 401.

11. Newburgh, 401.

12. Newburgh, 402: ". . . sed quaestionem suspicionemque auxit portenti."

13. The prodigy that William saw may very well have been an instance of the same phenomenon that A. H. M. Jones believes the Emperor Constantine probably saw: ". . . a rare, but well-attested, form of the 'halo phenomenon.' This is a phenomenon analogous to the rainbow, and like it is local and transient, caused by the fall, not of rain, but of ice crystals across the rays of the sun. It usually takes the form of mock suns or of rings of light surrounding the sun, but a cross of light with the sun in its centre has been on several occasions observed." *Constantine and the Conversion of Europe*, 96.

14. Newburgh, 482–83.

15. *The Peterborough Chronicle*, trans. H. A. Rositzke 133–34.

16. *Peterborough*, 134.

17. Newburgh, 401.

18. Devizes, 35–36.

19. *Peterborough*, 139.

20. Devizes, 18–19, 72–73.

21. *Peterborough*, 160; and Henry's denial, 277.

22. Huntingdon, 123, 167, 242–43, 251–52.

23. Newburgh, 329.

24. Newburgh, 329–30.

25. Newburgh, 318.

26. For an excellent discussion of the fading of the distinction between popular and educated belief as reflected in historical writing, see A. D. Momigliano, "Popular Religious Beliefs and the Late Roman Historians," *Studies in Church History* 8 (1972): 1–18.

27. Otto of Freising, the self-proclaimed, if mistakenly so, Augustinian historian, is the prime example of an historian willing to work at interpretations; his cultural significance, however, is odd in that he appears to have done what modern scholars think medieval historians *should* have been doing but, on the whole, were not; see Felix Fellner, "The 'Two Cities' of Otto of Freising and Its Influence on the Catholic Philosophy of History," *Catholic Historical Review* 20 (1934): 154–74. Fellner deplores the fact that contemporaries refused to follow Otto's example. See also R. D. Ray's discussion of the problems Orderic Vitalis encountered when he assumed that his monastic brothers knew how to "read" Christian significance into history for themselves—when they, apparently, wanted it all spelled out by the author: "Orderic Vitalis and His Readers," *Studia Monastica* 14 (1972): 17–33.

28. Huntingdon, 128.

29. Huntingdon, 4.

30. Antonia Gransden, "Realistic Observation in Twelfth-Century England," *Speculum* 47 (1972): 29–51.

31. I follow the *Oxford English Dictionary* for matters of this sort.

32. Newburgh, 297–98.

33. Newburgh, 298.

Bibliography

Primary Sources

Addison, J. *The Spectator.* Edited by D. F. Bond. 5 vols. Oxford, 1965.

Aelred of Rievaulx. *Speculum caritatis.* In *Corpus Christianorum continuatio mediaevalis, Aelredi Rievallensis opera omnia.* Edited by A. Hoste and C. H. Talbot. Turnhout, Belgium, 1971.

———. *Works. Historiae Anglicanae scriptores,* vol. 10. London, 1652.

Alexander Neckham. *De naturis rerum.* Edited by Thomas Wright. Rolls Series, 4. London, 1863.

Anglo-Latin Satirical Poets. Edited by T. Wright. Rolls Series, 59:2. London, 1872.

Annals of Winchester. Edited by H. R. Luard. Rolls Series, 36:2. London, 1865.

Anonymous of York. "*An liceat sacerdotibus inire matrimonium.*" *Monumenta Germaniae historica, libelli de lite,* edited by H. Boehmer. 3:645–48. Hanover, 1897.

Anselm. *Opera omnia,* vol. 4. Edited by F. S. Schmitt. Edinburgh, 1949.

Augustine. *De civitate Dei.* Vol. 40. *Corpus scriptorum ecclesiasticorum latinorum.* 1889.

———. *De divinatione daemonum.* Vol. 41. *Corpus scriptorum ecclesiasticorum latinorum.* 1900.

———. "*De genesi ad litteram.*" *Patrologia Latina* 34:245–486. [hereafter *PL*].

———. *Quaestionum in Heptateuchum libri VII.* Vol. 28. *Corpus scriptorum ecclesiasticorum latinorum.*

———. "*De Trinitate.*" *PL* 42:819–1098.

Bernard of Clairvaux. "*De Consideratione.* In *Sancti Bernardi Opera Omnia,* edited by J. Mabillon, 4th ed. 1:1005–96. Paris, 1839.

———. *De moribus et officio episcoporum, epistola XLII ad Henricum archiepiscopum Senonensem.* Vol. 1, *Sancti Bernardi opera omnia.* Edited by J. Mabillon. 4th ed. Paris, 1839.

The Book of Beasts, Being a Translation from a Latin Bestiary of the Twelfth Century. Edited and translated by T. H. White. London, 1954.

Boswell, James. *Boswell's Life of Johnson.* Edited by G. Hill; revision edited by L. F. Powell. 6 vols. Oxford, 1934.

Burchard of Worms. *"Decretorum liber."* PL, 140:537–1053.

Cartularium monasterii de Rameseia. Edited by William H. Hart. 3 vols. Rolls Series, 79. London, 1884–1893.

Chronicon abbatiae Rameseiensis, a saec. X usque ad an. circiter 1200. Edited by W. Dunn Macray. Rolls Series, 83. London, 1886.

du Méril, Edelstand. *Poésies popularies latines du moyen age.* Paris, 1847.

Eadmer. *Historia novorum in Anglia.* Edited by M. Rule. Rolls Series, 81. London, 1884.

Exordium Cisterciensis cenobii (exordium parvum). Edited by Philip Guignard. *Les Monuments primitifs de la règle Cistercienne.* Dijon, 1878.

Exordium Magnum. PL 185.

Feet of Fines: *A Calendar of the Feet of Fines Relating to the County of Huntingdon, Levied in the Kings Court from the Fifth Year of Richard I to the End of the Reign of Elizabeth 1194–1603.* Edited by G. J. Turner. Cambridge, 1913.

Florence of Worcester. *Chronicle.* Translated by T. Forester. Bohns Antiquarian Library. London, 1854.

Giraldus Cambrensis. *Itinerarium Kambriae.* Edited by J. F. Dimock. Rolls Series, 21 London, 1868.

Gratian. *Decretum.* PL 187.

Henry of Huntingdon, *Epigrammata seria.* Royal 13 C. II, B.M. ms.

———. *Historia Anglorum.* Edited by T. Arnold. Rolls Series, 74. London, 1879.

———. *Historiae rerum Anglorum, ad annum Regis Stephani decimum tertium.* Libri decem, sec. XIII, Arundel 48, B.M. ms.

Historia Ramesiensis. Edited by Th. Gale. *Historia Britannicae, Saxonicae, Anglo-Danicae scriptores.* Oxford, 1691.

Hugh of Kirkstall. *Narratio de fundatione Fontanis monasterii in comitatu Eboracensi.* Edited by J. R. Walbran. *Memorials of the Abbey of Saint Mary of Fountains,* Surtees Society Publications, 42. Durham, 1863.

Isidore of Seville. *Isidori Hispalensis episcopi etymologiarum sive originum.* Edited by W. M. Lindsay. 2 vols. Oxford, 1911.

Ivo of Chartres. *"Decretum."* PL 161:59–1022.

Jessop, Augustus, and Montague James, eds. and trans. *The Life and Miracles of Saint William of Norwich.* Cambridge, 1896.

Jocelin of Brakelond. *The Chronicle of Jocelin of Brakelond Concerning the Acts of Samson Abbot of the Monastery of Saint Edmund.* Translated by H. E. Butler. London, 1949.

John of Salisbury. *Frivolities of Courtiers and Footprints of Philosophers.* Translated by W. R. Trask. Princeton, 1953.

————. *Historia pontificalis.* Translated by Marjorie Chibnall. London, 1956.

Johnson, Samuel. *A Dictionary of the English Language.* 2 vols. London, 1755.

Josephus. *The Jewish War.* Translated by H. St. J. Thackeray. The Loeb Classical Library, London, 1927.

Liber Eliensis. Edited by E. O. Blake. London, 1962.

Mansi, J. D. *Sacrorum conciliorum nova et amplissima collectio.* 4 vols. Paris, 1776 (facsimile ed. 1903).

Map, Walter. *De Nugis Curialium.* Edited by E. S. Hartland; translated by M. R. James. London, 1923.

A Medieval Bestiary. Translated by T. J. Elliot. Boston, 1971.

Morey, Adrian, and C. N. L. Brooke. *Letters and Charters of Gilbert Foliot.* Cambridge, 1967.

Obituary of Lincoln Cathedral. In *Opera Geraldi Cambrensis.* Edited by J. F. Dimock. Rolls Series, 21:7, appendix B. London, 1877.

Peter Damian. *"Liber Gomorrhianus." PL* 145:159–90.

————. *"Apologeticum de contemptu saeculi." PL* 145:251–92.

————. *"De fluxa mundi gloria et saeculi despectione." PL* 145:807–20.

The Peterborough Chronicle. Translated by H. A. Rositzke. New York, 1951.

Physiologus. Translated by Francis J. Carmody. San Francisco, 1953.

Rabanus Maurus. *"De magicis artibus." PL* 110:1095–1110.

Ralph of Coggeshall. *Chronicon Anglicanum.* Edited by Joseph Stevenson. Rolls Series, 66. London, 1875.

Registrum antiquissimum of the Cathedral Church of Lincoln. Edited by C. W. Foster and K. Major. *Lincoln Record Society.* Hereford. 1931–53.

Richard of Devizes. *Cronicon Richardi Divisensis de tempore Regis Richardi Primi.* Edited by John T. Appleby. London, 1963.

Richard the Canon. *Itinerarium Regis Ricardi.* Edited by W. Stubbs. Rolls Series, 38 (1864).

Robert de Monte, or Robert de Torigni. *The Chronicles of Robert de Monte.* Translated by J. Stevenson. *The Church Historians of England.* London, 1856.

Roger of Hoveden. *Chronica.* Edited by W. Stubbs. Rolls Series, LI51 (1871).

Symeon of Durham. *Symeonis monachi opera omnia.* Edited by T. Arnold. Rolls Series, 75. London, 1882.

The Travels of Three English Gentlemen, from Venice to Hamburg, being the Grand Tour of Germany in the Year 1734. In *The Harleian Miscellany* 4, pp. 365–77. London, 1809.

Vita secunda. Alanus Autissiodorensis. *PL* 185:469–524.
Vita tertia. Geoffrey of Clairvaux. *PL* 185:523–30.
Walter of Henley. *Walter of Henley and Other Treatises on Estate Management and Accounting.* Edited by Dorothea Oschinsky. Oxford, 1971.
Wilkins, David. *Concilia Magnae Britanniae.* 4 vols. London, 1737.
William of Newburgh. *Historia rerum Anglicarum.* Edited by Richard Howlett. Rolls Series, 82. London, 1884–1885.
————. *William of Newburgh's Explanatio sacri epithalamii in matrem sponsi, A Commentary on the Canticle of Canticles.* Edited by John C. Gorman. Fribourg, 1960.
William of Saint Thierry. "*Vita prima.*" *PL* 185:225–466.
Woolley, Reginald Maxwell. *Catalogue of the Manuscripts of Lincoln Cathedral Chapter Library.* London, 1927.

SECONDARY SOURCES

Amanieu, A. "Archidiacre." *Dictionnaire de droit canonique* 1. Paris, 1935.
Appleby, J. T. "Richard of Devizes and the Annals of Winchester." *Bulletin of the Institute of Historical Research* 36 (1963): 70–77.
Auerbach, Erich. *Mimesis.* Translated by W. Trask. Princeton, 1953.
Austen, Jane. *The History of England from the Reign of Henry the 4th to the Death of Charles the 1st, by a partial, prejudiced, and ignorant Historian.* Vol. 6. *The Works of Jane Austen.* Edited by R. W. Chapman. London, 1954.
Baker, Derek. "Viri Religiosi and the York Election Dispute." *Studies in Church History* 7 (1971): 87–100.
Baker, L. G. D. "The Desert in the North." *Northern History* 5 (1970): 1–11.
————. "The Foundation of Fountains Abbey." *Northern History* 4 (1969): 29–43.
————. "The Genesis of English Cistercian Chronicles: The Foundation History of Fountains Abbey I." *Analecta Cisterciensia* 25 (1969): 14–41.
Baldwin, John W. "A Campaign to Reduce Clerical Celibacy at the Turn of the Twelfth and Thirteenth Centuries." In *Études d'histoire du droit canonique dediées à Gabriel le Bras*, vol. 2, pp. 1041–53. Paris, 1965.
————. "The Intellectual Preparation for the Canon of 1215 Against Ordeals." *Speculum* 36 (1961): 613–36.
Baldwin, Marshall W. *Alexander III and the Twelfth Century.* In *The Popes Through History*, edited by Raymond H. Schmandt, vol. 3. New York, 1968.
Barb, A. A. "The Survival of Magic Arts." In *The Conflict Between*

Paganism and Christianity in the Fourth Century, edited by A. Momigliano, pp. 100–125. Oxford, 1963.

Barber, R. W. *Arthur of Albion*. London, 1961.

Baron, Salo W. *A Social and Religious History of the Jews*. 14 vols. 2d ed. New York, 1957.

Barraclough, Geoffrey. "The Making of a Bishop in the Middle Ages." *Catholic Historical Review* 19 (1939): 275–319.

Beddie, James S. "Libraries in the Twelfth Century: Their Catalogues and Contents." In *Anniversary Essays in Medieval History by Students of Charles Homer Haskins*, pp. 1–24. Boston, 1929.

Bernheimer, Richard. *Wild Men in the Middle Ages*. Cambridge, Mass., 1952.

Bethell, Denis. "The Fountains Abbey and the State of St. Mary's of York in 1132." *Journal of Ecclesiastical History* 17 (1966): 11–27.

———. "William of Corbeil and the Canterbury–York Dispute." *Journal of Ecclesiastical History* 19 (1968): 145–59.

Brandt, William M. *The Shape of Medieval History*. New Haven, 1966.

Brentano, Robert. *Two Churches*. Princeton, 1969.

Brooke, C. N. L. "Gregorian Reform in Action: Clerical Marriage in England, 1050–1200." *Cambridge Historical Journal* 12 (1956): 1–21.

———. "Heresy and Religious Sentiment: 1000–1250." *Bulletin of the Institute of Historical Research* 41 (1968): 115–31.

———. "Historical Writing in England between 850 and 1150." In *La storiografia altomedievale*. Settimane di studio del centro Italiano di studi sull'alto medioevo, 17. 2 vols. Spoleto, 1970.

———. "Married Men Among the English Higher Clergy, 1066–1200." *Cambridge Historical Journal* 12, no. 2 (1956): 187–88.

———. Note in *English Historical Review* 77 (1962): 554.

Brooke, Z. N. *The English Church and the Papacy from the Conquest to the Reign of John*. Cambridge, 1931.

Brundage, James A. *Medieval Canon Law and the Crusader*. Madison, 1969.

Bugge, Alexander. "The Norse Settlements in the British Islands." *Transactions of the Royal Historical Society*. 4th ser. 4 (1921): 173–210.

Bultot, Robert. *Christianisme et valeurs humaines; la doctrine du mépris du monde*. 4 vols. Paris, 1964.

Butterfield, Herbert. *Christianity and History*. London, 1949.

———. "Historiography." *Dictionary of the History of Ideas* 2 (1973): 464–98.

———. *Man on His Past*. Cambridge, 1955.

Cantor, Norman. *Church, Kingship, and Lay Investiture in England, 1089–1135*. Princeton, 1958.

273

Cartwright, John K. "St. Bernard and the Papacy." *The Catholic Historical Review* 9 (1923): 393–400.

Chambers, E. K. *Arthur of Britain*. London, 1927.

Cheney, C. R. "England and the Roman Curia under Innocent III." *Journal of Ecclesiastical History* 18 (1967): 173–86.

———. *English Bishops' Chanceries, 1100–1250*. Manchester, 1950.

———. *From Becket to Langton: English Church Government, 1170–1213*. Manchester, 1956.

———. "Legislation of the Medieval English Church." *English Historical Review* 50 (1935): 193–224, 385–417.

Cheney, Mary. "The Compromise of Avranches of 1172 and the Spread of Canon Law in England." *English Historical Review* 56 (1941): 177–97.

———. "The Recognition of Pope Alexander III: Some Neglected Evidence." *English Historical Review* 84 (1969): 474–97.

Clay, C. T. "The Early Abbots of the Yorkshire Cistercian Houses." *Yorkshire Archeological Journal* 38 (1952): 8–43.

———. "Master Aristotle." *English Historical Review* 76 (1961): 303–8.

Cohn, Norman. *The Pursuit of the Millennium*. Rev. ed. New York, 1970.

Conkin, Paul K. "Causation Revisited." *History and Theory* 13 (1974): 1–20.

Constable, Giles. "The Second Crusade as Seen by Contemporaries." *Traditio* 9 (1953): 213–79.

Cooke, Alice M. "The Settlement of the Cistercians in England." *English Historical Review* 8 (1893): 625–76.

Cronne, H. A. *The Reign of Stephen 1135–54: Anarchy in England*. London, 1970.

Crosby, Everett U. "The Organization of the English Episcopate under Henry I." *Studies in Medieval and Renaissance History* 4 (1967): 1–88.

Curtius, Ernst. *European Literature and the Latin Middle Ages*. New York, 1953.

Darlington, R. R. "Ecclesiastical Reform in the Late Old English Period." *English Historical Review* 51 (1936): 385–428.

Deanesly, Margaret. *Sidelights on the Anglo-Saxon Church*. London, 1962.

Dickins, Bruce. "A Yorkshire Chronicler." *Transactions of the Yorkshire Dialect Society* 5 pt. 35 (1934).

Dickinson, J. C. "English Regular Canons and the Continent in the Twelfth Century." *Transactions of the Royal Historical Society* 5th ser. 1 (1951): 71–89.

———. *The Origins of the Austin Canons and Their Introduction into England*. London, 1950.

Douie, D. L. *Archbishop Geoffrey Plantagenet and the Chapter of York*. St. Anthony's Hall Publications, no. 18. York, 1960.

Duggan, Charles. "From the Conquest to the Death of John." In *The English Church and the Papacy in the Middle Ages*, edited by C. H. Lawrence, pp. 63–116. New York, 1965.

———. "Richard of Ilchester, Royal Servant and Bishop." *Transactions of the Royal Historical Society*. 5th ser. 16 (1966): pp. 1–21.

———. *Twelfth-Century Decretal Collections and Their Importance in English History*. London, 1963.

Edwards, Kathleen. *The English Secular Cathedrals in the Middle Ages*. Manchester, 1949.

Fallow, T. M. "Priory of Newburgh." *The Victoria History of the County of York*, vol. 3, pp. 226–30. London, 1913.

———. "Cell of Hood." The Victoria History of the County of York, vol. 3, pp. 230–31. London, 1913.

Farmer, D. H. "Two Biographies by William of Malmesbury." *Latin Biography*, edited by T. A. Dorey, pp. 157–76. London, 1967.

Fellner, Felix. "The 'Two Cities' of Otto of Freising and Its Influence on the Catholic Philosophy of History." *Catholic Historical Review* 20 (1934): 154–74.

Fletcher, Robert Huntingdon. *The Arthurian Material in the Chronicles. Studies and Notes in Philology and Literature* 10. Boston, 1906.

Fliché, Augustin, and Martin Victor. *Histoire de l'église depuis les origines jusqu'à nos jours*, vol. 9, pt. 2, Raymonde Foreville, and Jean Rousset de Ana. Paris, 1953.

Foreville, Raymonde. *L'Église et la royauté en Angleterre sous Henry II Plantagenet*. Paris, 1942.

Frazee, Charles A. "The Origins of the Clerical Celibacy in the Western Church." *Church History* 41 (1972): 149–67.

Freeman, Edward A. "Mr. Froude's Life and Times of Thomas Becket." *The Contemporary Review* 33 (August-November 1878): 213–41.

Galbraith, V. H. "Good Kings and Bad Kings in Medieval English History." *History* n.s. 30 (1945): 119–32.

Gathorne-Hardy, G. M. *A Royal Impostor: King Sverre of Norway*. London, 1956.

Gay, Peter. *Style in History*. New York, 1974.

Gilson, E. "De la Bible à Francois Villon," and "Tables pour l'histoire du thème *ubi sunt*.'" in *Les Idées et les lettres*, pp. 9–38. Paris, 1932.

Goldsmith, Oliver. *The History of England*. 4 vols. London, 1771.

Gransden, Antonia. *Historical Writing in England c. 550 to c. 1307*. Ithaca, N.Y., 1974.

———. "Realistic Observation in Twelfth-Century England." *Speculum* 47 (1972): 29–51.

Grant, A. J. "Twelve Medieval Ghost Stories." *Yorkshire Archaeolog-*

ical Journal 27 (1924): 363–79.

Gréa, A. "Essai historique sur les archidiacres." *Bibliothèque de l'école des Chartres* 12 (1851): 39–67, 215–47.

Hanning, Robert W. *The Vision of History in Early Britain from Gildas to Geoffrey of Monmouth.* New York, 1966.

Hardy, Th. D. *Descriptive Catalogue of Materials Relating to the History of Great Britain and Ireland to the End of the Reign of Henry VII.* 2 vols. Rolls Series, 26. London, 1865.

Herman, Émile. "Célibat des clercs." *Dictionnaire de droit canonique,* vol. 3, pp. 132–56. Paris, 1942.

Hill, Bennett D. *English Cistercian Monasteries and Their Patrons in the Twelfth Century.* Urbana, 1968.

Holmes, Urban T. "Transitions in European Education." In *Twelfth-Century Europe and the Foundations of Modern Society,* edited by M. Clagett, G. Post, and R. Reynolds, pp. 15–38. Madison, 1961.

Howard, Donald R. "Renaissance World-Alienation." In *The Darker Vision of the Renaissance: Beyond the Fields of Reason,* edited by R. Kinsman, pp. 47–76. Berkeley, 1974.

―――. *The Three Temptations: Medieval Man in Search of the World.* Princeton, 1966.

Hunt, R. W. "English Learning in the Late Twelfth Century." *Transactions of the Royal Historical Society* 4th ser. 19 (1936): 19–42.

Hunt, Tony. "The Structure of Medieval Narrative." *Journal of European Studies* 3 (1973): 295–328.

Jacobs, Joseph. "Little St. Hugh of Lincoln, Researches in History, Archaeology and Legend." *Transactions of the Jewish Historical Society of England* 1 (1893–1894): 89–135.

James, M. R. "Twelve Medieval Ghost Stories." *English Historical Review* 37 (1922): 413–22.

Jolliffe, J. E. A. "Northumbrian Institutions." *English Historical Review* 41 (1926): 1–42.

Jombart, E. "Concubinage." *Dictionnaire de droit canonique,* vol. 3, pp. 1513–24. Paris, 1942.

Jones, A. H. M. *Constantine and the Conversion of Europe.* London, 1948.

Jones, Charles. "Bede as Early Medieval Historian." *Medievalia et Humanistica* 2 (1946): 26–36.

Kealey, Edward J. *Roger of Salisbury, Viceroy of England.* Berkeley, 1972.

Kemp, R. R. "Hereditary Benefices in the Medieval English Church: A Herefordshire Example." *Bulletin of the Institute of Historical Research* 43, no. 107 (May 1970): 1–15.

Knowles, David. "The Case of Saint William of York." *Cambridge Historical Journal* 5 (1936): 162–77, 212–14.

————. *The Monastic Order in England.* Cambridge, 1963.

————. "Some Developments in English Monastic Life." *Transactions of the Royal Historical Society,* 4th ser. 26 (1944): 37–52.

————. C. N. L. Brooke, V. London. *The Heads of Religious Houses in England and Wales, 940–1216.* Cambridge, 1972.

Kuttner, Stephen, and Eleanor Rathbone. "Anglo-Norman Canonists of the Twelfth Century." *Traditio* 7 (1949–1951): 279–358.

Langmuir, Gavin I. "The Knight's Tale of Young Hugh of Lincoln." *Speculum* 47 (1972): 459–82.

Langton, Edward. *Satan, A Portrait.* London, 1945.

Lawson, John C. *Modern Greek Folklore and Ancient Greek Religion.* Cambridge, 1910.

Lazzari, Francesco. *Il contemptus mundi nella scuola de S. Vittore.* Naples, 1965.

————. *Monachesimo e valori umani tra XI e XII secolo.* Milan, 1969.

Lea, Henry C. *An Historical Sketch of Sacerdotal Celibacy in the Christian Church.* 2d ed. Boston, 1884.

————. *Materials Toward a History of Witchcraft.* New York, 1957.

Leach, Henry Goddard. *Angevin Britain and Scandinavia.* Cambridge, 1921.

Lear, Floyd S. "The Medieval Attitude Toward History." Rice Institute Pamphlet 20 (1933): 156–77.

Leclercq, Jean. "L'Humanisme des moines au moyen age." *Studi Medievali,* 3d ser. 10 (1969): 69–113.

————. *The Love of Learning and the Desire for God.* Translated by C. Misrahi. New York, 1961.

————. "Monastic Historiography from Leo IX to Callistus II." *Studia Monastica* 12 (1970), 57–86.

Le Patourel, John. "The Norman Conquest of Yorkshire." *Northern History* 6 (1971): 1–21.

Levy, M. L. "As Myn Auctour Seyth." *Medium Aevum* 12 (1943): 25–39.

Liborio, M. "Contributi alla storia dell' 'ubi sunt.'" *Cultura Neolatina* 20 (1960): 141–209.

Liotta, Filippo. *La Continenza dei clierici nei Pensiero Canonistico Classico, de Graziano a Gregorio IX.* Milan, 1971.

Loomis, Roger Sherman. *Wales and the Arthurian Legend.* Cardiff, 1956.

Luard, Henry Richards. "Henry of Huntingdon." In *Dictionary of National Biography* 9. London, 1917.

Lunt, William E. *Financial Relations of the Papacy with England to 1327.* Studies in Anglo-Papal Relations During the Middle Ages 1. Medieval Academy of America Publications, no. 33. Cambridge, 1939.

McCulloch, Florence. *Mediaeval Latin and French Bestiaries.* University of North Carolina Studies in the Romance Languages and Literatures, no. 33. Chapel Hill, 1960.

McLaughton, T. P. "The Prohibition of Marriage Against Canons in the Early Twelfth Century." *Mediaeval Studies* 3 (1941): 94–100.

Maitland, F. W. "William of Progheda and the Universal Ordinary. In *Roman Canon Law in the Church of England*, pp. 100–131. London, 1898.

Mann, Horace K. *The Lives of the Popes in the Middle Ages.* 18 vols. 2d ed. London, 1925.

Markus, R. A. *Saeculum: History and Society in the Theology of St. Augustine.* Cambridge, 1970.

Megaw, Isabel. "The Ecclesiastical Policy of Stephen, 1135–1139: A Reinterpretation." In *Essays in British and Irish History in Honour of James Eadie Todd*, edited by H. A. Cronne, et al., pp. 24–45. London, 1949.

Momigliano, Arnaldo. "Pagan and Christian Historiography in the Fourth Century, A.D." In *The Conflict between Paganism and Christianity in the Fourth Century*, edited by A. Momigliano, pp. 79–99. Oxford, 1963.

———. "Popular Religious Beliefs and the Late Roman Historians." *Studies in Church History* 8 (1972): 1–18.

———. *Studies in Historiography.* London, 1966.

———. "Tradition and the Classical Historian." *History and Theory* 11 (1972): 279–93.

Moore, Arthur K. "Medieval English Literature and the Question of Unity." *Modern Philology* 65 (1968): 285–300.

Moore, R. I. "The Origins of Medieval History." *History* 55 (1970): 21–36.

Morenbert, T. de. "Éon de l'Étoile." *Dictionnaire d'histoire et de géographie ecclésiastiques*, vol. 5, p. 519. Paris, 1963.

Morey, Adrian. "Canonist Evidence in the Case of Saint William of York." *Cambridge Historical Journal* 10 (1952): 352–53.

———, and C. N. L. Brooke. *Gilbert Foliot and His Letters.* Cambridge, 1965.

Morris, Colin. "A Consistory Court in the Middle Ages." *Journal of Ecclesiastical History* 14 (1963): 150–59.

———. *The Discovery of the Individual 1050–1200.* London, 1972.

Mullin, Francis Anthony. *A History of the Work of the Cistercians in Yorkshire.* Washington, 1932.

Nelson, William. *Fact or Fiction.* Cambridge, Mass., 1973.

Nicholl, Donald. *Thurstan: Archbishop of York (1114–1140).* York, 1964.

Nineham, Ruth. "The So-called Anonymous of York." *Journal of Ecclesiastical History* 14 (1963): 31–45.

Norgate, Kate. "The Date of Composition of William of Newburgh's History." *English Historical Review* 19 (1904): 288–97.

———. "William of Newburgh." *Dictionary of National Biography*, vol. 21, pp. 361–62. Oxford, 1921–1924.

———. "William of Longchamp." Dictionary of National Biography.

Owen, Dorothy M. *Church and Society in Medieval Lincolnshire.* Lincoln, 1971.

Patrides, C. A. *The Grand Design of God: The Literary Form of the Christian View of History.* London, 1972.

Poole, R. L. "The Appointment and Deprivation of Saint William, Archbishop of York." *English Historical Review* 45 (1930): 273–81.

———. "The Early Lives of Robert Pullen and Nicholas Breakspear." In *Essays in Medieval History Presented to Thomas Frederick Tout*, pp. 61–70. Manchester, 1925.

Poulet, Georges. *Studies in Human Time.* Translated by E. Coleman. Baltimore, 1956.

Powell, D. L. "Little Stuckley." In *History of the County of Huntingdon.*, vol. 2, p. 235. London, 1932.

Powicke, F. M. "Aelred of Rievaulx and His Biographer." *Bulletin of the John Rylands Library* 6 (1921–1922): 310–51, 452–521.

Ray, R. D. "Orderic Vitalis and His Readers." *Studia Monastica* 14 (1972): 17–33.

Richardson, Henry. *The English Jewry Under Angevin Kings.* London, 1960.

Ritchie, R. L. Graeme. *The Normans in Scotland.* Edinburgh, 1954.

Robbins, R. H. *The Encyclopedia of Witchcraft and Demonology.* New York, 1959.

Roth, Cecil. *A History of the Jews in England.* Oxford, 1941.

Rousset, P. "La Notion de chrétienté aux XIe et XIIe siècles." *Le Moyen Age* 69 (1963): 191–203.

Roy, A. E., and E. L. G. Stones. "The Record of Eclipses in the Bury Chronicle." *Bulletin of the Institute of Historical Research* 43, no. 108 (1970): 125–33.

Runciman, Steven. *A History of the Crusades.* Vols. 2, 3. Cambridge, 1952–1954.

Russell, Jeffrey Burton. *Witchcraft in the Middle Ages.* Ithaca, 1972.

Russell, J. C. "The Renaissance of the Twelfth Century." In *The Development of Historiography*, edited by Matthew A. Fitzsimons, Alfred G. Pundt, and Charles E. Nowell, chap. 4. 1954.

Ryding, William W. *Structure in Medieval Narrative.* The Hague, 1971.

Salter, H. E. "William of Newburgh." *English Historical Review* 23 (1907): 510–14.

Sandford, W. A. C. "Medieval Clerical Celibacy in England." *The Geneologist's Magazine* 12 (1957): 371–73.

Sanford, Eva. "The Study of Ancient History in the Middle Ages."

Journal of the History of Ideas 5 (1944): 21–43.

Scammell, G. V. *Hugh de Puiset, Bishop of Durham.* Cambridge, 1956.

Scammell, Jean. "The Rural Chapter in England from the Eleventh to the Fourteenth Century." *English Historical Review* 86, no. 338 (1971): 1–21.

Smalley, Beryl. *Historians in the Middle Ages.* London, 1975.

―――. "Sallust in the Middle Ages." In *Classical Influences on European Culture,* edited by R. Bolgar, pp. 165–75. Cambridge, 1971.

Southern, R. W. "Aspects of the European Tradition of Historical Writing: 1. The Classical Tradition from Einhard to Geoffrey of Monmouth." *Transactions of the Royal Historical Society,* 5th ser. 20 (1970): 173–96.

―――. "Aspects of the European Tradition of Historical Writing: 2. Hugh of St. Victor and the Idea of Historical Development." *TRHS,* 5th ser. 21 (1971): 159–79.

―――. "Aspects of the European Tradition of Historical Writing: 3. History as Prophesy." *TRHS,* 5th ser. 22 (1972): 159–80.

―――. "Aspects of the European Tradition of Historical Writing: 4. The Sense of the Past." *TRHS,* 5th ser. 23 (1973): 243–63.

―――. "The Place of England in the Twelfth-Century Renaissance." *History* 45 (1960): 201–16.

―――. "The Place of Henry I in English History." *Proceedings of the British Academy,* 48 (1962): 127–69.

―――. *Saint Anselm and His Biographer: A Study of Monastic Life and Thought 1059–1130.* Cambridge, 1963.

Squire, Aelred. *Aelred of Rievaulx.* London, 1969.

Stubbs, William. Historical Introduction to the Rolls Series. Edited by A. Hassall. London, 1962.

Talbot, C. H. "New Documents in the Case of Saint Wiliiam of York." *Cambridge Historical Journal* 10 (1950): 1–15.

Taylor, J. *Medieval Historical Writing in Yorkshire.* York, 1961.

Thompson, A. Hamilton. "Diocesan Organization in the Middle Ages, Archdeacons and Rural Deans." *Proceedings of the British Academy* 29 (1943): 153–94.

Ullmann, Walter. *The Growth of Papal Government in the Middle Ages.* 3d ed. London, 1970.

―――. *The Individual and Society in the Middle Ages.* Baltimore, 1966.

Vacandard, E. "Les Origines du célibat ecclésiastique." In *Études de critique et d'histoire religieuse,* pp. 69–120. Paris, 1906.

Van Caenegem, R. "The Law of Evidence in the Twelfth Century: European Perspective and Intellectual Background." *Proceedings of the Second International Congress of Medieval Canon Law,* edited by S. Kuttner and J. Ryan, pp. 297–310. Vatican City, 1965.

Vaughan, Richard. *Matthew Paris*. Cambridge, 1958.

Venables, Edmunc. "Godfrey de Lucy, Bishop of Winchester." *Dictionary of National Biography*.

Vernet, F. "Éon de l'Etoile." *Dictionnaire de théologie catholique*. Paris, 1913.

Vinaver, Eugene. "Form and Meaning in Medieval Romance." Presidential Address of the Modern Humanities Research Association, 1966. Leeds, 1966.

―――. *The Rise of Romance*. Oxford, 1971.

Ward, Mary Augusta (Mrs. Humphrey Ward). *Robert Elsmere*. London, 1888.

White, Beatrice. "Medieval Animal Lore." *Anglia, Zeitschrift für englische Philologie*. 72 (1954): 21–30.

Wilkinson, Bertie. "The Government of England during the Absence of Richard I on the Third Crusade." *Bulletin of the John Rylands Library* 28 (1944): 485–509.

Willey, Basil. "How 'Robert Elsmere' Struck Some Contemporaries." *Essays and Studies 1957*, edited by Margaret Willy, pp. 53–68. London, 1957.

Williams, George. *The Norman Anonymous of 1100 A.D.: Toward the Identification and Evaluation of the So-Called Anonymous of York*. In *Harvard Theological Studies*, 18. Cambridge, Mass., 1951.

Williams, Gwyn A. *Medieval London*. London, 1963.

Witke, Charles. *Latin Satire*. Leiden, 1970.

Index